Is Nature Enough?

Is nature all there is? John Haught examines this question and in doing so
addresses a fundamental issue in the dialogue of science with religion. The belief
that nature is all there is and that no overall purpose exists in the universe is
known broadly as "naturalism." Naturalism, in this context, denies the existence
of any realities distinct from the natural world and human culture. Since the rise of
science in the modern world has had so much influence on naturalism's
intellectual acceptance, the author focuses on "scientific" naturalism and the way
in which its defenders are now attempting to put a distance between contemporary
thought and humanity's religious traditions. Haught seeks to provide a reasonable,
scientifically informed alternative to naturalism. His approach will provide the
basis for lively discussion among students, scholars, scientists, theologians and
intellectually curious people in general.

John F. Haught is Distinguished Research Professor of Theology at Georgetown
University. His area of specialization is systematic theology with particular
interest in issues pertaining to science, cosmology, evolution, ecology and religion.
He is the author of thirteen books and numerous articles and reviews.

Is Nature Enough?
Meaning and Truth in the Age of Science

John F. Haught

CAMBRIDGE UNIVERSITY PRESS
Cambridge, New York, Melbourne, Madrid, Cape Town, Singapore,
São Paulo

CAMBRIDGE UNIVERSITY PRESS
The Edinburgh Building, Cambridge CB2 2RU, UK
Published in the United States of America by Cambridge University Press,
New York

www.cambridge.org
Information on this title: www.cambridge.org/9780521609937

First published 2006

Printed in the United Kingdom at the University Press, Cambridge

A catalogue record for this book is available from the British Library

Library of Congress Cataloging in Publication data

Haught, John F.
    Is nature enough?: meaning and truth in the age of science / John F.
    Haught.
        p.   cm.
    Includes bibliographical references.
    ISBN-13 978-0-521-84714-8 (hardback) ISBN-10 0-521-84714-1 (hardback)
    ISBN-13 978-0-521-60993-7 (paperback) ISBN-10 0-521-60993-3
    (paperback)
    1. Religion and science. I. Title.
BL240.3.H38 2006   215–dc22   2005029841

ISBN-13 978-0-521-84714-8 (hardback)
ISBN-10 0-521-84714-1 (hardback)
ISBN-13 978-0-521-60993-7 (paperback)
ISBN-10 0-521-60993-3 (paperback)

To the memory of Pierre Teilhard de Chardin, SJ
(1881–1955)

Contents

Acknowledgments

I would like to express my gratitude to the John Templeton Foundation for the grant that allowed me to complete this book. Likewise I am indebted in a special way to Kate Brett, Gillian Dadd and Elizabeth Davey at Cambridge University Press for their skill and generosity in guiding the book to publication.

Introduction

In 1715 Isaac Watts wrote a Christian hymn beginning with this stanza:

> I sing the mighty power of God
> That made the mountains rise
> That spread the flowing seas abroad
> And built the lofty skies.
> I sing the wisdom that ordained
> The sun to rule the day;
> The moon shines full at his command
> And all the stars obey.

In 1975 Kenneth Boulding offered a new version:

> What though the mountains are pushed up
> By plate-tectonic lift,
> And oceans lie within the cup
> Made by the landmass drift.
> The skies are but earth's airy skin
> Rotation makes the day;
> Sun, moon, and planets are akin
> And Kepler's Laws obey.[1]

Boulding does not say whether the sentiments expressed in his update are really his own, but his rendition expresses succinctly the

---

[1] Kenneth Boulding, "Toward an Evolutionary Theology," in *The Spirit of the Earth: a Teilhard Centennial Celebration*, edited by Jerome Perlinski (New York: The Seabury Press, 1981), pp. 112–13.

worldview known as "scientific naturalism." This is the belief that nature is all there is and that science alone can make sense of it. Some scientific naturalists are willing to keep singing the old hymns. Even though the lyrics no longer ring true, they still warm the heart. Others, however, insist that it is time to stop singing them altogether. There can be no harmonizing of Watts' stanza with Boulding's. Nature is enough.

Is it time then to resign ourselves to this claim? In the following pages I intend to argue that there is no good reason to do so and that in fact the belief that nature is all there is cannot be justified experientially, logically or scientifically. In developing my response I shall be addressing fundamental issues in the dialogue of science with religion. Although this conversation has many facets, two large questions stand out: is nature all there is? And is there any point to the universe? I have addressed the second question often in previous writings, but until now I have not focused a book-length treatment on the first.

The belief that nature is all there is, and that no overall purpose exists in the universe, is known broadly as *naturalism*. Naturalism, at least as I shall be using the term, denies the existence of any realities distinct from the natural world, an unimaginably immense and resourceful realm of being that includes humans and their cultural creations. Naturalism either suspends or rejects belief in God and most other religious teachings. Hence it should be a topic of great concern to anyone who cherishes religions and the "wisdom of the ages." Since the rise of science has had so much to do with naturalism's intellectual acceptance today, the focus of these pages will be on *scientific* naturalism and the way in which some of its most ardent defenders are now seeking to put a distance between contemporary thought and humanity's religious traditions.

There are several ways of thinking that "nature is all there is," including classic forms of pantheism, but our focus here will be on science-inspired naturalism. Because of the growing academic sponsorship of this belief system, it is important that reasonable, scientifically informed, alternatives to naturalism and its burgeoning influence now become more visible. This book attempts to provide such an alternative. However, my approach will not be to mount an attack on science itself. Numerous books and articles expressing opposition to naturalism end up rejecting good science in the process. Some authors, for example, try to rout naturalism by throwing away conventionally accepted biological and paleontological information in their zeal to repudiate evolutionary materialism. Even a religious scholar as accomplished as Huston Smith weakens his case against naturalism when his anti-Darwinist polemic needlessly discards carefully gathered biological information.[2] Understandably, good scientists and other informed readers dismiss such criticism as not deserving a second look.

I believe there is an urgent need today for sensible alternatives to naturalistic belief, but they will never be effective as long as they edit defensively whatever seems *prima facie* religiously or theologically offensive in the accumulating mound of scientific information. In this book I shall lay out what I consider to be a reasonable, scientifically informed alternative to naturalism. It may seem that the two stanzas quoted above are contradictory, but I will try to show how they can be smoothly mapped onto each other without straining either science or religion. My approach will be to embrace the results of scientific research while simultaneously raising questions about scientific naturalism. I do so with the deepest respect for the body of established scientific knowledge as well as religious affirmations of ultimate meaning.

---

[2] Huston Smith, *Why Religion Matters: the Fate of Human Spirit in an Age of Disbelief* (New York: HarperCollins, 2001), pp. 75–78, 103–12, 178–82.

1 Is nature enough?

At the beginning of his popular *Cosmos* television series scientist and author Carl Sagan declared that "the universe is all that is, all there ever was and all there ever will be."[1] Sagan was a proponent of *naturalism*, the belief that nothing exists beyond the world available to our senses. There is no God, and hence no creative source of the world's existence other than nature itself. Nature, a term derived from the Latin word "to give birth," is self-generating. Nature is quite enough all by itself, and religions professing belief in God or gods are fictitious distractions at best.

To its adherents naturalism is not only intellectually satisfying but also emotionally liberating. It is a breath of fresh air in a world made stale by the obsessive recitations of religion. Naturalism boldly turns our attention toward the immensities of this world even as it embeds us within the cosmic processes that gave birth to life. It rescues adventurous souls from what they take to be the backwardness, irrelevance and oppressiveness of traditional forms of spirituality. Naturalism also has the advantage – or so it would seem – of being completely reconcilable with science.

Naturalism comes in many flavors, but the focus here will be on the specific variety known as scientific naturalism. Scientific naturalism assumes not only that nature is all there is but also that science is the only reliable way to understand it. This latter belief is commonly called "scientism." Scientism, the epistemic soul of scientific naturalism, claims that the experimental method that came to

[1] Carl Sagan, *Cosmos* (New York: Ballantine Books, 1985), p. 1. An earlier version of my reflections on Sagan's claim appears in "Is Nature Enough? No," *Zygon: Journal of Science and Religion* 38 (December, 2003), 769–82.

prominence in the modern period is sufficient to tell us everything factual about the universe. It is convinced that all religious visions of nature and humanity are now superseded by a superior way of understanding. Scientism does not always insist that science will answer every important question, but that it has a better chance of doing so than religion ever will. According to Richard Dawkins, one of the world's most noteworthy scientific naturalists, "it may be that humanity will never reach the quietus of complete understanding, but if we do, I venture the confident prediction that it will be science, not religion, that brings us there. And if that sounds like scientism, so much the better for scientism."[2]

The label "scientific naturalism" is apparently the invention of Charles Darwin's famous advocate Thomas H. Huxley (1825–95).[3] Although for Huxley scientific naturalism may have been more a method of inquiry than a worldview, this restraint is no longer always present. Today the term "naturalism" refers generally to a worldview that questions the existence of anything in principle inaccessible to ordinary experience or science. In fact, many scientific naturalists are now avowed atheists, although some, like Huxley, prefer to be called agnostics. Scientific naturalists, in any case, question whether complete understanding of the world requires reference to a creator or divine action. It seems more likely to them that nature is its own originator and that natural process is the sole author of life and mind as well. Life appeared by accident, as a purely physical occurrence, and then evolution took over. Random genetic changes, natural selection and an enormous amount of time have been enough to cook up all the diversity and complexity of life, including beings endowed

---

[2]   Richard Dawkins, "The Science of Religion and the Religion of Science," *Tanner Lecture on Human Values at Harvard University* (November 20, 2003). Cited on the *Science and Theology* website: http://www.stnews.org/archives/2004_february/ web_x_richard.html.

[3]   Ronald Numbers, "Science without God: Natural Laws and Christian Belief," in *When Science and Christianity Meet*, edited by David C. Lindberg and Ronald Numbers (Chicago: University of Chicago Press, 2003), p. 266.

with minds. Why then would reasonable people want to look beyond nature, or resort to theology, in order to understand things and events?

Richard Dawkins, going far beyond Huxley in the defense of naturalism, argues that deep cosmic time and blind evolutionary mechanisms are enough to explain life in all its complexity. In *Climbing Mount Improbable* the renowned evolutionist cleverly pictures life on earth as having made its way up a figurative mountain of time. On one side the mountain rises straight up from the plain below, while on the other it slopes gently from bottom to top. It is up the sloped side that life has made its long evolutionary ascent. If life had available to it only a biblical time-slot of several thousand years to mount the vertical side, a miraculous boost would have been needed to produce anything as complex as the eye or human brain so quickly. Natural explanations therefore would not be enough. But if the story of life in fact takes place very gradually, on a path moving back and forth up the gentler slope incrementally over a period of four billion years, then no supernatural assistance is required. Minute changes, together with the relentless weeding out of nonadaptive variations by natural selection in the course of *deep time*, are enough to account for the extraordinary variety and complexity of life. Nature, it would appear, is quite enough.[4]

The present book will be examining the claim that nature is all there is and that science is sufficient to understand it. It will be asking especially whether scientific naturalism is rationally coherent. I want to emphasize, however, that scientific naturalism is not by any means the same thing as science. Science is a fruitful but self-limiting way of learning some things about the world, whereas scientific naturalism is a worldview that goes far beyond verifiable knowledge by insisting on the explanatory adequacy of scientific method. Most reflective scientific naturalists will concede

[4] Richard Dawkins, *Climbing Mount Improbable* (New York: W. W. Norton & Co., 1996), pp. 3–37.

that they are indeed advocating a certain kind of belief, but they would add that their understanding of the world is still much more reasonable and fertile than any others. Indeed, for many inquirers today, scientific naturalism is the undebatable starting point for all reliable knowledge of anything whatsoever.

But does scientific naturalism hold up under careful scrutiny? I shall not be challenging science itself as a *method* of investigating the universe. As far as science itself is concerned, nature is indeed all there is. I agree with scientific naturalists that one should never introduce ideas about God, "intelligent design" or divine action into scientific work itself. As a theologian, I am happy to accept methodological naturalism as the way science works. But suppose there are dimensions of reality that science cannot reach. If there are, then scientific naturalism – the belief that scientifically knowable nature alone is real – is unreasonable since it arbitrarily cuts off access to any such precincts. And if scientific naturalism turns out to be at bottom an irrational set of beliefs, then the universe available to science may not be "all that is, all there ever was, or all there ever will be."

In addition to science there are other reliable ways of putting our minds, and hearts too, in touch with the real world. There may even be deep layers of the real world that we can see or encounter only by cultivating modes of exploration and cognitional habits that are not opposed to science but that are not themselves part of science. Is it possible that religion, even with all its perplexity and failings, still provides at least a dimly lit passage into depths of reality unapproachable by science?

IS NATURALISM SPIRITUALLY ADEQUATE?

There are, as I have noted, different kinds of naturalism. For example, one may distinguish between hard naturalism and soft naturalism.[5] Hard naturalism is roughly equivalent to scientific materialism. It

---

[5]   Holmes Rolston, III, *Science and Religion: a Critical Survey* (New York: Random House), pp. 247–58.

rules out the existence of anything nonphysical. Soft naturalism, on the other hand, allows that there may be aspects of the real world that hard naturalism leaves out. It proposes that nature consists of complex systems and organic wholes that cannot be accounted for exclusively in terms of their physical antecedents or atomic components. It suggests that "emergent" rules come into play spontaneously as the universe evolves in complexity. Yet these new ordering principles are in no way mystical or in need of theological explanation. They are simply phases of natural process.

A few soft naturalists like to be called *religious* naturalists. Religious naturalists do not believe that anything exists beyond the world of nature, but they often use religious terminology – words such as mystery and sacred – to express their sense that nature by itself is deserving of a reverential surrender of the mind.[6] Still, even to religious naturalists nature is all that exists. In philosophical discourse today the term "naturalism" generally signifies a godless view of the universe. For example, when the philosopher Owen Flanagan states that the mission of contemporary philosophy is to make the world safe for "naturalism," he clearly means safe for atheism.[7] More often than not the term "naturalism" entails the explicit rejection of the personal God of Judaism, Christianity and Islam. It means the denial of any sacred principle of being that is distinct from nature itself.[8]

There are still other ways of understanding naturalism, but most of them adhere minimally to the following core teachings:[9]

---

[6] Ursula Goodenough, *The Sacred Depths of Nature* (New York: Oxford University Press, 1998); Chet Raymo, *Skeptics and True Believers: the Exhilarating Connection between Science and Religion* (New York: Walker and Company, 1998). There are also soft forms of naturalism that seek an alliance with theistic religion. See, for example, David R. Griffin, *Reenchantment without Supernaturalism: a Process Philosophy of Religion* (Ithaca, N.Y.: Cornell University Press, 2001).

[7] Owen Flanagan, *The Problem of the Soul: Two Visions of Mind and How to Reconcile Them* (New York: Basic Books, 2002), pp. 167–68.

[8] This is the sense in which C. S. Lewis, for instance, understands naturalism in his passionate critique of it in *Miracles* (San Francisco: HarperSanFrancisco, 2001).

[9] This is an adaptation and expansion of Charley Hardwick's understanding of naturalism in *Events of Grace: Naturalism, Existentialism, and Theology* (Cambridge: Cambridge University Press, 1996).

1. Outside nature, which includes humans and their cultural creations, there is nothing.
2. It follows from #1 that nature is self-originating.
3. Since there is nothing beyond nature, there can be no overarching purpose or transcendent goal that would give any lasting meaning to the universe.
4. There is no such thing as the "soul," and no reasonable prospect of conscious human survival beyond death.
5. The emergence of life and mind in evolution was accidental and unintended.

What I am calling "scientific naturalism" accepts these five tenets, but adds two more:

6. Every natural event is itself the product of other natural events. Since there is no divine cause, all causes must be purely natural causes, in principle accessible to scientific comprehension.
7. All the various features of living beings, including humans, can be explained ultimately in evolutionary, specifically Darwinian, terms. I shall often refer to this belief as "evolutionary naturalism."

From now on I shall use the labels "naturalism" and "scientific naturalism" interchangeably unless otherwise indicated.

As I said earlier, I want to ask whether naturalism is a reasonable set of beliefs. Before beginning my reply to this question, however, I need to raise another. It concerns naturalism's *spiritual* adequacy. Can naturalism respond fully, in other words, to the human quest for meaning? Not all naturalists would consider this to be a relevant question, but it needs to be asked since they themselves sometimes claim that nature is quite enough to give our lives meaning as well as intellectual satisfaction.[10] Consort with nature, they insist, is *spiritually* adequate for humans. Some of the most

---

[10] See, for example, Flanagan, *The Problem of the Soul* and Goodenough, *The Sacred Depths of Nature.*

entrenched naturalists now admit that we humans possess ineradicably spiritual instincts as part of our genetic endowment. That is, we are meaning-seeking beings designed by evolution to seek communion with what is larger than ourselves. Our spiritual instincts need to be satisfied, and that is why our species has been so stubbornly religious, perhaps from the very beginning of the human journey on earth. So why cannot naturalism, a full-fledged belief system of its own, satisfy our native religious cravings for fulfillment? Is not nature itself resourceful enough to bring meaning, happiness and personal satisfaction to our brief life spans? Many naturalists, I have observed, are passionately religious, and their disillusionment with traditional creeds is often the expression of an abundance, not an absence, of spiritual longing.

Within the assembly of naturalists, however, some are sunny and optimistic – these are the religious naturalists – while others are more sober and pessimistic. Sunny naturalists hold that nature's overwhelming beauty, the excitement of human creativity, the struggle to achieve ethical goodness, the prospect of loving and being loved, the exhilaration of scientific discovery – these are enough to fill a person's life. There is simply no good reason to look beyond nature for spiritual contentment. Sober naturalists, on the other hand, are not so sanguine. They agree that nature is all there is, but for them nature is *not* resourceful enough to satisfy the voracious human hunger for meaning and happiness. In fact, they say, our species' religious appetites can never be satisfied since the finite universe is devoid of any discernible meaning, as cosmology and Darwinian science both now seem to confirm. If the universe is all there is, and if it is therefore devoid of purpose, then one must conclude that nature is *not enough* to fill our restless human hearts with the meaning we long for.

A literate representative of sober naturalism is the French writer Albert Camus. This famous novelist and philosopher freely acknowledges that humans have an insatiable appetite for ultimate meaning and eternal happiness. It would be dishonest, he says, to deny it. The hard fact, however, is that the universe can never satisfy such a craving. Eventually the world and each of us will end up in complete annihilation. If death is the final destination of all life, and if God and immortality do not exist – as for Camus they do not – then reality is absurd. Absurdity here means the incongruous union of a death-dealing universe on the one hand and the human passion for life on the other. Since these two sectors of reality will never mesh, their fatal conjunction is the very definition of irrationality. Moreover, no hope can ever surmount this situation. Hence the hero of the human condition is Sisyphus, the exemplar of all striving in the face of futility.[11]

A more scientific representative of sober naturalism is the physicist Steven Weinberg. In *Dreams of a Final Theory* he writes:

> It would be wonderful to find in the laws of nature a plan
> prepared by a concerned creator in which human beings played
> some special role. I find sadness in doubting that we will. There are
> some among my scientific colleagues who say that the contem-
> plation of nature gives them all the spiritual satisfaction that
> others have found in a belief in an interested God. Some of them
> may even feel that way. I do not.[12]

Like Camus, Weinberg takes seriously the question of God, and he is distressed that science has made atheism the only reasonable option today. Science provides no evidence of a purposeful universe, so the most one can salvage from our unhappy predicament is a sense of honor in facing up to the finality of tragedy.[13] Weinberg wants nothing to do with sunny naturalism and its shallow compromises with the bitter truth of our actual situation.

Were I to become a naturalist I confess that I would have to side, simply for the sake of logic, with the sober rather than the sunny

---

[11]   Albert Camus, *The Myth of Sisyphus, and Other Essays*, translated by Justin O'Brien
        (New York: Knopf, 1955), pp. 88–91.
[12]   Steven Weinberg, *Dreams of a Final Theory* (New York: Pantheon Books, 1992), p. 256.
[13]   Ibid., pp. 255, 260.

version. Sober naturalism is at least less cavalier about what all naturalists must acknowledge to be the ultimate truth about the universe and the human condition. As far as naturalism can tell, after all, science has shown the universe to be devoid of meaning. Is it candid, the sober naturalist asks, to pretend that humans could ever find lasting personal fulfillment in a pointless cosmos? If the option were forced, should not a concern for intellectual integrity lead one to take sides with the tragic realism of Camus and Weinberg rather than the groundless optimism of the more sprightly variety of naturalism? Fortunately, as I shall argue at length, there is a reasonable alternative to both sober and sunny naturalism.

The fact that naturalism is spiritually disproportionate to the fact of tragedy, of course, does not make it untrue. Let us concede for the moment that the tenets of naturalism listed above are indeed accurate. But if they are, then the philosopher John Hick is correct in pointing out that naturalism "is very bad news for humanity as a whole."[14] The physical pain, poverty and unbearable suffering of most people throughout history keep them from ever fulfilling their hopes within the limits of nature alone. "Even those who have lived the longest can seldom be said to have arrived, before they die, at a fulfillment of their potential." Naturalists, therefore, are hiding from the truth unless "they acknowledge the fact that naturalism is not good news for much of humanity."[15]

Hick is convinced that, whatever their truth-status, the classic religious traditions can rightly claim to respond to the deepest spiritual aspirations of people:

> We human beings are for so much of the time selfish, narrow-minded, emotionally impoverished, unconcerned about others, often vicious and cruel, but according to the great religions there are wonderfully better possibilities concealed within us . . . We see

---

[14] John Hick, *The Fifth Dimension: an Exploration of the Spiritual Realm* (Oxford: Oneworld Press, 1999), p. 22.

[15] Ibid., p. 24.

around us the different levels that the human spirit has reached, and we know . . . that the generality of us have a very long way to go before we can be said to have become fully human. But if the naturalistic picture is correct, this can never happen. For according to naturalism, the evil that has afflicted so much of human life is final and irrevocable as the victims have ceased to exist.[16]

Naturalists, therefore, need to be rigorously honest:

> [they] ought frankly to acknowledge that if they are right the human situation is irredeemably bleak and painful for vast numbers of people. For – if they are right – in the case of that innumerable multitude whose quality of life has been rendered predominantly negative by pain, anxiety, extreme deprivation, oppression, or whose lives have been cut off in childhood or youth, there is no chance of ever participating in an eventual fulfillment of the human potential. There is no possibility of this vast century-upon-century tragedy being part of a much larger process which leads ultimately to limitless good.[17]

IS NATURALISM REASONABLE?

Even if naturalism turns out to be spiritually inadequate, however, this alone does not make it untrue, as Hick would surely agree. But is naturalism true? That is, does it meet the human mind's best standards of understanding and knowing? Can naturalism, even in principle, ever provide an ultimately satisfying framework for making sense of every natural occurrence? Or does human reason have to appeal, at some point in its attempt to make *complete* sense of things, to something deeper than the natural world itself, something beyond the ambience of science?

Are naturalistic explanations ever going to be enough to explain *ultimately* why the universe would give rise to life, mind,

---

[16]   Ibid.   [17]   Ibid., pp. 24–25.

ethics, religion and scientific inquiry? Granted, science can say a lot about all of these, but can it say everything? Can one ever be certain that all causes are natural causes? Can science, for example, explain why there is anything at all rather than nothing? Even the astronomer Martin Rees, a devotee of scientific naturalism, places this big question outside the competence of science.[18] If there is nothing that lies beyond or deeper than the scientifically accessible world, then of course natural causes would be the ultimate and exhaustive explanation of everything. Scientific understanding would then amount to final or ultimate enlightenment. There would be no logical space left for theological interpretations of reality, and theology would stand in a competitive relationship to science. In such a set of circumstances it would be best for theology to fade away for good, an outcome that many naturalists fervently desire.

Fortified by the success of science, contemporary naturalists are confident that we can discover in nature alone the sufficient explanation of everything. Life can be completely broken down into chemical terms. Mind is the outcome of natural selection (Cziko). Language (Pinker), ethics (Ruse and Wilson) and even religion (Hinde, Boyer, Atran) can be understood fully in naturalistic terms.[19] Given the fact that naturalists deny the existence of anything other than nature, they are compelled logically to maintain that natural causes provide the final explanation of everything, including intellectual, ethical and religious phenomena. But can naturalism give an ultimate explanation of anything, let alone everything?

---

[18]   Martin Rees, *Our Cosmic Habitat* (Princeton: Princeton University Press, 2003), p. xi.
[19]   Gary Cziko, *Without Miracles: Universal Selection Theory and the Second Darwinian Revolution* (Cambridge, Mass.: MIT Press, 1995); Steven Pinker, *The Blank Slate: the Modern Denial of Human Nature* (New York: Viking, 2002); Michael Ruse and Edward O. Wilson, "The Evolution of Ethics," in *Religion and the Natural Sciences*, edited by James Huchingson (New York: Harcourt Brace Jovanovich, 1993), pp. 308–11; Robert Hinde, *Why Gods Persist: a Scientific Approach to Religions* (New York: Routledge, 1999); Pascal Boyer, *Religion Explained: the Evolutionary Origins of Religious Thought* (New York: Basic Books, 2001); Scott Atran, *In Gods We Trust: the Evolutionary Landscape of Religion* (New York: Oxford University Press, 2002).

Many evolutionists think it can. Today naturalistic confidence flourishes especially among Darwinians. Evolutionary naturalists are certain that the neo-Darwinian recipe – random (contingent) genetic changes (and other natural accidents) plus natural selection, along with a considerable amount of time to experiment – can account entirely for all the features of living beings. Is this confidence justifiable? As a theologian I am eager to have science push evolutionary understanding as far as it can legitimately go. And I agree that evolutionary science has to be an aspect of every serious attempt to understand life, consciousness, ethics and even religion. But are evolutionary explanations enough?

For example, beneath life's evolution there is the larger universe that consists of an exquisite blend of contingent unpredictability, lawful necessity and eons of time, features of nature that Darwinism appeals to but does not and cannot account for by itself. Life's evolution jumps astride this foundational cosmic mix. The essential ingredients for evolution had been laid out on the cosmic table long before life began to stew. Darwinism presupposes a specific cosmic setting, but it does not provide the grounds for it. The physical sciences may have something to say about this cosmic tableau, of course, but even after they are finished, the question will still remain: why is the universe such an exciting, adventurous mix of contingency, predictability and temporality that it can give rise to an evolutionary story at all? Why does the world remain open constantly to a new future? Why does it give rise to subjectivity, feeling and striving? Why does it eventually give birth to an insatiable passion for knowledge? And, of course, why does nature exist at all? Perhaps theology may have at least something to say in response to these questions without in the slightest way interfering or competing with scientific inquiry.

Darwinian naturalists, of course, will protest. Before Darwin came along appeals to theology might have been excusable, they admit, but does not evolutionary biology now provide science with the tools to get to the *ultimate* explanation of living phenomena without having to take flight into the superlunary world of religious understanding?

We shall see. But before going any further, I hope we may at least agree that in the final analysis there can be only one *ultimate* explanation of anything, whereas there can be many intermediate or secondary explanations. Darwinian explanations, I will argue, are intermediate, not ultimate. Naturalists put too heavy a burden on evolutionary science whenever they turn it into ultimate explanation. What I shall propose instead, as a way of giving a place to both science and religion, is *layered explanation*. By this I mean that everything in the universe is open to a plurality of levels of explanation. The alternative to layered explanation, or to explanatory pluralism, is explanatory monism, an approach dear to the heart of most naturalists.

Here is an example of what I mean by layered explanation. Suppose that a wood fire is burning in your backyard. Your neighbor comes over and asks you to explain why the fire is burning. A very good response would be: it is burning because the carbon in the wood is combining with oxygen to make carbon dioxide. This is an acceptable explanation, and for a certain kind of inquiry it is enough. Still, there can be other levels of explanation. For example, you might just as easily have answered your neighbor's question by saying: the fire is burning because I lit a match to it.

And a third answer might be: "The fire is burning because I want to roast marshmallows." Different levels of explanation, as is evident here, can coexist without conflict. "I want to roast marshmallows" does not in any way compete with physical explanations of the burning wood. I do not respond to my neighbor: "The fire is burning because of chemical combustion *rather than* because I want marshmallows." "I want to roast marshmallows," in fact, cannot be squeezed into the explanatory slot that focuses on the chemistry of combustion. And yet, there is no inherent contradiction between the chemistry of combustion and my overarching purpose of wanting something to eat.

Analogously, let us suppose that there is an ultimate reality which for some mysterious reason wants to create a life-bearing universe. We should not expect this divine intentionality to show up within a physical analysis of nature – including scientific speculations on the Big Bang and the origin of life – any more than we should expect to find "I want marshmallows" inscribed on the burning wood or molecules of carbon dioxide. And yet, it is just such direct "evidence" that scientific naturalists almost invariably demand from those who adopt a theological understanding of the universe. The usual reason naturalists give for their opposition to theology is that there is no "evidence" to support the latter's claims. The assumption is that if there were a deeper than natural explanation, it would still have to be *scientifically* available. And since it does not show up at that layer of explanation, it must not exist. Underlying this judgment, of course, is the more fundamental naturalistic assumption that there is really only a single legitimate explanatory slot available, one carved out to fit the contours of scientific method. So, if scientific discoveries now fill this niche, there is no room left over for theology.

Reasonable theology, however, allows for many layers of explanation. It argues that divine action or divine creativity stands in relation to nature – to such occurrences as the emergence of the cosmos, life, mind, ethics and religion – analogously to the way in which "I want marshmallows" stands in relation to the chemistry of burning firewood. It can embrace both Isaac Watts' and Kenneth Boulding's versions of the causes of natural events (see Introduction). It is not a case of God *rather than* nature. It is both. The ultimate explanation of natural phenomena will necessarily be hidden from view when science is focusing on physical explanations. Analogously, even the most painstaking investigation of the molecular movement in the fire will not reveal, at that physical level of scrutiny, the "ultimate" reason why the fire is burning. Likewise, even the most detailed scientific examination of natural processes may not be able to discover, nor indeed rule out, any more profound reason why the universe, life, mind, language, ethics, religion and scientific inquiry have come into existence. There is still plenty of room, logically speaking, for a theological understanding of the natural world alongside scientific accounts.

Of course, the naturalist will immediately reply that my desire for marshmallows can also be accounted for fully in terms of the mindless chemistry that underlies my brain and nervous system. For many a naturalist there can be only one level of explanation, and it must be purely physical at bottom. If this were the case, however, there would be no reason to take the criticism seriously, emanating as it does ultimately from the allegedly mindless physical causes that underlie the brain of my critic. The naturalistic view of reality, if taken consistently, leads to the self-subverting of all truth claims, including those of science. More on this later.

My wager in this book, then, is that adequate explanation runs endlessly deep and involves many levels. No one science, or even the whole set of sciences, can ever comprehend the rich *totality* of causal ingredients that underlie each cosmic event. Every branch of science, after all, works on the tacit premise that it does not have to account fully for everything. Each field of scientific inquiry, for the sake of clarity, has to leave something out. In fact, the individual sciences can reach toward exactness only by *abstracting from* most of nature's causal depth. The real world is fuzzy and indistinct, so achieving Cartesian clarity in scientific thinking is not a sign that one has arrived at deep understanding.[20] Conversely, the deepest explanations – precisely because they leave less out – will inevitably be the least clear and distinct. This is why theological explanations will always have a vagueness that frustrates the scientific naturalist.

Naturalism (once again, a term that I am using interchangeably with "scientific naturalism" throughout the book) typically insists that ultimate explanation be clear and distinct. In doing so, its devotees often appeal to the idea of Occam's razor, which asserts that

---

[20] Alfred North Whitehead, *Process and Reality*, corrected edition, edited by David Ray Griffin and Donald W. Sherburne (New York: The Free Press, 1978), p. 173.

explanations should not be multiplied without necessity. Accordingly, since Darwin's recipe can explain life, mind, behavior, language, ethics, religion, and so on, simply in terms of natural selection, the naturalist declares that there is no need to appeal to the obscure notion of an unseen divine creativity or purposiveness in order to make ultimate sense of these fascinating developments.

The promise of explaining all the great "mysteries" of life in terms of the economical notion of reproductive success is hard to resist. It has led to the cult of "universal Darwinism" and the belief that natural selection is the bottommost foundation of all the manifestations of life. This exclusionary singleness of mind, however, may be compared to explaining the fire in my backyard by leaving out as completely irrelevant the fact that "I want marshmallows." If we can reach a *simpler* explanation at the level of the fire's chemistry, why bring in the fuzzy idea that I would like something to eat? If one can explain why we have ears, eyes and brains in terms of natural selection, why bring up the possibility that a transcendent creative principle of care wants the universe to become sensitive, conscious and responsive? Would not such a proposal violate Occam's razor?

Occam's razor, I must point out, was never intended to suppress layered explanation as such, even though this is exactly how naturalists often tend to slice up the world with it. If life were as simple as evolutionary naturalists think it is, then of course Darwinian explanation would be adequate. Theological explanations of life would be superfluous. But William of Occam said that explanations should not be multiplied *unless they are necessary*. Sometimes multiple layers of explanation are necessary for deep understanding. So there is no justification, either in Occam's maxim or in science itself, for arbitrarily closing off the road to explanatory depth.

In the following pages I will attempt to show, by way of a number of examples, that the human mind must look beyond nature, as understood by science, in order to make *ultimate* sense of the world and ourselves. It is not the business of science, but of theology (or religious thought in a broader sense) to look for ultimate explanations.

In order to substantiate this claim, most of the following chapters will contain essentially three major elements, though not always placed in the same sequence: they will examine briefly some easily accessible feature of our world as known by immediate experience or by science; they will summarize what this phenomenon looks like from the point of view of scientific naturalism; and they will question whether a purely naturalistic understanding can ever lead to the fullest possible understanding of the particular phenomenon in question.

I will not lay out a series of arguments for the existence of God, nor try to make the idea of God function as an explanation in slots that belong appropriately to science. In fact, as one who is deeply appreciative of science, I shall persistently propose that we push scientific accounts as far as they can take us. However, I believe they can take us only so far. If its practitioners attempt to turn science into ultimate explanation – which is exactly what scientific naturalism attempts to do – science becomes twisted into a belief system that can only stand in a competitive relationship with other belief systems. This predicament in turn leads to senseless battles that often end up marginalizing science, especially in cultures or subcultures where belief in God is dominant. I believe that science will have an effective future only so long as it remains free from naturalistic attempts to make it function as fundamental or final explanation.

2 Religion

> There is communion with God, and communion with the earth, and
> communion with God through the earth.
>
> Pierre Teilhard de Chardin[1]

If nature is not all there is, then what else is there, and how do we
know about it? Religions are convinced that there is more, indeed
infinitely more, but they tell us we can know about it only if we are
disposed to receive it. The infinitely "more" cannot be known in the
same way that ordinary objects are known. In fact, religion is less a
matter of knowing than of being known. It is a state of being grasped
rather than of grasping. Not every person is ready for religion, and
even self-avowed religious believers cannot truthfully claim to be
ready for it most of the time. Indeed, much of what we usually call
religious life consists of avoiding or running away from the demands
of religion. Religious understanding – as most theologians see it – is
impossible without surrender, worship and prayerful waiting, along
with struggle and frustration. Yet, to those who wait, the rewards can
be peace and joy, as well as profound intellectual satisfaction.

Religion, at least in any conventional sense, cannot get along
with scientific naturalism, but it can get along quite well with science. Science deals with what can be sensed, or at least what can be
inferred from sensation. Religion is based in experience too, but of a
different kind from science. Religious people testify to having felt,
beneath all sensible appearances, the very real presence of an elusive
mystery that takes hold of them, invites them, sometimes unsettles
them and often reorients their lives. They profess to having been
carried away, as it were, by something "more" than nature. Their

[1]   Pierre Teilhard de Chardin, *Writings in Time of War*. translated by René Hague (New
York: Harper & Row, 1968), p. 14.

sense of a mysterious presence beyond the world, beneath the surface of life, or in the depths of the universe, evokes responses of vague anxiety mixed sometimes with overwhelming excitement and the impulse to worship. Religion often also involves the encounter with unseen agents, powers and personalities, but these are experienced as emerging out of the background of a more fundamental transcendent mystery. Religion, taken here in a very broad sense, is a *conscious appreciation of and response to the mystery that grounds, embraces and transcends both nature and ourselves.* There are other ways of defining religion, of course, but the issues raised by scientific naturalism have to do especially with religion's bold claims that there is *more* than nature, and a good name for this *more* is "mystery."

Religion, therefore, means that the universe available to science and ordinary experience is *not* "all that is, all there ever was, and all there ever will be." To most religious persons there is something *other* than the physical universe. This mysterious presence is not separate from the universe, but it is not identical with it either. It simultaneously penetrates, encircles, grounds and enlivens nature without being reducible to nature. Religions are convinced that reality does not end at the limits of nature, but instead includes an incomprehensible dimension that extends beyond the scientifically knowable world. The infinite scope of mystery provides religious devotees with a permanent reason for hope and a sense of freedom. It allows for limitless breathing room in the face of nature's obvious constraints and ultimate perishability.

It is especially those whose thoughts and passions reach toward infinite mystery who are most prone to feel imprisoned by naturalistic doctrine. Religious believers, unlike naturalists, do not look to nature for either ultimate fulfillment or ultimate explanation. Still, a wholesome communion with ultimate reality can take place *through* nature. Healthy religion is gratefully aware of the riches of life and the resourcefulness of the natural world. It is appreciative of science as well. But it also senses that nature imposes obvious limits on life, most notably suffering and death. Religion then is a kind of route-finding that looks for pathways beyond the boundaries that nature places on life.[2]

It is imperative that naturalists be fully sensitive to this point even if they vehemently disagree with it. Religious persons may turn out to be wrong, but clearly they are seeking ways to get beyond what they take to be the natural limits on life. This does not mean that they have to despise the world – although in some cases they do – but that they relativize it. They do not take nature to be ultimate nor do they see science as ultimate explanation. Characteristically, no matter how large science has shown the universe to be, religious people look upon the claim that "nature is enough" as itself an arbitrary confinement that they must get beyond.

To religious ears, including those attuned to the monumental scale of contemporary cosmology, the assertion that "nature is enough" sounds like a prison sentence. This is because religious awareness generally involves a sense that the human mind (or spirit) has already transcended the limits of nature, not finally or decisively, but at least by *anticipation*. In the next chapter I will show that human intelligence, in spite of all attempts to understand it naturalistically, extends itself beyond the limits of nature in every act of questioning, understanding and judging. Religion is inseparable from the intellect's anticipation of an infinite fullness of being. In biblical circles religious anticipation of this fullness of being takes the form of *hope*. So, to those who hope for final transcendence of death and suffering, naturalism is the most dreary and suffocating of dogmas. Instead of limitless horizons, naturalism offers only an ultimate captivity, unbearable to those who sense that at the core of their being they are *capax infiniti* – open to the infinite.

Of course, to the naturalist, religion is fully part of nature and, like everything else, it must submit to being explained naturalistically.

---

2   John Bowker, *Is Anybody out There?* (Westminster, Md.: Christian Classics, Inc., 1988), pp. 9–18, 112–43.

There must be a purely scientific answer to the question of why so many humans have longed for the infinite and thereby experienced nature as a limit. To many naturalists these days it is evolutionary biology that seems best equipped to provide the deepest account of humanity's persistent religious tendencies. If evolutionists can come up with a purely natural explanation of the habit that religious believers have of looking toward limitless horizons, then this will supposedly expose infinite mystery itself as empty fiction rather than ultimate reality. And the most efficient way to disabuse religious people of the illusion that there is anything beyond the limits of nature, therefore, is to explain in purely scientific terms how that illusion could have arisen in the first place. Nowadays Darwin's idea of natural selection, brought up to date by genetics, seems to provide the best, perhaps even the ultimate, explanation of the human conviction that reality overflows nature's boundaries.

Naturalists today often attempt to explain not only religion but also morality in Darwinian terms (see chapter 9). There was a time not long ago when the moral instincts of people seemed to be the best evidence for God's existence. Indeed, moral aspiration was a clear indication of the direct imprint of a transcendent divine goodness on each soul; and conscience was the stamp of God's will on the inner core of each personality. Hints of an infinite perfection could be found in the insatiable anticipation of goodness, truth and beauty that drives the questing human heart. Humans were said to be restless only because infinite goodness, truth and beauty had already tacitly entered into their moral, intellectual and aesthetic sensibilities.

The scientific naturalist, however, will have none of this, at times even rebuking religious people for being so "greedy" as to look for fulfillment beyond the limits of nature. In a book whose every page chastises those of us with cloudier images of reality than his own, the philosopher Owen Flanagan asserts that there is nothing beyond what scientific naturalism is able to discern. How he knows this he does not say, but he is certain that people who look beyond nature for fulfillment "are still in the grip of illusions." "Trust me," he says, "you can't get more. But what you can get, if you live well, is enough. Don't be greedy. Enough is enough."[3]

My own work brings me into contact with many good scientists and philosophers from all over the world. Some are religious, but many others are naturalists like Flanagan. Naturalism is now so entrenched in science and philosophical faculties around the globe that it constitutes one of the most influential "creeds" operative in the world today. Scientific naturalists are still a small minority in the world's overall population, but their influence is out of all proportion to their numbers. Generally speaking, their beliefs quietly determine what is intellectually acceptable in many of our universities. Naturalism has now spread from science and philosophy departments into social studies and the humanities. Even departments of religion are no longer immune.

The academic world now harbors numerous scientific naturalists who prefer to keep a low profile in order to avoid controversy wherever religion is considered important. Flanagan wants them to come clean. Likewise the Pulitzer Prize-winning science writer Natalie Angier believes that most scientists are closet naturalists but are reluctant to state openly what they really think about religion and theology. In a recent issue of *The American Scholar* she cites studies showing that as many as 90 percent of the members of the elite National Academy of Sciences are nontheists, and less than half of other scientists believe in a personal God. She upbraids scientists for not being more vocal in criticizing the "irrationalities" of religion in all of its forms. Most scientists are no longer afraid to state publicly that Darwinism has made creationism obsolete, but Angier is annoyed that they pass over in silence the larger body of religious illusions. In her own opinion the entire history of human religiousness is a preposterous mistake – since there is no

---

[3] Owen Flanagan, *The Problem of the Soul: Two Visions of Mind and How to Reconcile Them* (New York: Basic Books, 2002), p. 319.

scientific evidence for its empty musings. She is agitated that most scientists refuse to wear their *de facto* naturalism on their sleeves.[4]

It is annoying to scientific naturalists such as Flanagan and Angier that religious people cannot come up with "evidence" for what they take to be more than nature. But to religious experience this "more" will always be something that grasps us rather than something we can grasp. We can know it only by surrender, not possession. It will never have the clarity of scientific evidence, nor should it be presented as an alternative to science. The most immediate "evidence" for it is the fact of our own anticipation of more truth, deeper goodness and wider beauty, an insatiable reaching out toward a fullness of being that is by no means illusory but instead the very core of our rationality. Biblical religions refer to this transcendent dimension as God. And they think of God as possessing the most noble of attributes: infinite goodness and love, unsurpassable beauty and splendor, the fullness of being and truth. God is also the epitome of fidelity, creativity, freedom, healing, wisdom and power. As one who allegedly makes and keeps promises, this God is also understood to be "personal" as well, since only persons can love and make promises.

Naturalists, on the other hand, consider such a belief untenable, especially after Darwin. To them the universe is at heart utterly impersonal. Their persistent question is: where is the *evidence* for God in this imperfect world? Religious people, however, do not usually claim to be able to *see* the mystery of God directly – "nobody can see God and live." God is the light that lights up everything else, but one cannot look directly into that primordial illumination without being blinded. Yet, even though the human person cannot grasp God, many people testify to being grasped by God. For them the powerful sense of being carried away by something of ultimate importance is evidence enough. To take them at their word, they have

---

4   Natalie Angier, "My God Problem – and Theirs," *The American Scholar* 72 (Spring, 2004), 131–34.

surrendered their lives and hearts to an irresistible presence and power that receives them into its compassionate embrace. It is not that they have comprehended the overwhelming divine mystery of beauty, goodness and truth. Rather, they have been comprehended by it. They express their response to this experience in acts of worship, prayer, praise and gratitude, as well as in distinctive ways of living and relating to the world. That this is not wishful thinking can be demonstrated if it turns out that our longing for the infinite is supportive of what I shall call "the desire to know," the very heart of human rationality. Subsequent chapters will develop this proposal.

As Flanagan and Angier illustrate, however, the naturalist ideal is to bring the totality of being out into the clear light of daytime consciousness, so that there is nothing left for religions to talk about. And if theology wants to be respected intellectually, so says the naturalist, it must also adduce the right kind of evidence, namely scientific. This does not necessarily mean that all naturalists demand that God show up among the objects available to empirical inquiry. But there must be visible and unambiguous tracks of divine reality in the natural world if scientifically educated people are to pay any attention to theology. If science comes across anything in nature that cannot be fully explained naturalistically then there might be good reason to invoke the causal powers of a deity. Today, however, naturalists are eager to demonstrate that everything that formerly gave the appearance of being a trace of the divine can now be explained in natural terms. Not only the "apparent" design in living organisms but also the ethical and mystical inclinations of human beings can be "naturalized." And if science can account sufficiently for even the holiest of phenomena, there is no need any more for theology.

THE OUTLINES OF A RESPONSE

The goal of scientific naturalism is to explain everything, insofar as it can be explained at all, in terms of natural processes. This would include the mind itself, which is part of nature. Human intelligence arose by way of a natural process that can be accurately laid out in Darwinian terms. But, as we shall see, the actual performance of human intellection (and later I shall include moral aspiration) is such that it will forever overflow the limits of naturalistic understanding, no matter how detailed scientific understanding becomes in the future. I shall propose that the concrete functioning of intelligence cannot in principle, let alone in fact, be fully captured by the objectifying categories of any science. In other words, the natural sciences cannot account completely for what I shall be calling *critical intelligence*. If this claim turns out to be true, it will be necessary to go beyond naturalism in order to arrive at an adequate understanding of the universe.

In order to present my argument as clearly as I can, I shall be inviting you, the reader, to place yourself in the mindset of the naturalist, even if ordinarily you are not quite at home there. Then I shall ask you, if only as a thought experiment, to try to provide adequate justification *on naturalist premises* for your own mental functioning. I do not believe you can do so in all honesty. As a naturalist you already claim that your mind is fully part of nature. But your naturalistic worldview, as I hope I can lead you to acknowledge, is too restrictive to account fully for your own cognitional activity. And if your mind and your view of nature do not fit each other, then something has to give. My suggestion is not to abandon scientific explanations of mind, but to accept them as intermediate rather than ultimate. By itself science cannot justify the spontaneous trust you have placed in your own mind even as you seek to arrive at scientific truth. To justify your implicit trust in the possibility of arriving at truth, you will need to look for a wider and deeper understanding of the universe, a more expansive worldview, than naturalism has to offer. My proposal is that your own mind's spontaneous and persistent trust in the possibility of reaching truth is itself a hint that the physical universe, at least as naturalism conceives it, is only a small fragment of all that is, all there ever was and all there ever will be.

I shall begin this inquiry by inviting you to look closely at your own experience of critical intelligence (chapter 3). At first this may seem to be a most subjective and anthropocentric way to begin looking at nature, but it is not. My objective throughout the book is that of understanding the universe, not just human consciousness. Every conscious event, after all, is also an event occurring within and not outside the natural world. Science rightly situates the birth of critical intelligence within an unbroken series of natural occurrences, and much can be learned from scientific accounts about the emergence of mind. There is nothing unseemly in explaining mind and even morality and religion, as far as it is possible to do so, in a scientific way. However, once science has locked our minds into the chain of natural events, a close-up examination of human cognition will then stretch the naturalistic understanding of the entire world beyond the breaking point. Only the horizon of infinite being can be the appropriate setting for a universe that harbors critical intelligence.

What naturalism overlooks, and what I shall emphasize instead, is that you can understand the universe in depth only if you take into account, starting with yourself, the subjective "insideness" of nature that science usually leaves out of consideration. A full understanding of the universe is inseparable from the project of coming to terms with your own critical intelligence. By following a few basic ideas of the philosopher Bernard Lonergan I hope to convince you, beginning in the following chapter, that you can reasonably be led beyond the naturalist enclosure into a more encompassing view of reality.[5]

From there this book's reflections will go on to consider a number of other natural phenomena in light of their intrinsic connectedness to critical intelligence. These are: life (chapter 4), emergence

5   Bernard Lonergan, SJ, *Insight: a Study of Human Understanding*, 3rd edn. (New York: Philosophical Library, 1970); Bernard Lonergan, SJ, "Cognitional Structure," *Collection*, edited by F. E. Crowe, SJ (New York: Herder and Herder, 1967), pp. 221–39.

(chapter 5), purposiveness (chapter 6), seeing (chapter 7), the cosmic process (chapter 8), morality (chapter 9), suffering (chapter 10), death (chapter 11) and, in the end, anticipation itself (chapter 12). My proposal is that all of these phenomena can be understood in terms of science, but that after science has finished and even finalized its accounts of them, their natural linkage to critical intelligence demands that we situate the *totality* of natural process within a wider metaphysical setting than science itself is able to lay out.

Finally, I should add that my own proposed alternative to scientific naturalism will not be a simplistic "supernaturalist" worldview, where the infinite and ultimate reality is situated in a realm above, apart from or alongside the created world, essentially untouched by what happens in the cosmos. God is not to be encountered or loved "*above* all things," so much as "*in* and *through* all things."[6] Because of the presence of the infinite in nature, and because nature itself may sometimes give the impression of being infinite, humans can easily be attracted to pantheism, the view that nature *is* God. But the pantheistic identification of nature with God allows no room for anything other than nature. It is no more able to explain, in an ultimate way, intelligence and the other phenomena we shall be looking at than is scientific naturalism.

When I speak in this book of a "theological" understanding of nature I have in mind especially the biblical view of God as a creator who is both distinct from nature and deeply involved with it, a God who makes and keeps promises and is thereby intent on liberating humans and opening up the whole universe to a future of new creation. I embrace the view that God is the creator and savior of the world, but I would emphasize that God creates and saves by calling the world into a new and unprecedented *future*. This God can be approached only by way of anticipation and hope, not as a

---

6   Pierre Teilhard de Chardin, *Toward the Future*, translated by René Hague (New York: Harcourt Brace Jovanovich, 1975), p. 211.

present cognitive or religious possession. But precisely in being known by anticipation, God can function reasonably as the ultimate explanation of nature, and of the life and mind that have emerged in evolution.

Above all, I shall be arguing that only a religiously grounded worldview can provide a suitable domicile for critical intelligence as it actually functions. Scientific naturalism's point of departure in its understanding of everything is the settled past. It explains present phenomena only in terms of what is earlier and simpler. But there is more to nature than such an approach by itself can allow one to see. There is also an *anticipatory* aspect to natural processes, one that you can experience directly in your own cognitional and moral life, but which is also a filament visible at least faintly within natural process considered more generally. In each mind's native openness to the future there lies a gateway to an understanding of dimensions of nature that scientific naturalism characteristically ignores. When understood in terms of its linkage to your own intelligent functioning, each of the specific phenomena subjected to scrutiny in the separate chapters ahead will be shown to have an anticipatory aspect that cannot be fully naturalized, in spite of strong protests to the contrary by scientific naturalists. The anticipatory aspect of nature – most explicitly realized in the human desire to know – requires a general view of reality that will expose the limitations of naturalistic belief. Nature, even in all of its depth and expansiveness, as I hope you will come to see, is not nearly enough.

3 Intelligence

> [W]ith me the horrid doubt always arises whether the convictions of man's mind, which has been developed from the mind of the lower animals, are of any value or at all trustworthy. Would any one trust in the convictions of a monkey's mind, if there are any convictions in such a mind?
>
> Charles Darwin[1]

Is naturalism reasonable? In approaching this question let me assume, for the sake of discussion, that you are a scientific naturalist, and allow me to speak to you directly. As you have been reading this book your mind has been following an invariant sequence of cognitional acts. (1) You have *attended* to and experienced the words and sentences on each page. (2) Then you have tried to *understand* what I am saying, looking for something intelligible. You may or may not have found it so far, but I think you will agree that you have at least attempted to understand my ideas. (3) Finally, if you have understood anything so far, you have probably also asked whether my understanding is correct, or at least whether your own understanding of my ideas is accurate. In either case you have spontaneously subjected your understanding and mine to reflective, critical questioning. And your spirit of criticism may have led you to the *judgment* that I am either right or wrong.[2]

So your mind has spontaneously unfolded in three distinct acts of cognition: experience, understanding and judgment. Since you are capable not only of insight and critical reflection but also of action, you are also called upon at times to make decisions. So *decision* is a fourth cognitional act. I shall say more about decision when we come to the question of whether naturalism can provide an adequate

[1]   Letter to W. Graham, July 3, 1881, *The Life and Letters of Charles Darwin*, edited by Francis Darwin (New York: Basic Books, 1959), p. 285.
[2]   See Bernard Lonergan, SJ, "Cognitional Structure," *Collection*, edited by F. E. Crowe, SJ (New York: Herder and Herder, 1967), pp. 221–39.

account of morality (chapter 9). But for now our focus will be only on the first three levels of cognition.

You may never have noticed it before, but your mind *cannot help* passing through the three distinct but complementary acts: experience, understanding and judgment. This is because there are persistent and ineradicable imperatives at the foundation of your consciousness. These imperatives, along with the associated cognitional acts are these:

(1)   Be attentive! —>   experience
(2)   Be intelligent! —>   understanding
(3)   Be critical! —>   judgment

The fourth set (which I shall examine in chapter 9) is:

(4)   Be responsible! —>   decision

The cognitional acts, along with the imperatives that give rise to them, make up what I shall be calling *critical intelligence* (following Bernard Lonergan). It is not enough to call your mental functioning simply "intelligence," since you can be intelligent, insightful and even ingenious without being right. It is your *critical* intelligence, concerned as it is with *true* understanding, that I wish to highlight. An even fuller designation of your mental life would be "open, critical and responsible intelligence," but for the sake of economy I shall be satisfied with the simpler label for the time being.

The imperatives to be attentive, intelligent and critical flow from a single deep longing that lies at the heart of each person's intellectual life. Since ancient times this longing has been known as *the desire to know*. It is the root of science and all other rational pursuits. Science, for example, begins with *experience*, propelled by the imperative to be open and attentive. We may call this the empirical imperative. Experience provides data that scientists seek to understand. And if they reach insight into, or *understanding* of, the data, they express it in propositions known as hypotheses and theories. But science does not stop there, since not every bright idea is a true idea. A third imperative – be critical! – prods the scientist to reflect on whether the hypotheses or theories are correct. Scientific understanding must be subjected continually to verification (or falsification) procedures. Only after undertaking a rigorous criticism of one's ideas, usually requiring evaluation by others or publication in peer-reviewed journals, will it be appropriate to render at least a tentative *judgment* that one's scientific hypotheses or theories are true or false.

Science, of course, is much more nuanced than this. My point is only that the scientific process illustrates how closely the human mind adheres to the threefold cognitional structure and its persistent imperatives. But this invariant pattern is also operative in common sense, philosophy and other forms of cognition. It has been operating in you while you have been reading this chapter. You have experienced the words on the page in front of you – following the imperative to be attentive. You have then tried to understand the words – following the imperative to be intelligent. And now – in obedience to the imperative to be critical – you are asking whether what I am saying is true. So you can immediately identify the threefold cognitional pattern in the actual performance of your own critical intelligence. For the moment it does not matter how your mind evolved, or what were the cultural factors in its genesis. These are important matters also, but for our immediate purposes it will be helpful to focus only on how your critical intelligence is functioning presently.

Perhaps you have never attended to your mental operations in this immediate way before. You may never have turned your attention to the fact that your mind is continually prodded by hidden imperatives. Yet even if you have never adverted to them earlier, you will now discover that you cannot escape them. You may at times have failed to obey the imperatives to be attentive, intelligent and critical, but their presence has been operative even when their voice has been muffled. If you are now doubting what I have just said it is because you are being attentive, intelligent and critical – in response to your own mind's imperatives. No matter how many doubts and uncertainties you have about everything else, you cannot deny the threefold cognitional structure of your own critical intelligence without employing it even in the act of doubting it.

The next point I want to make, then, is that you cannot help *trusting* in the imperatives of your mind. Without having made a tacit act of faith in your own critical intelligence you would not have bothered to follow me up to this point. You would not have asked whether I am making any sense, or whether I may be pulling the wool over your eyes. Once again, perhaps you may never have noticed that your whole cognitional performance depends on a deeply personal confidence in your own intelligence and critical capacities. But unless you had already placed a certain amount of trust in your cognitional ability you would hardly even have bothered to ask any questions at all.

I can imagine that seasoned philosophers or scientific thinkers, after reading this chapter, will try to refute the claims I am making here. But such refutation will arise only because my critics also will have trusted their own minds' imperatives to be attentive, intelligent and critical. They will not be able to measure the value of my argument without obediently following their own desire to know as it issues the injunctions that unfold in the three cognitional acts. Any attempted rebuttal of my depiction of human mentality will inevitably mirror the depiction itself. The invariant threefold pattern of cognitional functioning is inescapable, as all attempts to renounce it will demonstrate.

Even the effort to deny that the imperatives are present in your own intelligence requires a deeply personal trust in the three imperatives at the root of your consciousness. Adherence to your mind's invariant directives, however, is not a sentence to mental imprisonment. Placing yourself trustfully in the hands of your mind's mandates is in fact a recipe for freedom. They intend the ongoing expansion of your consciousness and a richer relationship of your mind to the real world. For present purposes, a self-conscious embrace of your desire to know and its imperatives will place you in a position to make an informed and responsible judgment as to whether nature is all there is.

IS NATURALISM TRUE?

What the preceding exercise is leading up to is an invitation to pose the following question to yourself as honestly as you can: *is the creed of naturalism consistent with the trust that you are now placing in the imperatives of your mind?* It has been said that we should never deny in our philosophies what we affirm in our hearts.[3] I am not sure that this is always good advice, but what I am sure of is that you should never deny in your philosophical claims what you implicitly affirm in your every act of knowing. There must be a coherence between your worldview and the critical intelligence by which you experience, understand and know the world. Otherwise your worldview is an illusion. Consequently, if you judge a particular belief system to be reasonable or true, there must be nothing in that belief system that is inconsistent with how your own critical intelligence actually works. To test the worthiness of your formal beliefs, you need to ask whether they are in harmony with your desire to know. If they are not, then they can be called unreasonable.

If you embrace the belief system known as scientific naturalism, therefore, have you ever asked whether it coheres logically with the invariant structure of human cognition? Let me put my question another way: is the essentially mindless, purposeless, self-originating, self-enclosed universe of scientific naturalism large enough to house your own critical intelligence? If not, truthfulness compels you to conclude that nature is not enough, and that naturalism is an unreasonable creed. Your formal understanding of the world – your worldview, if you will – must not be such as to contradict the way the mind functions when it seeks knowledge of the world. Nor must your worldview have the effect of subverting the confidence that

---

[3]   "Let us not pretend to doubt in philosophy what we do not doubt in our hearts." Charles Sanders Peirce, *Selected Writings* (New York: Dover, 1966), p. 40.

underlies the thought processes that give rise to that worldview. That Charles Darwin himself considered this to be a serious consideration is evident in the citation given at the head of this chapter.

Does scientific naturalism support or subvert your desire to know? I do not know what your own response will be, but after struggling with this question for many years, I have concluded that the universe as conceived by scientific naturalism is quite clearly incompatible with the critical intelligence with which I attempt to understand the universe. More strongly stated, a consistent acceptance of scientific naturalism logically impairs the very trust that underlies my attempts to understand and know the world. In the rest of this book I will be setting forth my reasons for having reached this conclusion. I shall propose that only those views of reality that are logically consistent with, and lend support to, the desire to know and the mind's imperatives can be called truthful.

The desire to know is the intangible source of the precepts that urge each of us to open ourselves to the world and seek truthful understanding of it. We may call it the *pure* desire to know in order to emphasize its difference from the many other desires we also have, desires that are not interested in truth. For example, we long for pleasure, consolation, power and meaning, but these desires can all be satisfied by mere illusions. They are not natively interested in truth, and in fact they can at times drown out the desire to know. However, the pure desire to know, the craving that issues the precepts to be attentive, intelligent and critical, is never satisfied with illusions. It seeks the truth, no matter what the cost. My question, then, is whether naturalism is supportive of or contrary to this pure desire to know that we can identify at the foundation of our own critical intelligence. This can be a most reliable test of whether naturalism is a truthful belief system.

I am now in a position, then, to state more formally what is meant by truth. *Truth* can be defined as the objective or goal of the pure desire to know. In one sense truth is equivalent to *being* or *what is*. In another sense it is a property of statements that correspond to *what is.* In either case, by truth I mean what is sought out by the desire to know as distinct from what other desires seek. It is true that there are alternative ways of understanding truth – for example, truth as the power of disclosure or truth as coherence or right action. But even in the act of telling us that truth corresponds to these other meanings, philosophers are implicitly using "truth" as what is intended by the desire to know.

Illusion, by contrast, is the product of a desire for pleasure, consolation, power, or even meaning, insofar as these desires are functioning independently of the desire to know. For example, you may wish so badly to be a great philosopher that you end up thinking of yourself as one when in truth you are not. Your wishing can produce illusions. Your desire to know, on the other hand, cannot settle for illusions. It is willing to embrace the truth, even when it means going against the grain of your other longings. If you are now wondering whether this is true, you prove my point. Sooner or later you can come to recognize the difference between the truth-seeking desire to know and other desires that remain satisfied with mere imaginings. And once you have identified your mind's imperatives and the relentless desire to know that underlies them, you will be in a position to examine whether your worldview is consistent with truth.

This may not be easy, however, since truth cannot be bottled and capped. Truth is the *goal* of the mind's imperatives, and its complete capture always eludes the desire to know. Truth can never be possessed, only pursued. Consequently, for the human mind to set arbitrary limits on what can be taken as real or true is to repress the desire to know. Restricting the desire to know is an act of violence toward the very core of one's being and consciousness. In my view scientific naturalism, as I will be arguing at more length, entails just such a subjugation of the desire to know, so I shall be obliged to judge it unreasonable. Perhaps you will not agree, but I hope you will follow my argument and test whether it conforms to the imperatives of your own mind and your own desire for truth.

Throughout the book, in conscious obedience to my own mind's imperatives, I shall also subject to constant criticism the preliminary assessment of naturalism that I have just laid out. I shall do so by giving ample voice to naturalists' own thoughts as I look into a variety of phenomena that are currently of interest to scientists and that may seem at first to allow for a completely naturalistic reading. I shall be citing some of the most respected representatives of the naturalistic creed, setting forth their challenges to theology. Then I shall raise critical questions about the assumptions underlying their challenges. I hope to show that even though critical intelligence is fully part of nature, its own quest for a *fullness* of truth is a reasonable clue that the world of being is infinitely larger than what naturalism is able to acknowledge.

THE COURAGE TO KNOW

I take it that even at this early stage of my assessment of naturalism you have attained a palpable sense of the active desire to know expressing itself through the imperatives you have identified at the ground level of your own *critical intelligence*. By becoming explicitly aware of your desire to know, you have arrived at a standpoint from which you may be able eventually to judge whether naturalism is a reasonable set of beliefs. At the very least, in order to pass the test of reasonableness, any belief system that you cling to must be congruent with your desire to know and the imperatives of your mind. If a specific set of beliefs fails to support the interests of your desire to know, or if it undermines the confidence and trust in the cognitional imperatives that lead you toward open-minded and critical exploration of reality, then it is inconsistent with the fundamental criterion of truth, namely, fidelity to the desire to know.[4]

---

[4] As I have mentioned already, my whole inquiry is guided by Bernard Lonergan's ideas even though my terminology and applications of his theory of knowledge are not always his.

To be truthful, I repeat, means to be faithful to the desire to know. But can you consistently and coherently claim to be both a naturalist and, at the same time, completely faithful to your own desire to know? Not only naturalists but also religious believers who may be reading this book need to ask whether their explicit beliefs correspond to the interests of their desire to know. If not, then these beliefs must be declared unreasonable also, and lovers of truth must disown them. What one believes to be ultimate reality must not function in such a way as to contravene the restless longing for truth that I have just identified as the desire to know. Hence, one might also examine religious beliefs, and not just naturalism, from the point of view of whether and how these may be serving the interests of desires other than the desire to know. Not a few studies have argued, after all, that religion can indeed satisfy the desire for pleasure (Freud), consolation (Marx), revenge (Nietzsche) or meaning (Frankl, Berger, Shermer).[5] And the severest critics of religion have argued in effect that if belief in God is inconsistent with the desire to know, then it must be abandoned. I would agree. Seldom, however, has scientific naturalism been subjected to the same rigorous standard of authentication.

The desire to know is distinguishable from all other strivings in that it can never be satisfied with illusions. It is characteristic of the desire to know to cut through what all our other passions and longings would *prefer*, and to settle only for *what is*. In order to do so, however, courage is necessary, and courage sometimes fails. This is a fact that demonstrates the inseparability of virtue – in this case the cardinal virtue of fortitude – from the human process of knowing.

5   Sigmund Freud, *The Future of an Illusion*, translated and edited by James Strachey (New York: Norton, 1989); Karl Marx, *Early Writings*, translated and edited by T. B. Bottomore (New York: McGraw-Hill, 1964); Friedrich Nietzsche, *The Birth of Tragedy and The Genealogy of Morals*, translated by Francis Golffing (New York: Anchor Books, 1990); Viktor Frankl, *Man's Search for Meaning* (New York: Pocket Books, 1959); Peter Berger, *The Sacred Canopy* (Garden City, N.Y.: Anchor Books, 1990); Michael Shermer, *How We Believe: the Search for God in an Age of Science* (New York: W. H. Freeman, 2000).

I shall say more about the connection of virtue to knowing in chapter 9. For now, however, let it suffice to say that if courage and trust fail you, your desire to know also begins to flag. Then other impulses, powerful drives that have no interest in truth, come flooding in to fill the void.

In real life, as each of us knows, the desire to know must continually compete with opposing tendencies. While it is essentially pure and detached, in our actual existence the desire to know is always entangled with other longings. We have to struggle throughout our lives to decouple the innate intentionality of the desire to know from other urges that promise easy but evanescent satisfaction. As the Danish philosopher Søren Kierkegaard puts it, "it is far from being the case that men in general regard relationship to the truth as the highest good, and it is far from being the case that they, Socratically, regard being under a delusion as the greatest misfortune."[6] Nonetheless, it is possible, as you can tell from the exercise with which I opened this chapter, to identify the imperatives of your own mind and their intention to put you in touch with reality. In fact, *reality* means that which is intended by your desire to know. If you are still questioning whether this is true, it can only be because your own desire to know is at this moment seeking to know what is *really* the case. So, once again, the evidence is right there in front of you at this very instant.

Moreover, as a little reflection will show, the desire to know intends nothing less than the *fullness* of being. This is why any arbitrary imposition of boundaries on the desire to know is an act of violence, inconsistent with truth-seeking. Even the human capacity to experience limits as limits – for example, to suspect that nature is all there is – is due to the fact that the desire to know always reaches out *beyond* the confines of what is actually known. The desire to know is *anticipatory* rather than possessive. It is most at home where there is an openness to a limitless horizon of being, and

---

6   Søren Kierkegaard, *The Sickness unto Death*, translated by Walter Lowrie (Garden City, N.Y.: Doubleday Anchor Books, 1954), pp. 154–55.

it begins to feel cramped whenever it hears phrases such as "enough," "nothing but" or "all there is." Because the dynamism of the desire to know always carries the mind beyond actual cognitional achievements, the full sweep of reality can reveal itself to knowledge only incrementally. It is felt first in our *desire* for truth rather than in any possession of it.

The horizon of being and truth toward which the desire to know extends itself is unrestricted. And it is only our mind's reaching out toward an endlessly wider plenitude of being that exposes, by way of contrast, the poverty of what we have actually comprehended. The limits of cognitional achievement cannot be recognized as such unless the mind has already transcended those limits in some way. Consequently, there is something immediately unseemly about the naturalist claim that nature is all there is. For how could one know that reality ends at the boundaries of nature unless the naturalist's own mind has also quietly extended itself beyond that limit? Can the mind know a limit as a limit, G. F. Hegel and other philosophers have asked, unless the same mind has already somehow – courageously – transcended that limit?

FIELDS OF MEANING

Critical intelligence intends the truth even if it never fully captures it. If you are questioning this claim, is it not because your own intelligence spontaneously wants to know the truth and distinguish it from illusion? But the road to the real is not always easy and direct. Since the world has many aspects it requires different avenues of approach. I suggest that there are at least five fields of meaning through which the desire to know must travel if it is to encounter the rich texture of the world's being. These avenues are: affectivity, intersubjectivity, narrativity, beauty and theory. Science falls predominantly in the last, the realm of theory, but it is not through science alone that the mind comes into contact with reality.

Affectivity

Appropriate modes of feeling must accompany different kinds of understanding and knowing. There are circumstances in which the affects of warmth, anxiety, levity, joy or sadness are indispensable to grasping what is going on in the real world. In many situations I would lose touch with reality if the right mood were missing. For example, if I approached the funeral of a friend with the same emotional tone I usually carry to a birthday party, I would miss out on the drama unfolding before me. Surely, being in touch with reality does not always require the complete suppression of the passions. To approach the entire range of my experiences with the same suspension of desire that I practice in the laboratory would be not only pathological but also epistemically crippling. The desire to know must clothe itself in a wide spectrum of feelings if it is to reach toward its goal, the fullness of being and truth.

Religion, for example, is inconceivable apart from feeling. And one may assume that if there is anything of substance to religious experience, the sense of being grasped by, and surrendering worshipfully to, a sacred mystery, would elicit feelings unlike any others. But the fact that deep feeling is present cannot as such be taken as a reason for suspecting that religion is illusory. Even in ordinary experience some feelings, after all, are cognitively indispensable, so in religion many different shades of affectivity will also be relevant: joy, sorrow, remorse, dependency, fascination, excitement, anxiety, love, hope, confidence, reverence, and suchlike.

Because of the intensity and variety of the emotions involved in religious experience, modern scientific naturalism has questioned religion's objectivity. Should not objective knowledge put aside all feelings? And because it is so much a matter of feeling, is not religion completely subjective, and therefore cognitionally suspect? Religious people often claim to be in touch with a personal God, but is not their clothing of reality in the apparel of personality a clear sign of religion's tendency to overlook the real impersonality of the universe? Are not theists, for example, simply projecting their desire for divine companionship onto the indifferent mindlessness of the actual world? Does not religion, as naturalists claim, arise from wishes that have no interest in truth, rather than from the pure desire to know? Naturalistic literature is full of affirmative responses to these questions.[7]

However, the scientific naturalist's own elevation of the theoretic, subject-object, field of meaning to the status of supreme arbiter of all correct knowing is itself sodden with passion. There is a high degree of emotional investment in the naturalist's own personal commitment to scientific knowing as normative. In order to confirm this point all you need to do is have a serious conversation with an entrenched scientific naturalist. Naturalism is no more separable from feeling than are any other kinds of belief. This is because the desire to know can never be severed from the affectivity that carries along any passionate longing.

Yet, as we also know, passions can also divert the desire to know from its natural orientation toward truth. Some kinds of feeling can allow illusory longings to usurp first place in one's relation to the world. The question then still remains as to what precise feelings or affects are most appropriate to activate and energize the desire to know. I would suggest that those feelings associated with the postures of humility, gratitude and trust – fundamental religious virtues – will be a very good place to begin a liberation of the desire to know from passions that suffocate it.[8]

Intersubjectivity

Our world is made up not only of objects but also of other people, and we cannot hope to approach the fullness of truth without interacting with and learning from them. The desire to know is not

---

[7] Several recent examples are Owen Flanagan, *The Problem of the Soul: Two Visions of Mind and How to Reconcile Them* (New York: Basic Books, 2002); Tanor Edis, *The Ghost in the Universe* (Amherst, N.Y.: Prometheus Books, 2002); Sam Harris, *The End of Faith: Religion, Terror, and the Future of Reason* (New York: Norton, 2004).

[8] See my book *Religion and Self-Acceptance* (New York: Paulist Press, 1976).

completely private. Human existence is essentially a being-with-others, so the desire to know must be permitted to make contact with the subjective reality of these others. In order to do so one needs to adopt a kind of empathy, a capacity to indwell the world of the other person. An acknowledgement of the world of subjects is not explicitly operative in scientific knowing, although it is tacitly so even there. But in nonscientific cognition the desire to know must suspend the sterilizing approach it rightly employs in the field of science or theory. Instead it must adopt a posture of receptive open-ness to the unobjectifiable world of the other. This means that it must put on those virtues that allow the other subject to be another subject and not a mere object. Incidentally, this posture is one that applies also in some sense to our relationship to nonhuman living subjects. The fact that in modern times so many enlightened humans have treated animals as well as other humans as objects to be ma-nipulated and even destroyed, rather than as subjects to be respected, is a habit that has drawn considerable support from the assump-tion that only objects, and not subjects, are really real. The sorry twentieth-century history of atrocities, it is important to realize, has not occurred independently of the scientistic belief that the only field of meaning in which the desire to know can operate properly is that of theory, where everything shows up only as pure object and no room is allowed for the reality of subjects.

The assumption that knowledge is most realistic when it is impersonal actually amounts to a smothering rather than a purifying of the desire to know. The reality of other subjects, to repeat, simply cannot show up at all in the world of scientific objectification. This is a major reason why religious belief in a personal God seems so utterly misguided to the scientific naturalist. After all, there is no space for any subjects, let alone a divine subject, in the theoretic (objectifying) field of meaning, which for the strict scientific natural-ist is apparently the only world wherein raw contact with reality can take place. Of course, there is no objective, theoretical justification for this claim either.

Narrativity

For human subjects the world is not experienced, at least in a rich or interesting way, apart from stories. Even evolutionary science and cosmology today grasp our attention because of their narrative character. There is a narrative quality to all of our experience, and it is from stories, whether mythic or historical, that we acquire any sense of reality at all.[9] It is not surprising then that "story" is the form in which humanity's religious encounter with mystery has received its primordial expression. Because narrative is at the nucleus of human awareness it is where religious sensibilities first take up residence. The feeling of the sacred is sculpted especially in myths that bear the local stamp of specific cultures. By situating our lives and all events within the setting of stories, religions bring coherence to the moments that make up our lives. Our feelings, aesthetic preferences and intersubjective encounters conform to the narrative tone of our experience. So significant are stories that without them our lives would be empty of content, and moral aspiration would be either tenuous or nonexistent.

However, naturalism views most of our stories, especially religious ones, as nothing more than human fabrications superimposed on the senseless substratum of physical reality first fully exposed by science.[10] Even if stories respond to our desires for consolation and meaning, it is doubtful according to naturalism that they can satisfy the desire to know. Stories can give us a sense of reality, scientific naturalists generally agree, but they cannot give us reality. Only theoretic, objectifying consciousness can be trusted to deliver the *real* world to us. Stories, along with our feelings, subjectivity and aesthetic impressions, are filmy coatings that we employ to cover up the stark impersonality of the real world. They may have been adaptive in the

---

[9] Stephen Crites, "The Narrative Quality of Experience," *Journal of the American Academy of Religion* 39 (1971), 291–311.

[10] A classic example is Freud's *The Future of an Illusion.*

Darwinian sense, but they are now epistemologically dubious and can therefore be ignored.

At least this is the dominant view of contemporary scientific naturalism. However, close examination will show that the naturalistic dismissal of the cognitive (as distinct from emotive) function of story, a denial that undergirds much contemporary academic life, is itself borne aloft on the wings of a firmly established cultural narrative of its own. It is empowered by the myth that trustworthy consciousness came into the world only with the birth of objectifying scientific method during the sixteenth and seventeenth Centuries. It is a story laced with abundant accounts of heroic explorers and their own struggles toward the light. All over the world initiates to objectifying consciousness imbibe the myth of science's ascent and its exalted ethic of knowledge. Nothing provides clearer evidence of the inescapability of story than the modern attempts to escape it.

Beauty

The desire to know also clings closely to our appreciation of beauty. Feeling, intersubjectivity, narrative and even theory are all overlaid with what strikes us as more or less beautiful. In other words, there is an aesthetic aspect to all knowing. Beauty, as philosophers have often noted, is inseparable from truth, and this is why the desire to know always has some degree of aesthetic interest. The quest for beauty gives zest to the search for truth, as many good scientists will also attest. Without it the desire to know can hardly become active at all.

Consequently, when people respond to a worldview, whether naturalistic or religious, they do so only if it has at least some degree of aesthetic as well as intellectual appeal. If a vision of the world is unnecessarily monotonous or disorderly we are not drawn to it. Because beauty and truth are so closely associated, inquiry into the truth-status of naturalism demands that we also ask about its aesthetic qualifications. Is scientific naturalism a vision of reality that can satisfy our longing for beauty as well as the pure desire to know?

Naturalism, as I see it, implicitly subverts the significance of our aesthetic longing when it dismisses beauty in effect as a human projection, and hence as not having any reality independent of human construction.[11] By privileging the theoretic (objectifying) field of meaning, naturalism in its modern scientific transformations has taught that reality, beneath all its outward appearances, is essentially predictable and routine. Whatever beauty exists in nature, at least according to materialist versions of naturalism, comes from the inventive human mind. Most naturalists understand beauty not so much as having the status of truth but as an illusory human concoction. Beauty is not really real, but the product of our own creativity. Nature cannot be beautiful in itself, but is instead a monotonous canvas onto which we humans paint or project our own aesthetic preferences. Beneath its apparent aesthetic appeal, the fundamental layer of all being is the dead world of primary qualities, the scientifically knowable quantitative stuff that we overlay with the secondary qualities of our five senses. As Alfred North Whitehead has rightly stated, the prevalent modern view of nature has been one in which the underlying world is "a dull affair, soundless, scentless, colorless: merely the hurrying of material, endlessly meaninglessly."[12] Thus the materialism underlying most modern naturalism ironically exhibits an aggressively anthropocentric bias even while denying in effect the real existence of human subjectivity. By theoretically isolating our subjectivity from its own world, it unthinkingly enshrines humans in a position of creative supremacy over the rest of the world.

Theory

Our critical intelligence is wrapped up in a bundle of spontaneities that are mostly pre-theoretical and nonscientific. Each of us is

---

[11] For a critique of the modern conviction that beauty (along with other values) is our own creation alone, rather than a quality inherent in nature, see Alfred North Whitehead, *Science and the Modern World* (New York: The Free Press, 1967), esp. pp. 39–94.

[12] Ibid., p. 54.

engaged in the world through the mediation of moods or feelings, aesthetic sensitivities, intersubjective involvements and narratives about where we came from and where we are going. We may call these *primal*, as distinct from theoretic, fields of meaning. These are all pathways traversed by the desire to know, even though they are trodden by less noble desires as well. Without them we would be out of touch with reality altogether, so it is wrong to view them as inevitably deviating from true knowledge. But in the sentient, inter-subjective, narrative and aesthetic fields of meaning our critical in-telligence is still so intimately and personally entangled with its world that a clear distinction between the subjective knower and the objective world "out there" has not yet emerged clearly. In moments of anxiety and joy, for example, the character of the uni-verse itself seems inseparable from our subjective moods. To a de-pressed person the world seems empty and the future bleak, whereas to a happy person it may seem filled with meaning and overflowing with possibility. In our experience of beauty we can be carried away by the aesthetic object in such a way that our separate subjectivity seems to dissolve. Furthermore, for most of us the world takes shape in accordance with historic or mythic narratives that color our whole sense of reality with cultural and psychic specificity.

It will seem to the scientific naturalist that the four primal fields of meaning – the affective, intersubjective, aesthetic and narra-tive – are so private or personal that they are more likely to conceal than reveal the real world. This is not necessarily the case at all, for there can be both realistic and unrealistic feelings, stories, intersub-jective involvements and aesthetic preferences. Nevertheless, scien-tific naturalism is inclined to think of all pre-theoretic modes of involvement in the world as cognitionally suspect since they lack the *objective* detachment practiced by science. The primal fields of meaning can give us mere illusions, it would seem, whereas only science can deliver the *real* world to us.

Science can be realistic, we are told, because it belongs to the wider world of *theory*. The theoretic field of meaning is one in which the knowing subject seeks personal detachment from what is known. Theory idealizes *impersonal* knowing, so some of its most devoted servants generally dismiss the primal fields as cognitionally useless. And since religion has made the primal fields its original dwelling, the theoretician is often inclined to dismiss its claims to truth as unwarranted. However, in doing so the theoretician has also stepped back into the primal fields. The dismissal of religion as mere illusion usually comes from persons who are fully immersed in the heroic narrative that tells how genuine enlightenment can come about only by way of the asceticism of impersonal knowledge.[13] And this very modern myth tends to mold passions, shape intersubjective involvements and determine aesthetic preferences among naturalists in no less forceful a fashion than religions have always done with their own adherents.

As long as theoretic knowing is employed as one among other ways of unleashing the desire to know, it is absolutely essential to our openness to the real. However, theory no less than the primal fields can be taken captive by the will to power and other less worthy desires. Even though a scientist, for example, may be emotionally detached while working *within* the theoretic mode of knowing, he or she is hardly emotionally uninvolved in the act of choosing or defending scientific method as essential for scientific knowledge. And in the case of scientific naturalists, who view the primal modes as factories of fiction, theoretic detachment becomes the criterion of all acceptable cognition. Ironically, though, the *exclusivist preference* for theory may itself be a consequence not so much of the pure desire to know as of other cravings.

It is questionable, in any case, whether impersonal, subject-object detachment can put us in touch with everything the desire to know intends. Clearly there are kinds of knowing, for example in the area of our intersubjective or aesthetic involvements, in which a

---

[13]   See Michael Novak, *The Experience of Nothingness* (New York: Harper Colophon Books, 1971), pp. 17–18.

calculated suppression of feeling would interfere with our contacting reality. There is a deep sense in which the desire to know must always remain pure. But purity does not mean affective deadness. Rather it often means searching for the depth and quality of passion that can most effectively move us toward the rich tapestry of the real world.

Not every kind of detachment, after all, requires emotional neutrality. The whole enterprise of knowing, as we have seen above, is undergirded by *desire*, a quality hard to imagine apart from passion. Moreover, the fundamental criterion of truth is fidelity to our passionate desire to know, not emotional detachment from it. Even when we are doing science we cannot shut down the underlying affective dynamism of the desire to know and its persistent imperatives. And to suffuse the primal modes of knowing with the detachment characteristic of theory would drown out the *eros* for the real that undergirds theory itself. Cool-headed aloofness is appropriate in some fields of meaning but out of place in others.

CONCLUSION

When I speak of critical intelligence in the remainder of this book I have in mind not only the desire to know and the imperatives of the mind, but also the complex web of five intentional fields that I have just sketched. It is not necessary at this point to say anything about the evolutionary, cultural, historical and social processes that went into the making of this critical intelligence, important and fascinating as this may be. For now it is sufficient simply to be fully aware, first, of the presence of a desire to know at the core of your own being and, second, that this desire is as much a part of the natural world as are trees and toads. Your critical intelligence is not hovering somewhere outside nature. It *is* nature, in the same way that stars and rivers are nature. It should not be hard for the naturalist to accept this premise, since nature is supposedly all there is. However, since critical intelligence is so intimately entangled with the rest of nature – a point that both evolution and cosmology have confirmed in great detail – what we can find out by looking closely at critical intelligence will also be relevant to our understanding of the whole natural world with which it is so intimately interlaced.

I suggest that the richest point of entry and the most illuminating access each of us has to the natural world are the portals of our own critical intelligence. At the very least, it is at least one such doorway. So why would we want to leave this emerald of evolutionary construction out of our picture of nature as though it were not part of it? Science generally does just that, and for its limited purposes such exclusion of our subjectivity seems appropriate. But how could we profess to be *fully* open to the data of experience, in obedience to the mind's first imperative, if we deliberately refused to focus on what is to each subject the most precious of all nature's products? (For one last time, if you are still doubting that critical intelligence is something you deeply value, this doubt itself is "evidence" of your valuing it.)

Yet, as we shall see later on, if we do attend fully to our critical intelligence, and if we seriously try to integrate it into our understanding of nature, then the naturalistic approach to the world will be exposed as insufficiently attentive, intelligent and critical. In the final analysis, scientific naturalism turns out to be only half-heartedly empirical, too narrow in its vision, and too deficiently intelligent and critical to satisfy the mind's imperatives fully. It looks away from critical intelligence, refusing therefore to appreciate the latter's implications for a rich understanding of nature. And it fails to reflect on the relative poverty of a method of inquiry that places in brackets evolution's most exquisite outcome. The scientific method enshrined by naturalism as the privileged road to the real is by definition not interested in subjects, only objects. Subjectivity of any sort does not show up on its radar screen, even when it tries to understand minds. Scientific naturalism's world, at least in its typically materialist versions, is a world without subjects.[14] So, if one asks the naturalist how to

---

[14] Alan Wallace, *The Taboo of Subjectivity: Toward a New Science of Consciousness* (New York: Oxford University Press, 2000).

explain the immediately obvious fact of critical intelligence, the only conceptual tools available to do so are already denuded of the very categories that might illuminate it.

Naturalism attempts to enclose consciousness within a dominantly scientific way of understanding. I will not deny that consciousness is part of nature or that the sciences, including evolutionary biology and paleontology, can help us understand it. What I will deny is that a *complete* understanding of consciousness and the natural world that gave birth to it can ever come from science alone. In terms of natural history, our critical intelligence emerged from a universe that earlier lacked any actual intelligence and even life. It now appears that a formerly lifeless and mindless universe is the historical matrix of mind. To admit this much is necessary in the light of current scientific information about the universe and evolution. But there is more to a birth process than the moment of conception and the period of gestation. It is not enough to assert that the ultimate ground of the desire to know is a lifeless and mindless causal past. If the ultimate cause of mind is mindlessness, we would still need to look for reasons to trust our minds here and now, as Darwin himself seemed to realize. Fully justifying the obvious acts of faith that we place in our critical intelligence requires that we situate human cognitional life, and along with it the whole universe, in a more spacious environment than the one laid out by scientific naturalism. I believe it will be essential to call upon theology to accomplish this expansion.

However, in moving toward a theological vision I shall not be looking at reports of supernormal phenomena, mystical experiences, miracles, private revelations, parapsychological and transpersonal excursions, or anything beyond the ordinary. Most of us have little or no experience of these marginal phenomena anyway. And even though I keep an open mind to their possible occurrence, I intend this book's reflections to be fully consistent with an honest doubt that such extraordinary events ever happen at all. Instead in each separate chapter I shall focus on a particular phenomenon that is readily available to ordinary experience or scientific investigation. Then I shall argue that making more than superficial sense of this readily observable phenomenon requires a view of reality that transcends the world as conceived by scientific naturalism. In this way I hope to show that abundant room remains open in an age of science for plausible religious and theological interpretations of nature.

In order to do so, I need to underline once again a fundamental theological principle: If there *is* a "more-than-nature," it could never be grasped cognitionally in the same way that things in nature are mastered by science. Transcendent reality would first come to our awareness in the primal regions of knowing – affective, intersubjective, narrative and aesthetic – rather than in the theoretic or objectifying field. This is because religion is less a matter of grasping than of *being grasped*. Religious experience leads to knowledge, but it is a knowledge of being comprehended more than a comprehending kind of knowledge. So its elemental language will be symbol, metaphor and analogy. Religious experience is not entirely unlike the naturalist's own sense of being taken captive by truth, by the quiet call to surrender the mind to *what is*. Only if such a pre-theoretical surrender takes place can science get off the ground to begin with. Yet there is no objectifiable scientific evidence for the horizon of truth that invites the surrender. Even more in the case of theology, therefore, it makes no sense to suppose that supporting "evidence" for its claims could ever be squeezed into the domain of things that can be subjected to scientific control.

Having looked briefly at critical intelligence, I shall now turn my attention to some other natural phenomena that will also call out for a larger setting than naturalism provides.

4 Life

There's not a plant or flower below
But makes thy glories known;
And clouds arise and tempests blow
By order from thy throne.

Isaac Watts, 1715

There's not a plant or flower below
But DNA has grown;
And clouds arise and tempests blow
By laws as yet unknown.

Kenneth E. Boulding, 1975[1]

Except perhaps for critical intelligence, nothing stands out from the rest of nature more impressively than the life-world. And nothing provides more occasion for wonder. Especially interesting is the question of how life began. In fact, the question of life's origin is still one of the most challenging and exciting in all of natural science. Proposals about how life emerged from non-living physical antecedents are as abundant as they are unconfirmed. Did life begin, for example, with cycles of self-replicating RNA? Or from a prebiotic protein matrix? Did it emerge in direct continuity with the self-organizing tendencies of physical processes? Is the origin of life perhaps just one step in a whole series of emergent stages in cosmic process?[2]

Whatever the chemistry, physics and mathematical principles that underlie the origin of life may be, it still remains puzzling that in the arrival of living beings the universe made an abrupt and radical departure from the inanimate physical routines that had prevailed

---

[1]   Kenneth Boulding, "Toward an Evolutionary Theology," in *The Spirit of the Earth: a Teilhard Centennial Celebration*, edited by Jerome Perlinski (New York: The Seabury Press, 1981), pp. 112–13. Once again, I do not consider Boulding to be a scientific naturalist. He was much given to humorous rhyme, but he captures well the naturalist perspective.

[2]   Harold Morowitz, *The Emergence of Everything: How the World Became Complex* (New York: Oxford University Press, 2002).

beforehand. Life is so unlike nonliving states of being that our religious ancestors spontaneously attributed its existence to a mysterious divine agency. Quite understandably pre-scientific humanity interpreted life as a perpetual miracle. Even today it seems to countless people in the world that the existence of life requires the ongoing intercession of God. However, scientific naturalism insists that life and its origin require no special causal factors unspecifiable in physical terms. Life, it contends, came about naturally *rather than* by divine influence. And life persists not because of any special spiritual energy but ultimately because of impersonal physical and chemical processes. Theological explanation is unnecessary.

But do we have to choose *between* scientific and theological accounts, between Watts' lyrics and Boulding's (playful) revision? Science, it is true, can and should try to understand all phenomena without reference to God. But are scientific accounts *alternatives* to theological ones? Theology does not usually consider itself to be a rival to scientific explanation. Yet scientific naturalists typically assume that the more room one gives to theological explanation the less will be left for science. At the same time, religious believers often fear that the more impressive scientific explanations become, the less reason there will be for invoking the idea of divine creativity in accounting for life.

The beginning of life, according to scientific naturalism, was a purely natural occurrence. It may even have been inevitable since the universe is old enough to have allowed chance and physical laws ample time to experiment with different chemical and environmental combinations. So why look for any supernatural causal agency as a factor in the birth of life? Such a superfluous supposition would only distract science from inquiring into the *physical* causes of life. In any case, if a creator had wanted to bring life into being, why did it take so long after the beginning of the universe for it to happen? To a neutral observer the first instance of life would have looked like a chemical accident, an anomalous convergence of lines of causation that may just as easily not have met at all. Science, especially in its disclosure of the enormous depth of cosmic time and empty space, seems to have shown that the universe is *essentially* lifeless. Only the most unlikely chain of contingencies could have allowed life to arise at all.

And after it appeared, further accidents in the historical unfolding of life only add to the naturalist's suspicion that the story of life on earth follows no eternal plan. For example, the random fusion of bacteria with protocells, possibly a major step in the complexification and diversification of life, must have involved numerous near misses.[3] Such accidents refute the expectation that life's unfolding follows an intelligently devised plan. And as Darwinians have pointed out, serendipity is operative at every twist and turn in life's ongoing evolution.

By all scientific accounts, then, the origin and development of life seem to have been unintended. In order to visualize the apparent absence of intelligent design in natural history, imagine that you have on your bookshelf a set of thirty large volumes. Each is 450 pages long, and every page represents a million years of cosmic time. Taken together, the thirty books tell the story of our approximately fourteen-billion-year-old universe. The Big Bang takes place on page 1 of volume I, but puzzlingly – that is, if you are theologically inquisitive – the next twenty-two volumes are utterly lifeless. It is possible, of course, that life has appeared earlier in other parts of the universe, but, even so, such occurrences would still have had to wait until galaxies formed and heavy chemical elements, especially carbon, were created. This could only have taken place some billions of years after the Big Bang. So the question remains: why so long? By the latest estimates, life on earth does not even make its debut until about 3.8 billion years ago. And even after life appears, it is not in a hurry to achieve anything spectacularly interesting until around the end of volume XXIX, when the so-called Cambrian Explosion takes place. Then life begins to complexify with relative rapidity. Still, the earliest emergence of

3   Lynn Margulis and Dorion Sagan, *Microcosmos: Four Billion Years of Evolution from Our Microbial Ancestors* (New York: Simon & Schuster, 1991).

"thought" has to wait until the last few pages of volume XXX. And, finally, the history of modern humans takes up only the last paragraph or so of the very last volume.

If there were anything other than purely natural agency at work in this story, then why has there been so much randomness, awkward engineering, wasted experiments and "fooling around" until the cosmos became complex enough to be endowed with life, sensitivity and consciousness? And if any conceivable deity is involved at all in these cosmic proceedings, what can one learn about the creator from all the accidents, struggle, pain, and especially the prebiotic epochs of purely physical activity that took place before life entered into the universe? Is not the new scientific picture of life's unheralded debut just one more reason to embrace scientific naturalism?

It might be, except for the fact that life has led, by one route or another, to a most unexpected outcome, namely, a species driven by a passion to understand and know.[4] Even after Darwin and the discovery of deep time, it does not seem foolish to ask just how mind could ever have emerged out of utter mindlessness. The story of life has had many other amazing results, of course, and even aside from the fact of critical intelligence it is not certain that science can penetrate to the very bottom of what may be working itself out in the universe. But it may nonetheless prove instructive in a special way to ask what the fact of critical intelligence's recent emergence in evolution implies about life as such. I shall be focusing on this question more explicitly in the chapters ahead. Here I shall take only a modest step toward that larger discussion by asking whether science, as enshrined by naturalism, can give an adequate account of life and its origin.

THEOLOGY AND LIFE'S ORIGIN

Was the origin of life a purely natural occurrence or was divine influence also at work? This question provides the opportunity not only to

---

[4]   This is not to deny, of course, that life itself, even independently of the emergence of intelligence, is of great theological interest.

examine the specific issue of theology's relevance to an understanding of the origin of life, but also to reflect on a more fundamental issue raised by the present book: does the idea of divine action have any legitimacy at all in view of the strong claims by naturalists that science is enough to explain all phenomena satisfactorily by itself? Modern science suggests that nature can accomplish great feats of creativity on its own, including giving birth to life and evolutionary diversity, without any divine accompaniment. To the naturalist, any kind of belief in divine creativity is completely uncalled for. The rigorous Darwinian Gary Cziko, to cite just one of many possible examples, maintains that evolutionary biology now functions as a superior substitute for the unilluminating idea of "divine providence" in the explanation of adaptations.[5] Indeed, according to him and many other evolutionists, science has now replaced the idea of divine providence as the most plausible way to explain all the features of living organisms. Consequently, one must choose between science and theology, and there is no question as to which option the naturalist will embrace.

Such a forced option, however, is indicative of a serious misunderstanding of theological explanation. Theology, without at all encroaching on scientific levels of understanding, can find legitimate space for the idea of divine action within the wide range of explanatory levels available to human inquiry. Theology need not be seen as a rival account to scientific inquiry into natural causes. Even some deeply religious medieval thinkers encouraged philosophers to push naturalistic explanation of events as far as they could. In no way did they consider such accounts contradictory to theology.[6] Unfortunately, however, many scientifically thoughtful people today are inclined to place theology in an imaginative joust with science.

<hr />

[5] Gary Cziko, *Without Miracles: Universal Selection Theory and the Second Darwinian Revolution* (Cambridge, Mass.: MIT Press, 1995).

[6] See Ronald Numbers, "Science without God: Natural Laws and Christian Belief," in *When Science and Christianity Meet*, edited by David C. Lindberg and Ronald Numbers (Chicago: University of Chicago Press, 2003), pp. 265–85.

Theological explanation can coexist quite comfortably and non-competitively with scientific explanation. How so? To begin with, theology does not emulate the kind of explanation that science gives with respect to natural causes. Although theology must be conversant with the methods and fruits of scientific discovery, it cannot imitate the scientific way of explaining things without losing its own identity. Discourse about divine action, moreover, must begin with metaphor or analogy, or else it is likely to appear as though the notion of divine creativity is competing with scientific accounts of natural causes. A major reason why "Intelligent Design Theory" draws so much justified animosity from both scientists and theologians today is that it attempts to situate divine action, barely disguised as "Intelligent Design," in an explanatory slot that is customarily reserved for science. Theology has a legitimate explanatory role in an extended hierarchy of explanations, but it is not an alternative to scientific understanding.

According to naturalism, however, science has now *replaced* religion and theology in the task of making sense of life. How did this insurgency come about? There are many ways of telling the story, but one of the clearest versions is that of the philosopher Hans Jonas. To our pre-scientific ancestors, Jonas observes, the entire world was saturated with life. Not only plants and animals, but the whole cosmos, including the sun, moon and stars, pulsed with life. "Panvitalism," the belief that everything is somehow alive, was the norm. But if life was present everywhere how could there be any room for death? The answer is that death simply had no intelligible place in the panvitalist ontology, so it must be an illusion. And in order to bolster the impression that death was unreal, our panvitalist ancestors came up with the notion of a "spirit" or "soul," expressing their conviction that the core reality of the deceased still lingered on somewhere else in the wide world of life.[7]

---

[7]   Hans Jonas, *The Phenomenon of Life* (New York: Harper & Row, 1966), p. 9.

The idea of a distinct animating principle allows for the existence of life beyond death, and, of course, the expectation of subjective immortality has provided consolation to literally millions of people all the way down to the present. But after modern geology and astronomy exposed the vast expanses of lifelessness in the physical universe – and by contrast the paltry amount of life here on earth – there is no wider world of life left to give domicile to departed souls as the panvitalists had believed. Life is a deviant exception, so lifelessness has gradually come to replace it as the fundamental reality. As Jonas puts it, "the lifeless has become the knowable par excellence and is for that reason also considered the true and only foundation of reality."[8]

From this ironic turn of events has emerged the contemporary naturalistic agenda: "It is the existence of life within a mechanical universe which now calls for an explanation, and explanation has to be in terms of the lifeless."[9] Living organisms must be reducible ultimately to earlier and simpler nonliving components. The ideal of explaining life in terms of what is lifeless (and mindless) continues to motivate much modern scientific research. If life is made up ultimately of inanimate matter, then the truly explanatory sciences must be physics and chemistry rather than biology. The hierarchical boundaries that traditionally situated humans, animals, plants and minerals on separate levels of being and value have vanished, and the idea of pure, lifeless and mindless "matter" is now taken as foundational in naturalistic attempts to understand life and mind. Although some naturalists have recently grown uneasy with the cruder versions of materialist reductionism, generally speaking it is still accurate to say that the metaphysical backdrop of contemporary biology, as well as the sciences of mind, is very close to what both Jonas and the theologian Paul Tillich have called an "ontology of death."[10] Lifelessness seems more real than life. Jonas is aware that he is using the

---

[8]   Ibid., pp. 9–10.   [9]   Ibid.
[10]   Ibid.; also Paul Tillich, *Systematic Theology*, vol. III (Chicago: University of Chicago Press, 1963), p. 19.

term "death" here when others would simply call it "the mere indifference of matter." But he goes on to insist that "the cosmos once *was* alive as perceived by man," and it has since died in our hearts and minds.[11] What has taken its place is a "panmechanistic" worldview in which lifelessness is the ground state of all being. The earlier panvitalist concern about how to explain death if everything real is alive has now been replaced by the puzzle of how to explain life if being is essentially dead.[12]

According to Jonas, it was the emergence of dualistic myths and philosophies that made this metaphysical inversion possible.[13] The first shoots of dualism originally sprouted in panvitalistic soil in the form of the idea of a soul or spirit. But then, especially in modern times, dualism came to divide up the world ever more strictly between life, mind and soul on one side, and mindless and lifeless "matter" on the other. This worldview received its full-blown expression in René Descartes' famous separation of thinking substance (mind) from extended substance (matter). Dualism has been attractive to countless religious people because by separating soul from body, and linking bodiliness to the "evil" realm of materiality, it provides tidy answers to the question of why we die, suffer and have evil thoughts. But it has had the unhappy consequence also of robbing most of the universe of the vitality, sentience and mentality that all animals and humans feel immediately in their organic existence. A major outcome is the peculiarly modern belief that our own critical intelligence is not part of nature at all.

Naturalism in principle denies that there is anything apart from the material world. But many naturalists nonetheless treat our own critical intelligence as though it were not part of the natural world after all. Some even deny that such a thing as mind really exists. The modern divorce of the mind from nature has had the logical effect

---

11   Jonas, *The Phenomenon of Life*, p. 12.
12   Ibid., pp. 9–12.   13   Ibid., p. 12.

of rendering the earlier and simpler realm of "matter" completely mindless. And once matter has been pictured as utterly foreign to "mentality," it is only a small step further to empty nature of "vitality" also. Having exorcised the cosmos of life and mind, the modern ontology of death has bequeathed to science the logically impossible assignment of explaining life and mind completely in terms of what naturalists take to be an *essentially* lifeless and mindless universe. One side of Descartes' dualism has now been stripped off, and all that remains is the side consisting of lifeless matter. Nature can now be viewed more simply as an atomic, molecular and historical continuum in which each level of being is reducible to its historical antecedents and physical constituents. The former boundary between life and nonlife has dissolved. Any proposal that the origin and early development of life involved a great "leap" beyond its physical precursors must be rejected as regressive supernaturalism. As Darwin himself insisted, there can be no big leaps in nature (*natura non facit saltum*).[14]

THE LEAP OF LIFE

What has complicated the naturalist program, however, is that in the emergence of life from its cosmic antecedents nature appears after all to have indulged just the kind of leap that science, at least until recently, has precluded.[15] Today, as we shall see in chapter 5, scientists propose that the sharp discontinuity evident in "emergent" phenomena is a purely natural development. But the leap that nature makes in giving rise to life still seems extraordinary. The impression of life's discontinuity stems from several obvious features that make living beings stand out in sharp relief from their nonliving physical

---

[14]   Charles Darwin, *On the Origin of Species* (New York: Random House, 1993), p. 246.

[15]   An earlier version of some material presented in this chapter first appeared in my De Lubac Lecture at St. Louis University, published as "Science, Theology and the Origin of Life" in *Theology Digest* 49 (Winter, 2002), 334-46. Here, however, the content has been considerably revised.

predecessors. For example, organisms clearly have a capacity to *strive* and *feel* in ways that rocks and liquids do not.[16] These subjective marks are not easily measured, however, so science typically ignores them. Another distinctive mark of life, one that seems less subjective and more measurable than sentience and striving, is life's capacity to carry information. But by endowing life with a prodigiously "informational" signature, nature seems to have taken, quite suddenly, as large a leap as any supernaturalist might have hoped for.[17]

Can the origin of information in the universe, then, be given a purely naturalistic explanation? Or do we have in the informational aspect of life a novel phenomenon that invites us to break through the naturalistic enclosure? I believe theology must pursue such a proposal with great circumspection, since it is also easy for philosophers and scientists to understand information, like everything else, in a purely naturalistic way. "Information," as I understand it here, means the set of instructions required to form a specific pattern. In biology today information is especially conspicuous in cellular DNA. Since the 1950s biology has shown how a strand of DNA, featuring the four "letters" A T C and G, functions as a code that carries a complex "message" or set of directives. This message in turn tells cells how to manufacture and guide the proteins that build up into the various kinds of organisms.

But where did DNA's own specific pattern of instructions come from? It seems accurate to say that the question of the origin of life coincides in great measure with the fascinating question of the origin of coded information in the cell.[18] This is why Manfred Eigen proposes that the task of science is "to find an algorithm, a natural law

---

[16]   Michael Polanyi, *Personal Knowledge* (New York: Harper Torchbooks, 1964), pp. 327ff.

[17]   While it is true that inanimate artifacts such as computers also have an informational character, they are themselves extensions of *life*, manufactured by living beings whose own characteristics, including the capacity to create computers, is dependent upon the informational sequencing of their own genetic constitution.

[18]   Berndt-Olaf Küppers, *Information and the Origin of Life* (Cambridge, Mass.: MIT Press, 1990).

that leads to the origin of information."[19] The revered biologist George Williams has gone so far as to insist that matter and information are "two separate domains of existence, which have to be discussed separately, in their own terms." "Maintaining this distinction," he adds, "is absolutely indispensable to clarity of thought about evolution." And, he continues, "in talking about things like genes and genotypes and gene pools, you're talking about information, not physical objective reality."[20] In view of this new version of dualism it seems as difficult as ever to understand life completely in terms of physics and chemistry alone.

Is it perhaps in the logical partition between mindless physical reality on the one hand, and coded information on the other, that theological explanation of life becomes appropriate? Is the special place for divine action, as the scientist and theologian John Polkinghorne suggests, that of introducing into nature the nonphysical realm of information?[21] It seems undeniable that with the arrival of information in life, nature has made a great leap. The information-processing that codes for specific outcomes in organic life, no matter how gradual its arrival on earth may have been and regardless of how simple the first cells were, renders life logically and ontologically discontinuous with the inanimate world. *Natura facit saltum* (nature makes a leap) after all. The earlier and simpler world had no place for messages and meanings. At one time there was no coded information in nature, but now there is. And once information arrived, the face of nature was altered forever in a most dramatic way.

19   Manfred Eigen, *Steps towards Life: a Perspective on Evolution*, translated by Paul Woolley (Oxford: Oxford University Press, 1992), p. 12.

20   From an interview recorded in John Brockman, *The Third Culture: Beyond the Scientific Revolution* (New York: Simon & Schuster, 1995), p. 43.

21   John Polkinghorne, "Theological Notions of Creation and Divine Causality," in *Science and Theology: Questions at the Interface*, edited by M. Rae, H. Regan and J. Stenhouse (Grand Rapids: Eerdmans, 1994), p. 236. Arthur Peacocke expresses a qualified agreement with Polkinghorne in "A Response to Polkinghorne," *Science and Christian Belief* 7 (1995), 113.

And yet, information made its debut in such an unobtrusive manner that it disturbed none of the physical or chemical laws or processes already operative in the cosmos. There was no grand entrance accompanied by trumpet blasts. The introduction of information in the domain of life required no departure from the invariant habits of chemistry and physics. Carbon still bonded blindly with hydrogen, oxygen, nitrogen, and so forth, as it had done in organic molecules before the birth of self-replicating life. In the appearance of information there is no saltation detectable by chemistry alone. And yet, looked at in terms of information science, life clearly introduced a kind of discontinuity into the cosmos. When Francis Crick and James Watson contended that life is reducible to chemistry and physics, they overlooked the true role of information.[22] They failed to notice that information can be so important in life only because the *specific sequence* of letters in the nuclear DNA of any organism is *not* a matter of chemistry alone. The informational sequence is logically extraneous to the chemistry of the cell's DNA. If this were not the case, DNA could not be informational.[23] The fact that DNA is replete with instructions implies that there is obviously much more than chemical activity going on in living phenomena.

Nevertheless, would it be prudent on the part of theologians to make information the characteristic domain of divine action in the explanation of life? Is the discovery of information in living phenomena the theologian's opportunity to postulate some kind of nonscientific causation? Or does the fact of information perhaps mean only that we should now revise our understanding of nature itself so as to include an inherent informational resourcefulness that methodological materialism had previously left out? Is it possible, in other

---

[22] Francis H. C. Crick, *Of Molecules and Men* (Seattle: University of Washington Press, 1966), p. 10; J. D. Watson, *The Molecular Biology of the Gene* (New York: W. A. Benjamin, Inc., 1965), p. 67.

[23] Michael Polanyi, *Knowing and Being*, edited by Marjorie Grene (Chicago: University of Chicago Press, 1969), pp. 22–39, 229.

words, that taking stock of information leads only to a less materialist form of naturalism?

INFORMATION AS ANALOGY

The theologian, in any case, must be careful not to link information
too directly to divine action. Theology should have learned by now –
perhaps the hard way – to avoid seizing territory that may belong more
appropriately to scientific modes of explanation. It must not appeal to
any "God of the gaps," but instead allow science to push natural
explanations as far as these can go – as if God were not a factor – even
into the sphere of information. Theology should never give the
impression that it has any desire to intrude into, or set itself up
as an alternative to, scientific accounts. Instead it must look for a
way to hold together the two stanzas at the head of this chapter
without reducing one to the other.

This means, once again, that the theologian must be suspicious
of contemporary anti-Darwinian "Intelligent Design Theory," which
has now seized the freshly visible domain of information as an opportunity for inserting the category of "intelligence" into scientific work
as an explanatory category. Such a notion will inevitably be taken by
most scientists as just one more pointless metaphysical, if not theological, intrusion. Mathematician William Dembski would appear to
most scientists to be bringing in a category alien to science when he
accounts for the "specified" informational complexity of DNA in
terms of Intelligent Design.[24] If one were to understand intelligent
design as the characteristic mode of divine action in nature, such a
move, I believe, would be theologically suicidal. After all, the arrangement of genetic sequences does not rule out scientific explanations such as genetic drift or natural selection of random variations
in chains of DNA. Moreover, tying the notion of intelligent design
too tightly to specified informational sequencing risks attributing

---

[24] William Dembski, *Intelligent Design: the Bridge between Science and Theology*
(Downers Grove, Ill.: InterVarsity Press, 1999).

directly to God not only healthy but also diseased and "unfit" organisms that result from degenerate DNA chains.[25] This is not a move that a sound theology of nature would wish to endorse.

And yet, with these cautions in mind, I would suggest that the notion of information may still be employed fruitfully as an *analogy* for divine action in the origin and evolution of life. The quiet, unobtrusive way in which information insinuates itself into the chemistry of life serves to demonstrate that there can be a kind of influence operative in nature that is not reducible to sheer material force. By analogy, and only by analogy, divine influence could be said to be deeply influential in the universe and life without ever needing to display itself in such a crudely physical way that science could easily detect it. Life, as it is now plain to see, is most certainly not the outcome of physical and chemical processes alone. If George Williams is right, and information belongs to a realm distinct from sheer materiality, then science itself has now made room for nonmaterial forms of causation in the natural world.

The fact of information, however, does not require a reversion to anything like Descartes' dualism. It is closer to the role that "form" plays with respect to matter in Aristotle's philosophy. Informational causation, therefore, may be no less natural, and no more divine, than formal, efficient and material causation. Still, scientists' recent acknowledgement of the essential role of information in nature does indeed challenge crudely materialist interpretations of causation. It places in question the conventional naturalist view that life is fully explicable in terms of an earlier and simpler material makeup. The entrance of information into cosmic process points to a domain of unrealized possibilities that reside somewhere other than the purely material. Something quite natural, but nonetheless nonmaterial, is going on in the emergence of information. And from the

---

[25]   Resorting to the notion of a primordial Edenic "Fall" as an explanation of such evils may also appeal to anti-Darwinian Christians, but it will seem desperately defensive to most theologians and evolutionary biologists.

point of view of theology, any challenge to simplistic materialist naturalism is significant.

Consequently, I would advise against theology's locating divine action directly at the level of DNA's informational sequencing. This would introduce more problems than it could ever solve, given all of the monstrosities and maladaptations that occur in life's history. However, the powerfully effective but noncoercive way in which informational sequencing in DNA organizes organic life, without in any way disturbing chemical and physical laws and processes, certainly allows us to theorize that by analogy divine action could be of a kind that is deeply influential without ever making hugely interruptive waves on the surface of the physical world and without being strictly determinative. If information can do its "work" in such a quietly unobservable and unobtrusive way, then so also could divine agency.

LAYERED EXPLANATION

Where, then, if not as a direct source of information, may theology enter into the discussion of life's origins and evolution more prudently? A reasonable response to this question may have implications for the wider issue of how to understand divine action in a scientific age, generally speaking.

If it is to have any relevance at all, theology must first make room for what I earlier referred to as "layered explanation." By layered explanation I mean to emphasize that most phenomena admit of more than one level of understanding. I have already given an example of layered explanation in chapter 1, but let me now offer another.[26] Suppose a pot of water is boiling on my stove, and someone comes along and asks me to explain why it is boiling. I can respond at several levels. I might say, first, that it is boiling "because the molecules of H_2O are moving around excitedly, thus causing

---

[26] Here the example I am using and adapting is one that I believe I heard about first from John Polkinghorne.

the transition from a liquid to a gaseous state." This is a perfectly good explanation, and it should be pushed as far as it can go. But it does not rule out other ways of understanding what is going on. A second way to answer the question is to say the water is boiling "because I turned on the gas burner." And still a third response is to say that the water is boiling "because I want tea." Most people would agree that only this third explanation gets to the bottom of what is really going on in the single event of boiling water.

Here we have three logically distinct explanations. All are correct and relevant, but they cannot be reduced to or mapped onto one another. Each adds something important to an understanding of why the water is boiling, and it does so without conflicting or competing with the others. Of course, the persistent materialist will still try to reduce all three levels to atomic movement, but logically speaking the third-person language of physics and chemistry is not reducible to the first-person, subjective perspective of the "I want tea" that leads me to boil the water.[27]

Analogously, then, when people ask "why did life appear at all in the universe?," a perfectly good response is to recite the current physical and chemical explanations such as those mentioned briefly above. These accounts are highly complex and very tentative, of course, and scientists will surely continue to revise them. A theology comfortable with explanatory pluralism, furthermore, will encourage science to push purely natural explanations of life and its origin as far as possible. Theology must avoid any attempt to make room for divine action in yet uncharted scientific territory. But a sense of layered explanation can in principle make ample room for theological explanation at another level than that of science. Without contradicting or competing with elaborate physical and chemical explanations theology may be justified in claiming that life exists

---

[27]　The desperate claim by eliminative materialism that there is really no such reality as "subjectivity," as I shall show later, is the product of a failure to be radically empirical in one's approach to nature.

ultimately because of the infinite generosity and attractive power of God. Life is the consequence of physical, chemical and astronomical events at the level of "secondary causation," while also being willed, at the level of "primary causation," by a creator who longs for a universe that will emerge into being as much as possible on its own, accompanied by spontaneity, accident and ample temporal duration.

Scientific naturalism, however, is habitually disinclined to explain things in distinct layers. It prefers explanatory monism, often appealing spuriously to Occam's razor for justification. Yet, once an inquirer has adopted the style of explanatory pluralism, the quest to understand the origin of life becomes more interesting, even at the level of the natural sciences. Today, for instance, astrophysics adds its own insights into the origin of life to those of chemistry and conventional physics by taking into account the initial physical conditions and fundamental constants that have endowed the Big Bang universe with the very specific set of features that make life possible. In the first micro-second of cosmic existence a set of mathematical values came into play in such a precise way as to make for an essentially life-bearing universe.[28] Studies of the origin of life need to add this new layer of explanation to previous ones even though it is not logically reducible to them.

The astronomer Martin Rees, for example, finds "six numbers" in the physics of the early universe that had to have been set at just the right mathematical values if life was ever to emerge at all.[29] The fact that these six numbers came together at the beginning is highly improbable. If any of the six – for example, the expansion rate of the cosmos and the force of gravity – had been only infinitesimally different, life could never have occurred in our universe. How, then, are we to explain the precision with which the values are fixed? Have

[28]   Martin Rees, *Our Cosmic Habitat* (Princeton: Princeton University Press, 2003), pp. 123–40.
[29]   Martin Rees, *Just Six Numbers: the Deep Forces that Shape the Universe* (New York: Basic Books, 2000).

we found here at the edge of cosmology the ultimate limits of science and the right place to bring theology into the quest to understand life and its origin? Is God the cause of life because God is the direct cause of the improbable set of mathematical and physical features that make ours a peculiarly life-breeding cosmos?

While it may be tempting theologically to pursue this line of inquiry, I would prefer to heed Paul Tillich's admonition that one should avoid ever allowing theological explanations to appear as though they are making divine action part of a scientifically understandable causal series.[30] Consequently, it seems to me that Rees' appeal to the idea of a "multiverse" to account naturalistically for our life-bearing cosmos should not be dismissed abruptly. There may be, Rees speculates, an uncountable number of "universes," all invisible to us except our own. And the possibility that at least one of these will be ready for life can then be attributed to an *accident* that arises out of the play of immensely large numbers of them.[31] Moreover, Rees' multiverse theory appears to be compatible with certain interpretations of microphysics.

Theology, I would emphasize, does not have to be grudging in giving scope to the role of accident (or contingency) in natural process. If the natural world were perfectly directed or designed in every detail, after all, it could never become distinct from its creator. It would be a puppet. So the multiverse idea is completely compatible with the belief in an extravagantly generous creator. Nevertheless, I cannot help suspecting that beneath much of the growing interest in the idea of a multiverse there lies a naturalistic assumption that divine creativity can have no place at all in the explanation of life, at any level. Indeed, since there is no empirical evidence to support the theory so far, it is not unreasonable to ask whether it is scientific curiosity alone that fuels multiverse speculation. Or is it the prospect

---

[30]   Paul Tillich interprets the notion of first cause (*prima causa*) to mean the *ground* of the whole series of natural causes and effects, rather than the first in a series of causes: *Systematic Theology*, vol. I (Chicago: University of Chicago Press, 1951), p. 24.

[31]   Rees, *Just Six Numbers*, pp. 150-61; *Our Cosmic Habitat*, pp. 157–81.

that a multiverse would be *essentially* lifeless, as naturalism generally takes to be metaphysically true? And unless the universe is
thought of as essentially lifeless, might there not be a regressive
return to pre-scientific panvitalism?

There is, of course, something wholesomely scientific about
refusing to bring in God at explanatory levels where natural explanations belong. But Rees and others are doing more than protecting
science from theological meddling. The idea of a multiverse is attractive to their naturalistic philosophy because it allows the natural
world, now envisaged as an immense assembly of universes, to
remain originally and pervasively lifeless. After all, if our aberrantly
life-bearing universe were the only one available, naturalism might
be in trouble. Rees himself acknowledges that if our own "universe"
were alone, rather than being one among countless others, the coinci-
dence of the six numbers essential for life's emergence would seem
uncannily unnatural. The idea of a multiverse, on the other hand,
allows for a fundamental natural lifelessness to spread out over an
imaginably wider totality of being. This pervasive silence could then
be accidentally disturbed only momentarily by the rare, local and
unintentional fluctuation that takes the form of our own life-bearing
universe.

So panmaterialism would still be safe, rescued by the new
auxiliary hypothesis of a mindless multiverse. In such a setting, life
would never again have to be interpreted as a gift that arouses the
sentiments of worship and gratitude. Its obvious contingency would
not be a sign of grace but only of an underlying absurdity. One gets
the impression from reading Rees' work, and similar proposals, that
respectable thought must not allow that life and mind are somehow
built into the natural world in a *systematic* way. Naturalism cannot
in principle abide any openings for such a decay of thought.

Nevertheless, after expressing these suspicions, I want to emphasize once again that theology does not have any business in ever
functioning as an *alternative* to scientific explanation. It is never
good form for theology to object to any attempts to carry naturalistic

explanations as far as they can conceivably be taken.[32] It is not beyond the realm of plausibility, after all, that science may eventually be able to confirm (or falsify) the multiverse theory experimentally. Even though it is far from being able to do so at the moment, science must be given free rein to explore all explanatory possibilities.[33]

THE PLACE OF THEOLOGY

Why then bring theology in at all? For the same reason that it would considerably impoverish your understanding of why the pot of water is boiling on my stove if you failed to take into account the fact that I want tea. My telling you that the water is boiling because I want tea does not compete with scientific explanations of how liquid states are transformed into gaseous, but it certainly adds intelligibility to the scene. So also a theological claim that the terrestrial transformation of chemistry into living beings happened ultimately because of divine generosity does not have to be taken as a directive to stop looking for physical explanations of life – including possibly the complicity of a multiverse.

At the same time, however, it does not seem good form for naturalists to elevate chemical, physical, evolutionary or astrophysical accounts to the status of final or ultimate explanation of life. Such a claim, after all, may turn out to be analogous to the assertion that the water in my kettle is boiling because of molecular commotion *rather than* because I want tea. It is based on an unverifiable belief that physicalist accounts are final and that there cannot be many incommensurable levels of understanding. What the entire science and religion dialogue needs today, I believe, is the suppleness of mind to allow for richly layered explanation when trying to understand any set of complex phenomena.

---

[32] That Rees himself has arrived at the limits of scientific explanation is clear from his admission that science cannot answer the question of why there is anything at all: *Our Cosmic Habitat*, p. xi.

[33] Rees, *Our Cosmic Habitat*, pp. 157–81.

In this more expansive explanatory milieu theology should not have to apologize for using the vague language of symbol, metaphor and analogy in pointing to what it takes to be the ultimate explanation of life. From the perspective of theology, layered explanation laced with a generous amount of analogy is our best access to rich understanding of nature and life. The further theology drifts from the indigenously symbolic language of religion, the weaker and more superfluous its explanations will seem in comparison with those of science. Perhaps, then, the relationship of divine action to the origin of life on earth is *something like* the relationship of "I want tea" to the movement of molecules of boiling water in the teapot. Both levels of explanation are necessary for full understanding of why the water is boiling, but it is not helpful to collapse one layer directly into the other. Similarly a layered model of explanation allows theology to find its own depth so that it does not have to squeeze its accounts into the categorical slots carved out by the sciences.

In any case, attempts to be scientifically specific about how God acts in the world would be as futile as trying to show in serial detail exactly how "I want tea" affects the movements of molecules in the boiling water. Exactness here is not only unnecessary but logically self-subverting. It is obvious that there is an unspecifiable connection between the purposive "I want tea" and the causal movement of water molecules, but there is also a decoupling of causal levels that makes precipitous attempts to fold one directly into another ludicrous.

Let me put all of this another way. The fact that the water is boiling because I want tea does not logically exclude its boiling also because of the physical properties of H_2O. In Aristotelian terms, final causes are not rivals to efficient or material causes. Scientific naturalists, however, want nothing to do with the idea that purpose can be causal (see chapter 6), typically claiming that there can be only one explanatory level, and that this belongs to the efficient and material causal accounts proper to science. Scientific naturalism typically supposes that the more room we make for purposive (teleological) explanation, the less room will be left for physical, biological and other kinds of explanation, but I will argue later that there is no logical justification for this belief.

Finally, explanatory monism is a correlate of what Alfred North Whitehead has referred to under the general heading of "the fallacy of misplaced concreteness."[34] This is the illogical habit of identifying abstractions with concrete reality. Explanatory monism is rooted in the same modern failure to realize that adequate explanation may be deeply layered and that therefore any particular scientific explanation is inevitably an abstraction. This does not mean it is wrong, but every specific scientific account can provide access to only a very limited contemporary cross-section of the rich and inexhaustible causal depth that lies beneath, behind and within each cosmic occurrence. I hope this point will become clearer as we proceed.

---

[34]   Alfred North Whitehead, *Science and the Modern World* (New York: The Free Press, 1967), pp. 54–55; for fuller development see pp. 51–59.

5 Emergence

> In nature every moment is new; the past is always swallowed and
> forgotten; the coming only is sacred.
>
> Ralph Waldo Emerson[1]

Among the many scientific ideas that seem to support the naturalist
worldview that of *emergence* now holds an increasingly prominent
place. Emergence means the appearance in natural history of more
and more intricately organized physical and living systems over the
course of time. What is most remarkable about emergent systems is
that they display properties and functions that had not been operative
at earlier and less complicated chapters in cosmic history. Emergence
implies, at the very least, that the universe was not finished or fully
formed at the instant of its origin and that it takes time for its
potentialities to become actualized. Emergence also leaves open the
possibility that unpredictably novel modes of being are yet to be
realized in the cosmic future. There is no good reason to suspect that
emergence will not continue for billions of years to come. Even
while it is always subject to the laws of thermodynamics, the
cosmos remains open to surprising outcomes up ahead that will resist
entropy even as they feed on it.

However, in the end, will the story of cosmic emergence prove
to be nothing more than a fascinating but ultimately futile thrust into
the void? Or is it instead a meaningful series of responses to a
beckoning presence that addresses the universe from beyond, calling
it into a new future, and perhaps endowing it with permanent meaning? Scientific naturalism holds to the former, whereas a theology
rooted in the Abrahamic religions, with their sense of a creative and
promising God, must endorse the latter. The question of where the

---

[1]   Ralph Waldo Emerson, "Circles," *Emerson's Essays* (New York: Harper Perennial
Books, 1981), p. 226.

universe is heading – to ultimate extinction or final redemption – is one of the most divisive among thinking people today, so it is important to look at what science has to say about it all. Many who have focused closely on natural phenomena by way of scientific method have found little to encourage optimism. Others have not been so glum. For the cosmic optimists, the story of emergence is evidence of nature's essential inclination to move beyond the dullness of deterministic routine. The appearance of physical complexity, life, consciousness and other splendors in the history of natural process provides grounds for the expectation that even richer outcomes may arise in the future. Are there perhaps hints in emergence that nature is situated within a creative and redemptive mystery after all? Or does the prospect that the emergent universe will eventually culminate in catastrophe provide more reasons than ever for naturalistic gloom?

Biophysicist Harold Morowitz observes that in the history of the universe there have been no less than twenty-eight distinct stages of emergence.[2] The most eye-catching of these, of course, are the appearance of life on earth out of lifeless physical precursors 3.8 billion years ago, and then the relatively recent flowering of critical intelligence. But the emergence of increasingly complex systems has been occurring in less flashy ways from the first microsecond of cosmic origins. And as we stand here 13.7 billion years after the Big Bang, the adventure of emergence continues. Indeed, under our feet and behind our backs here on earth a new emergent reality is already taking shape in the form of a globalized human culture.

But why is the universe so restless to begin with? Why did not the initial cosmic burst of energy play itself out in a spasm of momentary duration and uncomplicated creation? Why did the universe go to all the bother of emerging gradually, so that by anyone's

---

[2] Harold Morowitz, *The Emergence of Everything: How the World Became Complex* (New York: Oxford University Press, 2002). See also Philip Clayton, *Mind and Emergence: From Quantum to Consciousness* (New York: Oxford University Press, 2004).

reckoning it has produced a stupendous increase in organized complexity and beauty, eventually accompanied by considerable tragedy as well, across a span of billions of years? Is cosmic emergence at bottom an empty plunge toward final nothingness, or a response to something like an invitation?

This is not a new question by any means, but over the last century science has altered the landscape on which it is being asked. On the heels of science's discovery of the energetic character of physical reality came a new awareness of matter's habit of undergoing unpredictable kinds of phase changes and emergent self-organization. If one is theologically inquisitive, the burning issue today is not only why anything bothers to exist at all but also why the universe has been so restless once it came into existence. Why does the universe emerge bit by incremental bit, amidst sputtering experimentation at every phase, and yet giving rise overall to something undeniably grand?

Presented with such a specter, even the most jaded naturalist is now forced to wonder. Yet, predictably, the wonder fades as soon as it arises. According to scientific naturalism, one of whose main objectives is to transform what seems initially remarkable into something causally unremarkable, the emergent universe does not have to be sparked by anything beyond itself in order to bring about inventive outcomes. If a sufficient number of constituent parts are available and time is plentiful, then ordinary physical and chemical routines can be swept up at critical junctures into new and more elaborate levels of being and functioning.[3] If new rules of governance come into play occasionally, this is not due to any special divine initiative. The mindless play of accident, blind physical laws and large numbers within a sufficiently long span of time are all that is needed. Somehow the earlier-and-simpler must already contain the full explanation of the later-and-more. New rules take over occasionally, but

---

3   See Stephen Johnson, *Emergence: the Connected Lives of Ants, Brains, Cities, and Software* (New York: Touchstone, 2001).

they were there all along *in nuce.* Emergence is neither mystical nor miraculous.

Nevertheless, emergent phenomena arouse our interest at all only because they give the impression of being systems in which "more comes out than was put in."[4] Given enough time, deadness comes to life and mud gives rise to minds. In emergence what is earlier-and-simpler gives way to the later-and-more. Scientists, who are people just like the rest of us, would never have noticed emergence did it not seem, at least at first sight, to violate the timeless principle of causality according to which an effect cannot be greater than its cause. Indeed, to say that "more comes out than was put in" makes emergence sound suspiciously like magic, a most unappealing option for the hardcore naturalist. So it does not seem out of order, in the interest of full disclosure, to ask where the admittedly unprecedented rules come from that allow for emergent novelty. Where are the higher-order regulative principles hiding before they become actual? Are deep time, elementary physical laws, large numbers and the play of chance enough to account fully for the organizing principles that impose themselves on subordinate levels of physical activity in each new stage of cosmic creativity?

To anyone who looks objectively at the history of nature it is obvious that, at least over the long haul, something *less* has given way to something *more.* For example, life and critical intelligence – infinitely more complex in their organization and functioning than rocks and liquids – have come to birth out of an originally lifeless and unconscious universe. Of course, some naturalists will deny that there is anything *more* or *higher* about human consciousness as compared to the mindless processes that led up to it. Such valuations, they say, have no basis in reality. Complexity, according to the

---

4   John Holland, *Emergence: From Chaos to Order* (New York: Perseus Books, 1999), pp. 15, 112, 225.

Oxford physical chemist P. W. Atkins, for example, is only a disguise for an underlying physical simplicity.[5] And apparently this principle must also apply to the emergence of the most complex of all natural phenomena, the human mind. It too must be simplicity "masquerading" as complexity. But to devalue our intelligence in this way only renders questionable any judgments that emanate from the mind as so construed, including that of the naturalist. To deny that critical intelligence is somehow "more" than the unintelligent processes that preceded it is to reduce all human cognition, including all of science, to mere chatter.

But where does the *moreness* of life and mind, as they now exist, come from? Has it always been present in nature but not fully revealed? Or does the novelty in emergence reside eternally in some reservoir of potentiality distinct from natural process itself?[6] Not yet actualized possibilities, it would seem, must reside somewhere before they are actualized. But where? Whatever answer one gives, there is no doubt that in the course of cosmic history a primordial sea of elementary waves and particles has given rise to a succession of new and more complex levels and systems, including eventually living and thinking systems. Perhaps, then, the fact that life and mind have emerged at all reveals something essential about the character of the whole universe. If so, these emergent realities cannot be put aside as incidental to an accurate understanding of the natural world.

The natural sciences are conditioned, however, to turn their attention away from the obvious *novelty* in emergent outcomes. They are tacitly aware of the novelty, but their focus is primarily on the material and efficient causes that historically led up to, or that

---

[5]   P. W. Atkins, *The 2nd Law: Energy, Chaos, and Form* (New York: Scientific American Books, 1994), esp. p. 200.

[6]   Alfred North Whitehead refers to these possibilities as eternal objects, and compares them to the Platonic forms that are also said to reside in God; e.g. *Process and Reality*, corrected edition, edited by David Ray Griffin and Donald W. Sherburne (New York: The Free Press, 1978), pp. 43–46.

now underlie, emergent outcomes, especially life and mind. That mind is indeed more than its mindless antecedents cannot be doubted without a discrediting of the minds that are doubting. Incontestably there is an element of *more*, at the very least in the emergence of critical intelligence. Naturalism has been satisfied to explain the more in terms of the less, and the later in terms of the earlier, but can it avoid a virtual appeal to magic in doing so? Where does the more come from? Simply denying that there is *really* any more in the outcomes of emergent process than "what goes in" leads logically to the subversion of the most impressive outcome of cosmic emergence, critical intelligence.[7] It is especially with reference to this most wondrous of all emergent phenomena that we need to test the intellectual integrity of naturalism.

When confronted with complex emergent phenomena, it is not surprising that the natural sciences try to make sense of them by digging back to a chronologically earlier and hierarchically subordinate simplicity. This is what science is supposed to do. Scientific explanation looks for the simplest and most economical algorithms to account for emergent complexity. According to mathematician Gregory Chaitin, "for any given series of observations there are always several competing theories, and the scientist must choose among them. The model demands that the smallest algorithm, the one consisting of the fewest bits, be selected. Put another way, this rule is the familiar formulation of Occam's razor: Given differing theories of apparently equal merit, the simplest is to be preferred."[8]

Scientifically speaking, I will concede that the explanation of emergent phenomena must begin with simplification. In computational language, accounts of emergent processes must determine

---

[7] As I shall continue to insist, however, the acknowledgment of information and intelligence in nature is no justification for the anti-scientific and anti-Darwinian interpretations of today's "intelligent design" advocates.

[8] Gregory J. Chaitin, "Randomness and Mathematical Proof," in *From Complexity to Life: On the Emergence of Life and Meaning*, edited by Niels Gregersen (New York: Oxford University Press, 2003), p. 23.

whether the latter are in any way algorithmically compressible. In other words, the mathematical operations that depict an emergent phenomenon must be simpler than the outcome itself or else emergence will have been only described, not explained. Scientific naturalism, however, goes beyond scientific method. It assumes that the only truly explanatory way to understand the specific features of organisms is to look backward into the historically antecedent evolutionary pruning that gradually sculpted the various species of life and their behavioral patterns. Simultaneously it may claim that understanding emergent complexity requires our looking downward into hierarchically lower degrees of organization in order to discover the simpler constituent elements and algorithms.[9] But is this adequate explanation?

I realize that there are some naturalists who would claim not to be so reductionistic, but I believe David Papineau is typical of most. He says:

> I take it that physics, unlike the other special sciences, is complete, in the sense that all physical events are determined, or have their chances determined, by prior physical events according to physical laws. In other words, we never need to look beyond the realm of the physical in order to identify a set of antecedents which fixes the chances of subsequent physical occurrence. A purely physical specification, plus physical laws, will always suffice to tell us what is physically going to happen, insofar as that can be foretold at all.[10]

Scientific naturalists are not satisfied unless nature's algorithms can be manageably reduced, since explanation means simplification.[11] If one can suppose that humans are just animals, then

---

[9]   Perhaps some naturalists would qualify this depiction of their belief system by insisting that information is also an ingredient in their understanding of nature. But then the question remains: is information really causal? Or is it purely epiphenomenal, in which case it would be an effect of material processes and not a cause at all.

[10] David Papineau, *Philosophical Naturalism* (Cambridge, Mass.: Blackwell, 1993), p. 3.

[11] E.g. Atkins, *The 2nd Law*, p. 200; and Werner R. Lowenstein, *The Touchstone of Life: Molecular Information, Cell Communication and the Foundations of Life* (New York: Oxford University Press, 1999), pp. 325–33.

understanding humans will be much simpler than if we viewed them head-on as critically intelligent subjects. And if one can view animals as mechanisms, and mechanisms as nothing more than embodiments of invariant physical laws, then explanation gets easier the further down inquiry goes. Scientific method, insofar as it simplifies and compresses understanding, quite correctly overlooks the novel, unprecedented, and possibly defining features of the emergent phenomena. But by laying out the earlier and simpler constituents as though these alone provide a pathway to exhaustive explanation, scientific naturalism in effect explains away the very complexity and novelty that attracted scientists' attention to emergence in the first place.

Once again, I am not objecting to *science's* search for simple explanations, at least as a first step in understanding. But it is still reasonable to ask whether simple explanations can ever be full and final. Scientific accounts are limited to explaining such captivating emergents as life and mind in terms of what is lifeless and mindless. However, since any abrupt transition from deadness to aliveness in natural history would appear magical, naturalists are obliged by their creed to look for ways to make the transition seem perfectly smooth and completely specifiable in physical and chemical terms. One way of doing so is to make lifelessness the pervasive natural state of being and deny that life has any distinct reality at all. Accordingly, one may suppose that an enormous amount of time – commingled with simple operations and the random play of large numbers – lets the transition from deadness to life unfold so gradually that any impression of magic is apparently eliminated. A series of small steps in place of one large leap makes the appeal to magic or divine creation superfluous. Put otherwise, a sense of deep time can protect the fact of emergence from the naive interpretations of supernaturalists.

By assuming that only mindless matter can be ontologically real, one may dismiss our initial sense of wonder at emergent mentality as naive "folk psychology." Mind, in this view, is just a tag for a certain kind of physical process. Daniel Dennett's manifesto on the complete reducibility of consciousness exemplifies this perspective:

there is only one sort of stuff, namely matter – the physical stuff of physics, chemistry, and physiology – and the mind is somehow nothing but a physical phenomenon. In short, the mind is the brain. According to the materialists we can (in principle!) account for every mental phenomenon using the same physical principles, laws and raw materials that suffice to explain radioactivity, continental drift, photosynthesis, reproduction, nutrition and growth.[12]

STARTING WITH CRITICAL INTELLIGENCE

Aware of the prima facie unbelievability of this kind of materialist reductionism, however, even hard naturalists these days are beginning to sound softer than before, and reductionists are taking pains to appear more moderate and less greedy.[13] Yet the old habits are hard to cure. E. O. Wilson, for example, argues passionately for a "consilience" of all disciplines, but it is clear that the synthesis for which he is searching can take place only by understanding everything in terms of the persistently materialist worldview that underlies all his work.[14] "Non-reductive physicalism," "supervenience" and even "emergence" are some of the labels being used by philosophers and scientific naturalists to express a growing uneasiness with materialist attempts to explain mind.[15] But such stretching of language cannot cover up the fact that the explanatory agenda is still the same as before: True novelty must be excluded or else a wider and deeper kind of explanation would have to be allowed in to share the load with science.

However, as I shall argue momentarily, the emergent fact of critical intelligence itself, the registry of scientific and all other modes of knowing, cannot be reduced logically to the earlier-and-simpler

[12]   Daniel C. Dennett, *Consciousness Explained* (New York: Little, Brown, 1991), p. 33.

[13]   Daniel C. Dennett, *Darwin's Dangerous Idea: Evolution and the Meaning of Life* (New York: Simon & Schuster, 1995), pp. 82–83.

[14]   Edward O. Wilson, *Consilience: the Unity of Knowledge* (New York: Knopf, 1998).

[15]   See Jaegwon Kim, *Philosophy of Mind* (Boulder, Colo.: Westview Press, 1996), pp. 211–37.

without losing, in the very process of such reduction, all authority to arrive at any reliable understanding of anything whatsoever. And when the actual performance of our minds is taken seriously as part of nature, reductionism, soft or hard, will be exposed as having only limited explanatory power.

Emergence at all levels of being, and not just at those of life and mind, requires that nature possess an anticipatory rather than simply a cumulative character. It must be open to a domain of potentiality that makes a quiet entrance – from the future as it were – and thus opens up the otherwise unbending fabric of things to the later-and-more. However, in order to comprehend the shift in worldview implicit here the point of departure once again must be my readers' own awareness of their own critical intelligence. The principles of explanation required to make sense of this most incandescent and anticipatory of all emergent phenomena can be applied also – in an analogous manner – to emergent process in general. Critical intelligence, as I have repeatedly noted, is fully part of nature, so it has relevance to our understanding of nature in a more general sense. Scientific naturalists should have no difficulty accepting this starting point, since they also agree that the human mind is completely continuous with the physical universe and its evolution. Hence it seems appropriate to commence our understanding of emergence by looking first at the most dazzling instance of it.

By taking this approach I shall have to follow, even more seriously than science does, the first imperative of the mind, namely, to be attentive and open. I have referred to it as the empirical imperative. Science is indeed empirical, but it does not attend to everything. In fact, scientific method deliberately leaves out some of the most immediately obvious data that present themselves to our experience. For example, biological science says little or nothing about, and is sometimes even embarrassed to mention, the purposeful, anticipatory *striving* characteristic of all living phenomena, even though the fact of striving is one of the traits that allows scientists to distinguish living from nonliving beings. The realm of biology was established separately from departments of physics and chemistry only because people understand intuitively that frogs and amoebas, and even plants in a way, can anticipate *more* being, and that they can therefore undertake a kind of *effort* in their environments that inanimate entities do not. Human persons apprehend, in an inarticulate sort of way, that living beings follow a "logic of achievement." Organisms are the kind of entities that can succeed or fail in their endeavors, whereas inanimate processes are incapable of effort, failure or success.[16] Striving is an emergent feature in nature, known tacitly by every biologist, but not focused on as such.

Ironically it is their implicit recognition of the distinct logic of achievement characteristic of living organisms that allows scientists to designate a whole region of natural reality as "alive." But having fenced off this domain and thereby secured the autonomous field of biology, biologists then usually ignore the purposeful striving that allowed them to put up the fence between the life sciences and the physical sciences in the first place. Instead, they now try typically to comprehend life completely in terms of the nonliving. Molecular biology and biochemistry, for example, focus on life's earlier and simpler lifeless constituents, turning their explicit attention away from the later-and-more of actually living and striving beings.

Science also filters out other kinds of information that bombard each of us in the affective, intersubjective, narrative and aesthetic regions of our experience. Because of its methodological self-limitations science cannot look squarely at what is truly emergent about natural phenomena. Indeed the theoretic mode of engagement with the world, generally speaking, diverts attention away from the primal fields of consciousness that opened us up to the reality of emergent novelty in the first place. In the contemporary outbreak of interest in emergence one can almost detect an unvoiced suspicion that ordinary scientific procedures have been leaving out

---

[16]   Michael Polanyi, *Personal Knowledge* (New York: Harper Torchbooks, 1964), pp. 327ff.

something vitally important in natural process. But any personal encounter with irreducible novelty remains formally unacknowledged by science insofar as the latter continues to explain things and predict future events in terms of the earlier-and-simpler.

If striving and novelty have been ignored by science, all the more so has the fact of subjectivity in nature. The sciences, including most of the human sciences, deliberately disregard the trait of "insideness" that each of us experiences immediately in our mental functioning. Even though our critical intelligence is no less part of the emergent universe than rocks and rodents, scientists' working assumption throughout the modern period has been to suppose that subjectivity of any sort is not part of the real world. One might have thought that the empirical imperative would have led scientific naturalists to attend more closely to the reality of their own cognitional performance, but just the opposite has been the case.

Why this oversight? Could it be that a thoroughgoing assimilation of critical intelligence into their picture of nature would require too radical a transformation of the naturalist creed? I believe so. A major reason for the modern refusal to allow for a richer and more generalized empiricism (such as Lonergan's), one that would view human subjectivity as a truly *objective* part of the universe, is that such an inclusion, if taken consistently, would burst open the tight enclosure within which naturalism has tried to corral the world. An honest embrace of critical intelligence as part of the natural world, on the other hand, would have the ironic effect of turning the whole universe literally inside out. To acknowledge that our critical intelligence is an emergent aspect of *nature*, and not an unnatural intrusion from some other world, would radically alter the set of categories needed to understand this world as it actually is.

Attending closely to our own desire to know, I want to stress, would not be a forsaking of the empirical imperative but a more thorough application of it. To take critical intelligence with complete seriousness, an exercise that I began in chapter 3, should even spell the end of naturalism as a plausible creed. Naturalists, of course, will vigorously deny that they have ignored the fact of critical intelligence. They will point out that cognitive science, neuroscience, evolutionary biology, paleontology, anthropology and other kinds of inquiry have long been studying the origins and properties of mind and that these disciplines are making great strides in understanding it. However, such fields of study alone can never fully escape an objectifying approach to "mind." They do not look at critical intelligence from the inside. Such an examination, after all, would call for a different kind of attentiveness, understanding and knowing from that employed by the natural sciences. I doubt that many of those I have been calling naturalists would be comfortable with the widening of our field of vision that I am proposing, even though such a shift would considerably enrich their understanding of nature. Naturalists write long books with audacious titles such as *Consciousness Explained*, but they seldom if ever attend closely to critical intelligence in the innovative and more empirical way that the sadly neglected philosopher Bernard Lonergan does.[17]

Some naturalists are very busy looking at the earlier evolutionary stages leading to mind, and others insightfully lay out the physical substructure of conscious functioning. But they all fail to notice or account sufficiently for the force of the imperatives operative in their own mental functioning here and now. The very fact that they are content with exclusively physicalist or evolutionary explanations of consciousness is indication that they have not attended closely to the mind's first imperative. If they had attended to it, they would have noticed the amazing degree of trust or confidence they have tacitly placed in their own minds' capacity to understand and make true judgments. As one can easily observe in their writings, scientific naturalists such as Dennett, Papineau and Atkins are exceptionally confident about their cognitional capacities. However, they almost

---

[17]   Bernard Lonergan, SJ, *Insight: a Study of Human Understanding*, 3rd edn. (New York: Philosophical Library, 1970); Bernard Lonergan, SJ, "Cognitional Structure," *Collection*, edited by F. E. Crowe, SJ (New York: Herder and Herder, 1967), pp. 221–39.

never turn around and take note of this confidence as a datum itself in need of deep explanation. Even if they did try to explain it, one can only assume that it would be in terms of the earlier-and-simpler, an approach that if taken consistently would subvert rather than justify their cognitional swagger.

If this last point needs any further amplification, let me simply restate what I have been saying all along. Naturalists, by decree, are limited to giving physicalist and evolutionary accounts as ultimate explanation – since there is nothing else, including human culture, that could possibly be appealed to as more fundamental. Hence they are obliged also to explain their own intelligent functioning in naturalistic terms, since intelligence is fully part of nature. But an application of naturalist explanation to the understanding of one's own cognitional performance still leaves us with the question of how to account for the indomitable trust that activates the desire to know and issues the mind's injunctions.

Even though physical and evolutionary explanations are necessary for any rich understanding of critical intelligence, these cannot be sufficient to explain the trust that any knower places in the imperatives of the mind. Later on, I will show how a shift in worldview can justify this confidence. For now, though, I simply ask that the reader consider this question: if intelligence were completely reducible to the earlier and simpler realm of mindless processes and physical elements that naturalists claim to be ultimate explanation, can we trust any mind that tries at this present moment to explain itself solely in such terms?

Some naturalists may see the point of the question, so they will look elsewhere than in earlier and simpler natural processes for an explanation of how they have acquired their cognitional pluck. Perhaps the basis of their confidence lies in the ways in which their minds have been molded by family life, human history and culture. If they have been educated into the "scientific worldview" they have been told stories about scientific heroes and bold adventures into the unknown. Their intellectual audacity is a psychological byproduct of being told stories that have built up their faith in scientific method. Or perhaps their mental poise has been behaviorally sculpted by an educational process that instills in them a sense of the practical power of science.

There is something to all of this, of course, but it is beside the point as far as the truth of naturalism is concerned. Because of the relativity inherent in all purely culture-based understanding, we cannot find an *ultimate* justification for our cognitional confidence there either. Even the judgment that enculturation is enough to ground our cognitional confidence would itself have to be the product of culturally conditioned consciousness, failing therefore to cure the logical circularity that surrounds such a proposal. No adequate justification of the trust we place in our mental functioning can be provided by going "outside nature" to culture since, for the naturalist, culture is locked inside nature anyway.

How then can we justify the spontaneous trust we all place in our critical intelligence and the imperatives of our minds? You will note that in asking this question I too am expressing confidence in my own mind, assuming that by obeying the imperatives to be open, intelligent and critical I may come closer to truth, to *what is*. If I lacked this spontaneous trust I would not be asking the question that begins this paragraph. And if any naturalists are reading this book, they will notice once again that their own sincere questioning of what I am writing here is also possible only because they too have already made an act of faith in the imperatives of their own minds to lead them to truth. But since the ultimate explanation of this firm intellectual faith cannot be supplied by either pure naturalism or pure culturism, any coherent grounding of our cognitional confidence – that is, of the trust we spontaneously place in our desire to know and its imperatives – requires that we turn somewhere else. But where?

I propose that the ultimate basis for our trusting the desire to know and the mind's imperatives can be found only in the mind's native anticipation of a transcending fullness of truth that has *already* grasped hold of us but which also escapes our grasp. Only if our minds already anticipate, and allow themselves to be carried away by, an infinite horizon of being and truth (later I shall add goodness and beauty), do we have any plausible reason for trusting our critical intelligence to take us deeper and deeper into the real. To anticipate a fullness of truth or being, however, does not mean to take a blind stab into the heart of total darkness. Anticipating truth is not the same as comprehending it, of course, but such expectancy would be impossible if the mind were totally untouched here and now by the fullness it is anticipating. Anticipation of truth's fullness is possible not because we can ever actually grasp this fullness, but only because we have the capacity to be grasped by it. Such a capacity cannot be actualized, however, without the practice of certain virtues such as courage and humility.

What I have been calling the "imperatives" of the mind, therefore, are not incentives to servility driven by a materially determined series of past causes. Rather they are at heart *responses* to a most compelling invitation that summons from a horizon up ahead. In spite of their persistence, the cognitional imperatives are not deterministic dictates but promises of the mind's fuller emancipation. The imperative to be open, for example, is the beginning of the mind's surrender to an enlivening wholeness or wideness of being that has already embraced it. The imperative to be intelligent is evoked by the inexhaustible intelligibility of being that frames both the cosmos and the finite human minds that have emerged from it. And the imperative to be critical arises because of the mind's instinctive awareness that no present hypothesis, theory or worldview can ever fully capture the fullness of being that has already begun to encompass the mind. It is only because our intelligent and critical mentality anticipates, and is already taken captive by, a fullness of intelligibility and truth that the imperatives of the mind are so eager to prod us toward deeper understanding and knowledge.

IMPLICATIONS FOR EMERGENCE

How then does our acknowledgment of critical intelligence's anticipatory ambience tie into this chapter's topic, that of emergence?

Once again, in responding to this question I take it for granted, along with the consistent naturalist, that our minds are completely continuous – physically and historically – with the natural world from which they have evolved. Since our own critical intelligence is the most luminous instance of emergence to which we humans have access, its characteristically anticipatory orientation may be understood as an intensification of, and not an exception to, nature's more general orientation toward a fullness of being and truth. The fullness of being and truth that arouses my own desire to know is the same horizon – or domain of potentiality – that awakens emergence in nature as such. In some sense the whole of emergent natural history, inseparable from the emergence of mind, has always anticipated the same fullness of being that my critical intelligence now reaches toward more explicitly. One may object to this conclusion, of course, but only by risking an even more questionable reversion to dualism, vitalism or materialism, each of which ends up artificially separating our minds from their natural habitat.

Since naturalist philosophers such as Dennett assume that the later-and-more must be accounted for exclusively in terms of the earlier-and-simpler, they are forced to eliminate from their naturalistic pictures of mind the very emergent qualities that call out for an explanation in the first place. What is "explained" in their writings, therefore, is not critical intelligence at all, but an abstraction in which the mind's anticipatory reaching toward truth has already been cut away as irrelevant. Consequently, the emergent reality most in need of explanation, the desire to know, is not explained at all. Biochemical and evolutionary accounts, indispensable though they may be, are not enough to do the job. It is logically contradictory to hold that critical intelligence, our best example of a later-and-more in all of natural history, can be fully accounted for only by following its tracks back into the murky mindlessness of what is earlier-and-simpler.

Furthermore, in attempts to explain emergence it does not help matters to appeal to gradualism or an abstract notion of time's enormity, as though a purely quantitative accumulation of moments could ever in billions of years add up to real agency. The mere transit of time, no matter how prolonged it may be, cannot by itself cause anything to happen. Something else has to be going on during the passage of evolutionary epochs in which quarks and atoms are being turned into minds. What time allows for is that the earlier-and-simpler has the opportunity to traverse a domain of anticipated *possibilities*, some of which may become actualized in the emergence of the later-and-more, and others not.

However, once again, where do these possibilities come from? Naturalism only assumes, and in no way accounts for the realm of potentiality into which temporal process travels. Nor does it spell out clearly why the universe is such that possibilities can be actualized only gradually rather than all at once. It is not enough to look only to the past for an understanding of emergence, although that too is an essential part of any full explanation. Rather it is primarily the power in possibility that accounts for the emergent character of the universe. The Latin word for possibility is *potentia*, and emergence cannot make good sense apart from what medieval philosophers referred to as "the possibles." These are realities that have not yet become actual. Expectedly, scientific naturalism will respond that the realm of the possible has no actual existence, and that therefore it cannot be explanatory in any sense. It will insist that the shape of the future is already fully determined *a retro*, that is, by a blind propulsion of events driven exclusively by material causes rooted firmly in the past. The future is pure emptiness. To the naturalist the unintelligent epochs of the earlier-and-simpler are explanation enough – even for the later-and-more of intelligence – if numbers are sufficient and time is profuse. So appealing has this worldview become that until emergence began to catch our attention recently there have not been many challenges to it in the modern and contemporary academic worlds.

However, the naturalist craft is logically shipwrecked on the emergent rock of critical intelligence from which it has tried so hard to steer clear. Even though the sciences provide undeniable evidence that our own intelligence has arisen historically from a natural process of evolution, by themselves they do not account fully for intelligence or even subjectivity as such. In the first place, methodologically speaking, both subjectivity and intelligence are concepts traditionally alien to natural science. For science to appeal to either of these as explanatory concepts would signal a dramatic departure from its accepted method of seeing and understanding. In the second place, neither cognitive nor evolutionary sciences can say why subjective experience ever entered the universe at all, or why the universe harbors a being with an insatiable desire to know.

There is a surplus in both subjectivity and intelligence that escapes even the Darwinian understanding that has lately become the court of final appeal in the life sciences. I would certainly allow that adaptation and even a degree of contingency are part of any full explanation as to why critical intelligence emerged in natural process. In previous books I have persistently expressed my general agreement with Darwinian biology, and I wish to reaffirm it here.[18] Our capacities to perceive, understand and know have come to birth from within the bowels of earth and evolution. Nevertheless, the evolutionary naturalist overlooks the fact that there is something stubbornly nonadaptive about critical intelligence, at least in terms of the universe as construed by naturalism. In fact, the anticipative restlessness of the desire to know can never feel completely at home in the naturalist's universe. If my desire to know is adapting me to anything at all it is not to naturalism's ultimately unintelligible universe but to an anticipated fullness of being, intelligibility and truth. An unrestricted desire to know could never find itself at home in a universe that is believed to be at bottom unintelligible or whose partial intelligibility is itself a mere accident.[19]

18 John F. Haught, *God after Darwin: a Theology of Evolution* (Boulder, Colo.: Westview Press, 2000); *Deeper than Darwin: the Prospect for Religion in the Age of Evolution* (Boulder, Colo.: Westview Press, 2003).

19 In chapter 9 we shall also see that the ethical sensitivities even of some prominent evolutionary naturalists are anything but adaptive to the Darwinian universe.

Therefore it is out of a sense of fidelity to my desire to know that I must now press on to find a more adaptive context for my critical intelligence than the one offered by scientific naturalism. I cannot find such an environment short of a worldview that looks upon nature as *completely intelligible*. And in the end, I believe, such a worldview must be a theological one, where the anticipated fullness of being, meaning and truth is ultimately nothing less than the eternal reality invoked by religions. Such a worldview is a much more encouraging setting for endless, ongoing scientific inquiry than is the naturalist belief that the universe "just is" and therefore is *ultimately* unintelligible.

SUMMARY AND CONCLUSION

This chapter has made two main points. The first is that critical intelligence provides an accessible key to understanding emergence as such. Let us recall once again that to each one of us the desire to know is the most immediately conspicuous emergent fact in the much larger cosmic unfolding. The mind is an extension of nature, and not something floating around outside it. Thus the anticipatory character of the desire to know tells us something important about nature in general: the world's full intelligibility is to be found only in terms of something that awaits it up ahead – in the later-and-more – and not in the earlier and simpler past that falls into isolated and more unintelligible fragments the further back we look. The emergent processes in nature as a whole receive their meaning and coherence not from the material past, but from a summons up ahead. The emergent world "rests on the future . . . as its sole support."[20] In biblical religions this future, in its ultimate reaches, is known as God.

If humans are part of nature, then their critical intelligence is also part of nature, as is the subjective experience of every other

---

[20] Pierre Teilhard de Chardin, *Activation of Energy*, translated by René Hague (New York: Harcourt Brace Jovanovich, 1971), p. 239.

sentient being. Of course, the scientific method of looking at what temporally precedes and physically constitutes life and mind is fruitful and illuminating. But if human inquirers want to understand in depth the *actual* universe, that is, the one that includes critical intelligence, they need to consider, in addition to what they can find out by way of a scientifically reductive analysis of subordinate particulars and historical precursors, what this particular emergent phenomenon is telling us about the natural world that gave birth to it. What it tells us is that the whole of nature is anticipatory.

My second point has been that critical intelligence cannot breathe or survive inside the boundaries of naturalism's understanding of the world. Obedience to the desire to know and the imperatives to be open, intelligent and critical can only lead to a disposition of discontent with naturalism's ultimately unintelligible universe. Only a world that I anticipate to be completely intelligible could ever be a fully adaptive environment for my desire to know. And only a completely intelligible world can ensure that science will have a future as well. Scientific naturalism cannot provide such a world. If taken consistently, it would suffocate critical intelligence. Fortunately, most self-avowed naturalists do not consistently follow their own creed.

6 Purpose

I sing the goodness of the Lord
That filled the earth with food;
He formed the creatures with his word
And then pronounced them good.

Isaac Watts, 1715

Is it the goodness of the Lord
That fills the earth with food?
Selection has the final word
And what survives is good.

Kenneth E. Boulding, 1975[1]

In contemporary conversations about the relationship of religion to science two questions stand out: is nature all there is? And does the universe have a purpose? The two issues are inseparable. For if nature is all there is, there could be no overall purpose to the universe. That is, there could be no goal beyond nature toward which the long cosmic journey would be winding its way. But if the logic here is correct, then the detection of an overarching purpose in nature would imply that nature is not all there is. In the broadest sense purpose means "directed toward a goal or *telos*." The question before us, then, is whether the cosmos as a whole is *teleological,* that is, goal-directed. Is there perhaps a transcendent goodness luring it toward more intense modes of being and ultimately toward an unimaginable fulfillment? How can we find out?

If cosmic purpose were to manifest itself palpably anywhere in nature, would it not be in the life-world? Yet contemporary biology finds there only an *apparent* purpose. Scientists, for the most part, seem to agree that there is indeed a kind of purposiveness, or

---

[1]   Kenneth Boulding, "Toward an Evolutionary Theology," in *The Spirit of the Earth: a Teilhard Centennial Celebration*, edited by Jerome Perlinski (New York: The Seabury Press, 1981), pp. 112–13.

teleonomy, in living phenomena.[2] The heart has the purpose of pumping blood, eyes of seeing, brains of thinking, and so on. Purposiveness in this sense is an indisputable fact of nature. However, the orientation toward specific goals in the life of organisms is not enough to demonstrate that there is an across-the-board purpose to the universe itself. Darwin's impersonal recipe for evolution now seems to be enough to account for what scientists used to think were signs in living organisms of a divine intelligence that orders all events toward a meaningful end. The adaptive complexity that gave earlier generations of biologists reason to believe in an intelligent deity now only *seems* to have been purposefully intended.[3] Blind evolutionary mechanisms are the ultimate explanation of purposive design.

In a recent interview the famous evolutionist Richard Dawkins states: "I believe, but I cannot prove, that all life, all intelligence, all creativity and all 'design' anywhere in the universe, is the direct or indirect product of Darwinian natural selection. It follows that design comes late in the universe, after a period of Darwinian evolution. Design cannot precede evolution and therefore cannot underlie the universe."[4] So purpose, at least in the guise of design, has apparently been fully naturalized by evolutionary science. Natural phenomena that formerly seemed to bear the direct imprint of divine intelligence are now exposed as outcomes of a completely mindless process. The adaptive design of organisms gives only the illusion of being deliberately intended. Purpose, at least in any theologically significant sense of the term, simply does not exist.

Dawkins is willing to grant that we humans have "purpose on the brain,"[5] and many other naturalists allow that we need a sense of purpose to live happy lives. But this does not mean that life at large

---

[2] E.g. Jacques Monod, *Chance and Necessity*, translated by Austryn Wainhouse (New York: Vintage Books, 1972).

[3] Michael Ruse, *Darwin and Design: Does Evolution Have a Purpose?* (Cambridge, Mass.: Harvard University Press, 2003), pp. 324–28.

[4] *New York Times*, January 5, 2005.

[5] Richard Dawkins, *River out of Eden* (New York: Basic Books, 1995), p. 96.

or the universe as a whole is in fact purposeful. Viewed from the perspective of evolutionary biology, the old human habit of looking for meaning in nature may be adaptive, but it is illusory. Nature itself has no goals in mind, and the purposiveness of organisms is no signal of an eternal divine plan. It is natural – even for naturalists – to seek purpose, but whatever purpose people seem to find in nature as a whole is in fact a purely human construct, not a reflection of the world as it exists "out there."

Biologically speaking, evolutionary naturalists emphasize, there is no significant difference between our own brains and those of our ancestors who sought purpose through religion. Our brains and nervous systems are built to look for meaning in things. But in an age of science the personal search for purpose can no longer presume the backing of the universe in the way that religions did in the past. After Darwin the ancient spiritual assumption that purpose is inherent in the natural world has been exposed as nothing more than an evolutionary adaptation.[6] Maybe the illusion of purpose was invented by our genes as a way to get themselves passed on to subsequent generations. Or, if not directly rooted in our genes, the human passion for purpose is a freeloading complex, parasitic on brains fashioned by natural selection ages ago for more mundane tasks.[7] By either account, the penchant for purpose is *ultimately* explainable in a purely naturalistic way. All human yearning for lasting purpose, whether in the universe or in our personal lives, is groundless. At best, religious myths about purpose are noble lies, perhaps convincing enough to help humans adapt, but too imaginative to be taken seriously in an age of science.[8]

[6]   Edward O. Wilson, *Consilience: the Unity of Knowledge* (New York: Knopf, 1998), p. 262; Walter Burkert, *Creation of the Sacred: Tracks of Biology in Early Religions* (Cambridge, Mass.: Harvard University Press, 1996), p. 20.

[7]   Scott Atran, *In Gods We Trust: the Evolutionary Landscape of Religion* (New York: Oxford University Press, 2002), pp. 78–79; Pascal Boyer, *Religion Explained: the Evolutionary Origins of Religious Thought* (New York: Basic Books, 2001), p. 145.

[8]   Loyal Rue, *By the Grace of Guile: the Role of Deception in Natural History and Human Affairs* (New York: Oxford University Press, 1994), pp. 261–306.

There is not the slightest evidence that the whole scheme of things makes any sense ultimately.

CAN PURPOSE BE FULLY NATURALIZED?

However, it is necessary to make two points here. First, it is not evolutionary biology, but *evolutionary naturalism* that rules out purpose. Dawkins himself, as we have just seen, admits that he *believes* – but cannot scientifically demonstrate – that evolution undermines any theological sense of purpose. Science as such, even the naturalist must agree, has nothing to say one way or the other about any overarching purpose in nature. Science, strictly speaking, is not preoccupied with questions about values, meanings or goals. Teleology is not its concern. My second point is that evolutionary naturalists, along with some religious believers, tend to confuse purpose with "divine intelligent design." And since Darwinism can explain local organic "design" naturalistically some claim there is no need any longer to look for purpose in the universe as a whole. To the pure Darwinian, organisms may seem to be designed, but divine intelligence is not the ultimate cause of their "apparently" purposive features.[9] Design is the outcome of an evolutionary recipe consisting of three *unintelligent* ingredients: random genetic mutations along with other accidents in nature, aimless natural selection, and eons of cosmic duration. This simple formula has apparently banished purpose once and for all from the cosmos.

However, the idea of purpose is not reducible to intelligent design. Design is too frail a notion to convey all that religions and theologies mean when they speak of purpose in the universe. Purpose does not have to mean design in the adaptive Darwinian sense at all. Rather, purpose simply means *the actualizing of value*. What makes any series of events purposive is that it is aiming toward, or actually bringing about, something that is undeniably *good*. Is it possible that the actualizing of value is what is *really* going on in the universe?

---

[9] Dawkins, *River out of Eden*; Ruse, *Darwin and Design*, pp. 268–70, 325.

And is not critical intelligence, with its capacity to know truth, direct evidence of it?

There is a close connection between purpose and value. Naturalists would agree with this point, but they doubt that values really exist anywhere independently of our human valuations. Obviously, most of them would agree, we humans have a sense of values that gives purpose to our lives. For example, I take my writing this book to be purposive since its intended goal is that of achieving something I consider good or worthwhile. Likewise, scientific naturalists consider their own intellectual efforts to be purposeful. They tacitly surrender their minds and hearts to the *value* of truth-telling, a cause they expect to outlive them and give significance to their work even after they are gone. If they did not consider truth-telling to be an enduring value worthy of the deepest reverence, they would scarcely care whether readers took them seriously, nor would they write books so earnestly instructing us that religions lead human minds away from the truth. Obviously evolutionary naturalists care about truth, and their lives are made meaningful only because truth functions for them as a value worth pursuing. So, in seeking what is unquestionably good, they too have "purpose on the brain." Were they to deny it, they would eviscerate their own intellectual achievements.

Naturalists maintain that there is a fully natural explanation for everything. But what about the value of truth itself, the value that gives meaning to their own lives? Can that too be explained naturalistically – as a purely human invention? If we really believed that truth is merely a human construct, then the pursuit of truth could no longer function to give purpose or meaning to our lives. To experience meaning in life, after all, requires the humble submission of our minds and lives to a value that pulls us out of ourselves and gives us something noble to live for.[10] It entails a commitment to something

---

[10] This is a point made emphatically by Viktor Frankl in *Man's Search for Meaning* (New York: Pocket Books, 1959).

greater than ourselves. Having a sense of meaning is the consequence of *being grasped* by a value or values that we did not invent and that will outlive us. If we sincerely thought that we were the sole creators of truth then truth could no longer function to give purpose to our lives, nor would it allow our intelligence to function critically. If evolutionary naturalists *consistently* thought that truth – along with other values – were nothing more than the products of genes, minds or cultures, then such a fabrication could no longer function to give meaning to their own lives either.

For a value to be the source of meaning it has to function as more than an arbitrary human invention. If I thought of truth as the product of human creativity alone, then there would be nothing to prevent me from deciding that deception rather than truth-telling should guide my life and actions. The naturalist of course will instinctively reject such a proposal. But why? What is it in the naturalist worldview that makes truth-telling an unconditional value, the absolute good that everyone is obliged to revere? If all the ideals that give purpose to one's life were seriously taken to be contingent concoctions of the human brain or cultural convention, it would seem inconsistent for naturalists to tell me in effect that I must treat the values of truth and truth-telling as though these were *not* also pure inventions.

In fact, however, naturalists are not consistent. Typically they deny in their philosophy of nature what they implicitly affirm in their actual ethical and intellectual performance. For example, evolutionary naturalists clearly treat truth as a value that judges their own work, and therefore as something they did *not* invent. Some of them even devote their whole lives to its pursuit. It is what gets them up every morning. In effect they are serving a cause that they tacitly know will outlast them. Their implicit sense of the lastingness of truth gives continuity to their efforts and satisfaction to their careers. Like the rest of us they are *grasped by* truth and have submitted their minds to it. At the same time, however, some of their own writings portray truth and other values as pure creations of human minds and, ultimately, of genes. They generally fail to see the logical contradiction between their almost religious obedience to truth-telling on the one hand and their evolutionary debunking of it on the other.

Since the universe itself is inherently valueless, their argument runs, people can all the more easily see that values and meanings must spring from their own creativity.[11] Owen Flanagan, for instance, says that "we have to find and make our meanings and not have them created and given to us by a supernatural being or force." Then he adds, "It seems like good news that meaning and purpose are generated and enjoyed by me and the members of my species and tribe, rather than imposed by an inexplicable and indefinable alien being."[12] However, Flanagan clearly performs professionally as though the truth-telling to which he apparently bows in writing his books, including the excerpt I have just quoted, is not simply "generated" by his or his tribe's inventive minds. If he seriously thought that he was the inventor of *all* the values he follows, among which truth-telling would have to take a prominent place, then it would seem unlikely that truth could function as a standard against which he could measure critically the content of his mind, or as something that could give his life significance.

Once again, then, naturalism proves to be too restrictive a worldview to contain the minds that thought it up. While Darwinian science can go a long way toward laying out the natural history that led up to the existence of our minds, it is too undersized to function as a worldview that accounts fully for why we are purpose-driven, meaning-seeking and truth-oriented beings. Darwinian explanations by themselves, after all, do not rule out the possibility that nature can create a kind of conscious organism that finds illusions more adaptive

[11] E. D. Klemke, "Living without Appeal," in *The Meaning of Life*, edited by E. D. Klemke (New York: Oxford University Press, 1981), pp. 169–72; Stephen Jay Gould, *Ever since Darwin* (New York: W. W. Norton, 1977), pp. 12–13.

[12] Owen Flanagan, *The Problem of the Soul: Two Visions of Mind and How to Reconcile Them* (New York: Basic Books, 2002), p. 12.

than truth. In fact, since truth can often be unsettling, and obedience to it demanding, the flight into fiction could conceivably be much more adaptive than facing up to facts. Some Darwinian naturalists understand religion in precisely this way. Religion is adaptive, they claim, because it allows people to avoid facing reality even while it is giving purpose to their lives.

Such a view, however, makes it all the more difficult to state in purely Darwinian terms how the naturalist's own mind came to be guided by an exceptionally pure passion for truth. What special events occurred in nature's normal course of making adaptive minds that allows one now to assume that the naturalistic belief system is not just one more way of adapting, no less illusory than all our other adaptive belief systems? As philosopher Richard Rorty admits, "the idea that one species of organism is, unlike all the others, oriented not just toward its own increased prosperity but toward Truth, is as un-Darwinian as the idea that every human being has a built-in moral compass – a conscience that swings free of both social history and individual luck."[13]

But perhaps, the naturalist might suggest, the passion for truth does not need to be explained in evolutionary terms after all. Maybe the naturalist's exceptional flair for truth-telling is the product not of natural, but of cultural evolution. Perhaps when humans came along in evolution they could learn to contradict what their genes dictate and thus elevate themselves to a new level of truthfulness and morality. Richard Dawkins insists that "we have the power to defy the selfish genes of our birth."[14] However, it is fundamental to the naturalist creed to insist that humans and their cultural creations are all ultimately part of nature. So it would be more consistent with evolutionary naturalism to insist that there has to be a purely natural

---

[13] Richard Rorty, "Untruth and Consequences," *The New Republic*, July 31, 1995, pp. 32–36. Cited by Alvin Plantinga: http://idwww.ucsb.edu/fscf/library/plantinga/dennett. html.

[14] Richard Dawkins, *The Selfish Gene*, 2nd edn. (New York: Oxford University Press, 1989), p. 200.

explanation of everything, including the urge to create culture. But let us suppose that the move by humans from nature into culture is so abrupt as to render evolutionary understanding irrelevant at a certain point. Perhaps, in other words, the naturalist's special ability to value truth is a skill that has been inherited through cultural influence rather than natural selection, since in the human arena Darwinism no longer works to explain everything very well. If so, however, this shift of ground only moves my question sideways. Can cultural influences, which we know to be riddled with relativity and historical contingency, explain any more substantially why the naturalist should have developed an exceptional talent for truth-telling? Dawkins, for example, does not provide a non-Darwinian explanation of why truth-telling is morally superior to deception either.

I doubt that moving over to the historico-cultural setting will make it any easier for the naturalist to say why truth-telling is an unconditional good. In any case, if truth were consistently thought of exclusively as either an evolutionary or a cultural invention it could no longer function as a beacon that arouses the imperatives of the mind or gives purpose to lives. Thus we need to consider another possibility: truth, in order to function as a value that gives meaning, must have its foundation in a region of being that transcends both nature and culture. Truth is best thought of as neither a natural nor a cultural creation, but as the anticipated goal of the desire to know. This is how truth functions in fact for naturalists whenever truth-telling gives zest to their lives. Truth is not something they possess, but something they anticipate. It is not something they concoct, but something that invites a surrender. What remains to be done, then, is for naturalists to bring their formal belief system into harmony with the way their minds actually work. What they tacitly affirm in every commitment of their minds to truth must no longer be denied when they articulate their worldview.

Truth, to reiterate my point, can function to give purpose to human lives only if it is encountered as a value distinct from or transcending our minds. Of course, human creativity enters into all our finite construal of truth, including this sentence. But even such constructs are responses to something like an invitation. We are addressed by truth even as we participate in its representation. There is no understanding of the world that is not in some measure a human construct, including those of both theology and naturalism. Every proposition can be subjected to layered explanation. At one level what I am saying now can be explained as a product of my own brain. At another level it can be explained as the result of my will to understand. But at still another it can be explained as my response to the attractive power of *what is*, that is, of being, reality, truth. By focusing only on the creative side of the mind's meeting with truth, naturalistic explanations fail to articulate what it is about truth that compels, persuades, makes us alive with excitement and gives purpose to our lives. To explain ultimately why truth has the power to attract and give purpose to our lives will require moving beyond the naturalistic worldview.

THE SELF-CONTRADICTION OF EVOLUTIONARY NATURALISM

Evolutionary naturalists, as a rule, do not seem to notice the logical inconsistency between their Darwinian accounts of value, truth and meaning on the one hand and their minds' actual performance on the other. They instinctively glorify the value of truth, especially scientific truth, as something to which the mind must bend. But their ultimately evolutionary explanations should lead them to doubt their minds' capacity to put them in touch with truth, as both Darwin and Rorty rightly point out. Assuming that their minds are a product of evolution, after all, there is nothing in the Darwinian recipe alone that would justify their trust that these same minds can reliably lead them to the truth rather than a state of deception. And if they took Darwinian naturalism as ultimate explanation they would have every reason to doubt that they have the capacity to know truth at all.

Even the late Harvard paleontologist Stephen Jay Gould, who was not a strict adaptationist, could not overcome the naturalistic inconsistency. For Gould, no less than for Flanagan, Dennett, E. O. Wilson and Dawkins, the ultimate explanation of every living phenomenon, including our capacity for truth, is evolution. Life's diversity and versatility is based on three general features of nature: accidents (undirected events), the law of selection (along with the laws of physics and chemistry) and lots of time. Gould gives more explanatory weight to contingency (especially accidents of natural history) than Dawkins and Dennett do, but the ultimate explanation of organic phenomena, including the brain, is still a combination of blind chance, impersonal necessity and deep time. As far as the present inquiry into the deepest ground of intelligence is concerned, it matters little what proportion is given to each ingredient. The point is that Gould's evolutionary naturalism views the ultimate explanation of mind – and this would have to include its tendency to value truth – as itself mindless and valueless.

Before Darwin, Gould says, we easily fell into the trap of think-ing that nature was inherently valuable and that values and meanings had a reality independent of us. But after Darwin,

> we finally become free to detach our search for ethical truth and spiritual meaning from our scientific quest to understand the facts and mechanisms of nature. Darwin liberated us from asking too much of nature, thus leaving us free to comprehend whatever fearful fascination may reside out there, in full confidence that our quest for decency and meaning cannot be threatened thereby, *and can emerge only from our own moral consciousness.*[15]

According to naturalism, there is nothing beyond nature that could conceivably give any value to the world. So it is left to our own human creativity to give value to things. But does this mean that it is also entirely up to us to decide that truth is a value? According to Gould, values and meaning have no objective status, either in nature

---

[15]   Stephen J. Gould, "Introduction," in Carl Zimmer, *Evolution: the Triumph of an Idea from Darwin to DNA* (London: Arrow Books, 2003), pp. xvi–xvii (emphasis added).

or God. The ultimate ground of value is not nature, evolution or God but our own "moral consciousness." And since there are no values "out there" in the real world, their existence can only be the result of human creativity solidified by cultural consensus. To be consistent, Gould would also have to claim that the value that naturalists accord to truth is dictated not by nature or God, since nature is valueless and God (probably) does not exist. And yet Gould's own life and work give evidence of a mind that *in fact* takes truth to be an intrinsic good. In his actual cognitional performance, both truth and his valuing of truth are irreducible to evolutionary or human creations. The unconditional value Gould finds in pursuing truth cannot be fully explained naturalistically or culturally without rendering that pursuit groundless.

Product of modernity that he was, Gould would probably respond that the naturalist's sense of human inventiveness allows us to recapture some of the self-esteem that our ancestors gave away to the gods. We can now take back what humans had forfeited during all those millennia when they naively assumed, in keeping with religions, that nature is intrinsically purposeful and that truth, value and purpose are not our own inventions. For Gould, the modern impression of a teleological void is an opportunity to fill the cosmos with our own values and meanings.[16] Once again, however, if we were fully convinced that the value we attach to truthfulness were no more than our own, apparently groundless, creation, then devotion to truth could no longer function as the source of meaning for our lives. Truth would be subordinate to the discretion of our own inventiveness rather than a torch that guides our minds more deeply into the marrow of the real. If evolutionary naturalists took their own doctrines seriously this would only have a corrosive effect on the trust they place instinctively in their own minds' imperatives to be open, intelligent and critical.

[16] Gould, *Ever since Darwin*, p. 12.

As a way of driving home this point, I shall ask you, the reader, to suppose once again that you subscribe to the tenets of *evolutionary naturalism*. Then I shall ask you whether the facts associated with the actual performance of your own mind are logically compatible with this naturalistic view of reality.

If you are an evolutionary naturalist, you will most probably account for living phenomena, including *your own mind*, ultimately in terms of the mindless Darwinian recipe for life. As an evolutionary naturalist you will also agree that the *ultimate* explanation of your various organs – your nose, mouth, eyes, ears and everything else functionally adaptive about you – is Darwinian natural selection.[17] And, to be completely consistent, you will be compelled to admit that your critical intelligence, which to the pure Darwinian is not a blank slate but has been molded to think the way it does by natural selection, can be explained ultimately also in terms of Darwin's recipe.[18] If you follow Gould, you may appeal too to the role of accidents in natural history, and not solely to selective adaptation, in explaining why you have a mind and why it works the way it does. But if you follow ultra-adaptationists such as Dawkins, then the ultimate explanation of your mind and all its features is the (mindless) natural selection of adaptive populations of related genes.

In either case, whether by Darwinian adaptation or by sheer accident (or a combination of the two), the *ultimate* explanation of your capacity to think is itself a set of mindless and unintelligent factors. But if this is right, then on what basis can you trust your critical intelligence, the outcome of an unintelligent process, to lead you to right understanding and knowledge of the truth at this instant? Darwin himself, as we have seen earlier, raised this troublingly subversive question, but he did not follow it up carefully. Evolution produced intelligence, declares Owen Flanagan, but evolution does

---

[17]   Gary Cziko, *Without Miracles: Universal Selection Theory and the Second Darwinian Revolution* (Cambridge. Mass.: MIT Press, 1995), p. 121.

[18]   Steven Pinker, *The Blank Slate: the Modern Denial of Human Nature* (New York: Penguin Books, 2002).

not require intelligence to produce intelligence. "Evolution *demonstrates* how intelligence arose from totally insensate origins."[19] But how then do you and Flanagan justify the confidence you *now* place in your mental functioning, especially if the ultimate ground of your intelligence is not only unintelligent but even insensate. If not by magic, then how did your dazzling intellectual prowess and the trust you place in it ever pop into this universe from a state of unutterable cosmic dumbness? It would appear, to me at least, that something momentous in the way of explanation has been left out here. A simplistic appeal to deep time and gradualism alone cannot bridge this explanatory gap since the passage of time itself does nothing to cure the fundamental blindness of the process.

If either aimless evolutionary selection or sheer contingency is the *deepest* possible explanation of your own mental endowment, then why should I pay any attention to you? How do I know – if I follow your own premises – that your mind is not just taking part in one more adaptive (and possibly fictitious) exercise rather than leading you and me to the truth? In company with Dawkins, Gould, Flanagan and others, you are telling me that a mindless evolutionary process (along with physical and chemical laws) is the *ultimate* explanation of your mind and its properties. Darwinism, you say, is true. I can agree with you scientifically speaking, but what I need to find out is how your mind's capacity for truth-telling slipped into the fundamentally unintelligent Darwinian universe that you started with. Although evolutionary explanation is essential, any attempt to answer this question in Darwinian terms alone will be circular and magical. In order to justify the assumption that your own mind is of such stature as to be able to understand and know truth, you will need to look for a kind of explanation that evolutionary science, at least by itself, cannot provide.

If you resort only to the idea of adaptation this will not work, since mindless adaptations, as you know well, can be illusory and deceptive. Perhaps then you will tell me that your highly prized human capacity for truth-telling is an incidental, unplanned byproduct of evolution. Perhaps it is something like what Stephen Jay Gould calls a "spandrel." That is, perhaps your cognitional talent is analogous to the arched surfaces (spandrels) that appear *incidentally* around the tops of columns whose main function is to hold up the roofs of cathedrals like San Marco in Venice. Such features are not the main architectural objective, but instead they simply appear, unintended in themselves, as the basilica is being erected. The spandrels, though unintended as such, may be taken as opportunities for great artists to cover them with frescoes or mosaics. And it may be the spandrels and the works of art, rather than the columns, that attract our focal interest as we enter the building.[20] Perhaps, in a similar way, your mind's capacity for truth-telling is a spandrel that just happened to show up as a contingent side-effect of the adaptive (and otherwise often deceptive and deluded) human brain.

Or, again, perhaps your critical intelligence is essentially the consequence of cultural conditioning that has little to do with natural selection. In any case, whether you interpret your capacity for truth-telling as a Darwinian adaptation, a spandrel, an accident of nature, or the consequence of enculturation, you will still have failed to justify the *trust* you are now placing – at this very moment – in your own intellectual activity. Both naturalistic and culturally relativistic explanations of mind provide too shallow a soil to ground the inevitable confidence that underlies your actual cognitional performance. Consequently, if up to this point you have professed official allegiance to evolutionary naturalism, you must now roam outside the circle of that creed in order to find a more solid reason for why your mind can be trusted to know and communicate the truth.

[20] S. J. Gould and R. C. Lewontin, "The Spandrels of San Marco and the Panglossian Paradigm: a Critique of the Adaptationist Programme," *Proceedings of the Royal Society of London*, Series B, vol. 205, no. 1161 (1979), 581–98.

If you are a Darwinian naturalist you will be given to making claims such as this one by biologist David Sloan Wilson: "Rationality is not the gold standard against which all other forms of thought are to be judged. Adaptation is the gold standard against which rationality must be judged, along with all other forms of thought."[21] I wonder, however, if Wilson is aware of how thoroughly his subordination of rationality to evolutionary adaptation logically undermines not only his claim but also the confidence with which his own mind makes such a claim. Assuming that the statement just quoted is one that comes from Wilson's own brain, and assuming also that his brain is the outcome of an adaptive evolutionary process, on what grounds can Wilson justify his assumption that readers should take his claim to be rational and true rather than simply an attempt to adapt? If a proposition contrary to Wilson's assertion had been the one to survive adaptively, then would it not have to be judged rational and true according to Wilson's proposal? If so, truth would have no stable meaning whatsoever, and pursuit of it could scarcely function to give purpose to one's life.

Are Darwinian selection, sheer contingency and the vicissitudes of enculturation, therefore, the best we can come up with by way of an ultimate account of intelligence? In particular, can evolutionary science, in any of its expressions, be the ultimate explanation of the spontaneous trust that all of us place in our rational faculties? Or is not Darwinism at best just one of several levels of explanation needed to understand critical intelligence? If the critical (truth-telling) aspect of our cognitional life could be explained ultimately in Darwinian terms, on what grounds can we trust it? We do not have to deny that physics, chemistry and evolutionary biology are all essential layers in the explanation of mind. But in order to account *fully* for the mind's natural longing for truth we have to move beyond naturalistic explanation.

---

21   David Sloan Wilson, *Darwin's Cathedral: Evolution, Religion and the Nature of Society* (Chicago: University of Chicago Press, 2002), p. 228.

PURPOSE AS ANTICIPATION OF TRUTH

Is it time then to call on theology? By no means, answers Richard Dawkins. Theology only complicates matters, doing nothing really to explain intelligence. After all, theology begins by assuming that there was *already* a creative intelligence operative in the scheme of things, namely, God. But, Dawkins insists, it is precisely creative intelligence that needs to be explained, not just taken for granted. And to the scientific mind any explanation of intelligence has to be in terms of what is unintelligent. Otherwise it is not an explanation. To explain anything scientifically means to simplify it. Before Darwin, Dawkins says, we had no simple and elegant explanation for intelligence, but now we do. "Darwinian evolution provides an explanation, the only workable explanation so far suggested, for the existence of intelligence. Creative intelligence comes into the world late, as the derived product of a long process of gradual change . . . After Darwin we at last have a universe in which creative intelligence is explained as emerging after millions of years of evolution."[22]

What I want to know, however, is how the evolutionary naturalist's own critical intelligence emerged with such pristine purity from utterly insensate origins. Dawkins' habitual appeal to gradualism here is no explanation. No matter how much time was available for intelligence to be cobbled together gradually (with the help of blind random variation and aimless natural selection), the question remains as to how naturalists' own minds acquired just those qualities that allow them to assume that they are in an especially advantageous position to contact *what is*. No matter how long it takes to bring intelligence into being out of absolute unintelligence, logically speaking this is still pulling a rabbit out of a hat. By appealing to time's fathomless depth – as though time itself were causal – Dawkins has not avoided magic either. His assumption is that an

---

[22] Richard Dawkins, "The Science of Religion and the Religion of Science," *Tanner Lecture on Human Values at Harvard University* (November 20, 2003). Cited on the *Science and Theology* website: http://www.stnews.org/archives/2004_february/web_x_richard.html.

enormous amount of time is explanatory, whereas a lesser amount is not.[23] But then where is the cut-off point? How many millions or billions of years of gradual change does it take before time ceases being a framework and becomes an efficient cause? And, again, how is magic to be avoided?

There is no denying, I must hasten to add, that evolutionary biology and the appeal to deep time can contribute much to an explanation of the origin and nature of the human mind. It is just that it cannot *fully* explain why the mind can know truth or why we should value truth-telling. I have no difficulty in accepting evolutionary accounts of mind, and I am willing to have the sciences push these as far as they can take us. However, I am questioning whether evolutionary accounts are *enough* to account ultimately for the trust that you, Gould, Flanagan, D. Wilson and Dawkins spontaneously place in your own minds to lead you (and me) to the truth. Darwinians, as I have already pointed out, even suspect that deception is one of life's most adaptive characteristics.[24] So if adaptive evolution, or accidents of nature, or social conditioning – or any other random or blindly material happenings underlying life – constitute the *ultimate* explanation of your own mental functioning, then why are you not suspicious right now that you may be deceiving me and yourself by claiming that naturalism is true?

What strikes me here especially is the degree of disconnection between the evolutionary naturalist's picture of nature's inherent unintelligence on the one hand, and, on the other, the especially prized scientific mind that has emerged from this foggy background already equipped with an amazing aptitude to understand and know the truth about things, including the truth of Darwinism. Something really big is missing from the evolutionary naturalist's account. The degree of separateness – between the primordial dumbness of nature

23   Richard Dawkins, *Climbing Mount Improbable* (New York: W. W. Norton & Co., 1996), pp. 3–37.
24   See Rue, *By the Grace of Guile*, pp. 82–127, for a convenient summary.

as depicted by naturalism, and the trustworthiness of critical intelligence as it is functioning now – is so severe that the very dualism of mind and universe that naturalism is supposed to have conquered has reasserted itself.

Evolutionary naturalism – as distinct from evolutionary science – must be rejected, therefore, because its method and claims are logically inconsistent with the trust that underlies the naturalist's own critical intelligence and the sense of purpose that comes with the pursuit of truth. On the other hand, a worldview in which truth is known by *anticipation* can explain this trust and sense of purpose, and it can do so without in any way contradicting the results of evolutionary science. It is because intelligent subjects can *be grasped by* truth that the surrender to this noblest of values – one that beckons the mind through the sacramental mediation of the natural and cultural worlds – can function to give our lives a purpose. Truth lights up everything and gives meaning to our lives not because it is created but because it is anticipated. And anticipation, in turn, entails a worldview in which the present state of nature is not only the sunset of the past, but the sunrise of an indeterminate future.

7 Seeing

> If the doors of perception were cleansed everything would appear . . . as it
> is: infinite.
>
> William Blake, "The Marriage of Heaven and Hell"

Organs and organisms act purposively. Even naturalists usually agree
that the life-world includes goal-directed functioning. The existence
of biology as a distinct discipline would never have come about
except for the fact that organisms and individual organs such as ears,
eyes and hearts have impressed people as having goals that nonliving
beings do not. It is especially our sense that living organisms
are able to strive, and that they can either fail or achieve success
in their pursuit of specific goals, that has allowed humans to distinguish living beings from inanimate.[1] It may seem somewhat ironic
then that naturalism today bases its claim that the cosmos is inherently pointless not so much on physics and cosmology as on
biology. The evolutionary blending of blind chance and impersonal
selection with an enormity of cosmic time seems sufficient to
account for the gradual, and hence nonmiraculous, emergence of
complex design, including minds. There is no need for, or any sign
of, any intentional cosmic agency guiding either life or the universe
as a whole. Individual aspects of organisms, including DNA, may be
functionally purposive, but this is not a good reason to suppose that
nature as a whole is teleologically guided. Purpose has now been
naturalized also.

Thus, it is evolutionary biology rather than physics that has
seemingly cleansed the last vestiges of intentional divine purpose
from the cosmos. Accordingly, naturalism now confidently invokes
the name of Darwin in its claims to have seen through the apparent

[1] Michael Polanyi, *Personal Knowledge* (New York: Harper Torchbooks, 1964),
pp. 327ff.

purposiveness in nature to the blind impersonality at the bottom of it all. Its devotees suspect that if it were not for the stubborn resistance by religious groups to Darwin's science, naturalism would quite possibly be now reigning triumphantly in human cultures.[2] Most naturalists are extremely critical of accounts of life that even so much as hint that the mechanism of natural selection, operating in league with contingent genetic variations and other undirected natural occurrences, may not be enough to explain evolutionary outcomes adequately. Efforts to dig deeper than Darwinian selection for complementary ways of understanding evolution seem only to open the door to the fog of mysticism.

To Darwinian naturalists the theological claim that purpose may be operative in the universe at large appears to rival rather than complement science. Final causal explanations seem to undermine the explanatory power of the mechanism of natural selection.[3] If we explain things in terms of purpose, the whole edifice of science comes crashing down. Evolutionary naturalists are critical even of common sense insofar as it usually looks for purpose in things and events. Thus, Harvard biologist Richard Lewontin:

> Our willingness to accept scientific claims that are against common sense is the key to an understanding of the real struggle between science and the supernatural. We take the side of science . . . because we have a prior commitment, a commitment to materialism. It is not that the methods and institutions of science somehow compel us to accept a material explanation of the phenomenal world, but, on the contrary, that we are forced by our *a priori* adherence to material causes to create an apparatus of investigation and a set of concepts that produce material explanations, no matter how

---

[2]   Daniel C. Dennett, *Darwin's Dangerous Idea: Evolution and the Meaning of Life* (New York: Simon & Schuster, 1995); Owen Flanagan, *The Problem of the Soul: Two Visions of Mind and How to Reconcile Them* (New York: Basic Books, 2002), pp. 43–50.

[3]   Michael R. Rose, *Darwin's Spectre: Evolutionary Biology in the Modern World* (Princeton: Princeton University Press, 1998), p. 211.

counterintuitive, no matter how mystifying to the uninitiated. Moreover, that materialism is absolute, for we cannot allow a Divine Foot in the door.[4]

The Divine Foot, of course, is shod with purposiveness. Lewontin assumes that the whole enterprise of science is powered by, and unintelligible apart from, an *a priori* commitment to materialist naturalism, a belief system that denies the presence of any overall purpose in the universe. Since material causes alone are explanatorily adequate, any alleged cosmic goal or final cause counts for nothing. As Lewontin concedes, however, his is not a scientific statement but a profession of faith. In fact, a more candid expression of the scientific naturalist's creed may be hard to come by. For Lewontin it is not science *per se*, but the belief that matter alone is real, that stands in contradiction to theological (and that includes teleological) explanation.

A RICHER EMPIRICISM

Since Lewontin's declaration is avowedly one of faith, and not a testable set of hypotheses, it is open to question whether his belief is a reasonable one. As I shall now argue, it is the naturalist's arbitrary suppression of alternative ways of *seeing* nature, and not the information gathered by science as such, that underlies the claim that evolution and the universe are pointless. Of course, any affirmation of purpose must be logically consistent with scientific experiment. In any quest to understand what is really going on in evolution the results of science must be taken fully into account. However, what exactly does it mean to *see*? According to naturalism, understanding must be tied to physical perception, knowledge to what is publicly testable, and prediction to what has happened already. I would agree that the empirical imperative to anchor thought in actual experience

---

4   Richard Lewontin, "Billions and Billions of Demons," *New York Review of Books* 44 (January 9, 1997), 31.

must reign over all trustworthy cognition. However, it is important to ask: just how thoroughgoing is science's own commitment to the spirit of empiricism? Can naturalists such as Lewontin claim justifiably that science and material explanations really see deeply into the heart of the real? Is scientific method the most foundational way of perceiving and understanding the world?

Science, I would submit, is not empirical enough to capture the most important things going on in evolution and the universe. Darwinian science is not wrong, but it cannot penetrate to the central core of life, mind and the cosmos.[5] In order to discern the presence of purpose, human inquiry must have access to other ways of seeing, understanding and knowing than those available to scientific inquiry. Science sees things more or less clearly, of course, but in arriving at clarity it forfeits the opportunity to penetrate to their ultimate depths. In fact, because science deliberately leaves out any concern with value, meaning, importance, subjectivity, intentionality or purpose, it cannot even in principle tell us whether or not these are features of the real world. The desire to know must engage what I have been calling the primal modes of experience (affective, intersubjective, narrative and aesthetic) if the cognitional imperative to be open and attentive is to contact those dimensions of nature that theoretic understanding cannot reach.

The naturalistic decree that cosmic purpose does not really exist, or that it is only a human construct, cannot be based on scientific observation alone. Scientific method, after all, deliberately blinds itself to any considerations of purpose. To assert that purpose is not really resident in nature, but is instead a human projection – since we have "purpose on the brain" – is no more rooted in scientific discovery than is Lewontin's declaration that science must begin by adopting a materialist belief system. Science's a priori self-blinding to teleology may be entirely appropriate methodologically speaking, but

---

[5] For a more thorough defense of this claim see my book *Deeper than Darwin: the Prospect for Religion in the Age of Evolution* (Boulder, Colo.: Westview Press, 2003).

only so long as scientists remain aware that their kind of inquiry has deliberately ignored the questions that most people of most times and places have considered all-important. Unfortunately, scientific naturalists seem to be unaware of how much of the real world science does leave out. And once naturalists identify the abstracted, quantitatively knowable aspects of the world with the totality of being, purpose is relegated to the status of fiction.

On careful inspection, however, the world that naturalism takes to be fundamental or concretely real turns out to be itself a construct built from the bottom up on a kind of faith and not on observation alone. Naturalism *assumes* that a kind of cognition that suppresses personal knowing, common sense and teleological considerations can be trusted to put us in touch with what is really real. It *believes* that the primal ways of knowing must take a back seat to the theoretic. As the above citation from Lewontin illustrates, naturalism cannot actually demonstrate that nature is devoid of purpose. Rather, it must *decree* dogmatically that purpose cannot be a real aspect of nature if we are to understand it. I believe, on the contrary, that it would be more consistent with the interests of the desire to know to avoid any such a priori declarations about the limits of either cognition or nature. The mind's first imperative is to open wide all the gates of experience, to cleanse the doors of perception, and only then to look at and try to understand what has been allowed to come in. Only after submitting to a richer empiricism shall we be in a position to say whether or not purpose is inherent in nature.

In submitting this proposal I have the backing of several philosophers who have recognized clearly the limits of science's own ability to see. They have instead argued for a wider and richer kind of empiricism, one that can pick up at least some of what science inevitably leaves out. Here I shall mention each briefly and then expand on the ideas of one in particular.

I am thinking, first, of the great French philosopher Henri Bergson (1859–1941), a broadminded scholar too easily dismissed as a vitalist and then discarded by most contemporary thinkers. Bergson insists on the penetrating power of the faculty of *intuition*. As compared to the less significant knowledge given by *intellection*, intuition can bring the mind into immediate contact with the facts of duration, life and creative novelty in evolution. Intuition also puts us in direct touch with levels of our own being that science keeps at a distance. Although an admirer of science, Bergson realizes that science generally employs a mathematical method of analysis that can provide only frozen and spatialized representations of the flux that makes up the real world. Science represents the dynamic actuality and striving of life only in a relatively shallow way. It pictures things in terms of lifeless units and thereby leaves out the pulsating actuality of the life world. Bergson has no objection to scientific method as a self-limiting way of making the world available to the intellect. But when its icy abstractions are not supplemented by a warmer intuition of the actual flow of life we end up with a stiff and distorted picture of the world.[6]

A second source of support for a wider view of seeing than the natural sciences utilize is the work of scientist and philosopher Michael Polanyi (1891–1976).[7] Polanyi emphasizes the power of *tacit knowing*, a kind of perception and cognition that is essential even for science, but which most scientific naturalists fail to notice because of their enshrinement of theoretic consciousness as exhaustive of human cognition. Polanyi is especially aware of the imperative to be attentive, but he emphasizes that attentiveness has two poles. In one sense we attend *to* things in a focal or explicit way. But in doing so we attend *from* their constituents in a tacit or inexplicit way. Attending has a "from-to" structure. For example, you are now attending *to* what I am writing on this page, but in doing so you are attending *from* the individual words that I am using in each sentence.

6   Henri Bergson, *An Introduction to Metaphysics*, translated by T. E. Hulme (New York: G. P. Putnam's Sons, 1912); *Creative Evolution*, translated by Arthur Mitchell (New York: Modern Library, 1944).
7   Michael Polanyi, *Personal Knowledge*; and *The Tacit Dimension* (Garden City, N.Y.: Doubleday Anchor Books, 1967).

While reading this page you have not been focusing on or attending *to* the individual words but instead to their joint meaning. If you had focused your attention only on the individual words you would have been so distracted that you would have missed their overall point. In order to apprehend what I am saying you have to relax your focus on the individual components of this page. You must tacitly "indwell" the particular words, sentences and paragraphs, suspending any inclination to focus *on* them, in order to integrate them into an explicit or focal knowledge of this page's content.

Likewise, if you are going to be able to see any meaning in nature you would have to learn to relax your attention *to* its separate parts. In fact, the more you focus on atoms, molecules, cells or other units, the less you will be able to discern any overarching meaning in their togetherness in the universe. To see the purpose of anything requires that you attend *from* the particulars *to* the overall meaning. Since science is generally concerned with breaking emergent phenomena down into their earlier and simpler components and attending *to* these atomic units, it does not as such attend *from* them to any possible significance the emergent universe may have as a whole. Science seeks focal knowledge of atomic particulars, so, by definition, it cannot say anything about cosmic purpose. In Polanyian terms, therefore, scientific naturalism's rejection of purpose in the cosmos is a function of its more fundamental overlooking of the from-to structure of attentiveness. It is the consequence of a failure to *see* fully what is going on in the universe as well as in the process of perception.

A third important advocate of our wider empiricism is the mathematician and philosopher Alfred North Whitehead (1861–1947). Whitehead argues that the human organism is equipped with the capacity for a *primary perception* that is able to make contact with depths of nature that sense perception, or what I shall call *secondary* perception, leaves out.[8] At the primary pole of perception each of us

---

8   Here I am simplifying Whitehead's much more complex way of putting things: Alfred North Whitehead, *Process and Reality*, corrected edition, edited by David Ray Griffin and Donald W. Sherburne (New York: The Free Press, 1978), pp. 117–21, 168–83.

feels our bodily entanglement with nature in a powerful and immediate way. But in this primary perception our experience is tied into the flux of nature in a perceptually vague fashion. The function of sense perception (or secondary perception), therefore, is to filter out a more manageable set of data from the wide world apprehended in primary perception. The five senses perform this work of abstraction. In doing so they put us in touch with the real world, but only by leaving out most of what is obscurely present to our experience at the pole of primary perception. The senses give us only a contemporary cross-section of a world that in fact runs much deeper than the surface features conveyed by secondary perception.

But does not natural science put us in immediate touch with nature? Whitehead, a scientifically educated philosopher himself, would say no. The world that natural science delivers to us is an abstract rendition of what the five senses have already narrowed down. Science leaves out not only most of the information given in primary perception, but also our subjective sensation of color, sound, texture, smell and taste. By attending mostly to what is objectively measurable, science turns out to be doubly abstract. The point is, therefore, that science cannot see nearly as deeply into the fabric of the universe as naturalists have generally assumed to be the case. Science's obedience to the empirical imperative is not as thorough-going as the modern intellectual world has supposed. It purchases clarity only at the price of looking away from layers of nature available to other kinds of experience.

Seeing the world in perceptual depth, therefore, requires that we adopt a wider or deeper empiricism, a way of retrieving the data of primary perception that have been left behind by both the senses and science. In my view, one of the functions of religious symbolism, analogy and metaphor is to pull us toward dimensions of cosmic reality that escape more ordinary ways of seeing. They do so only obscurely, and at times misleadingly, but in religious experience idealizing the kind of clarity that we associate with science and secondary perception would actually prevent an encounter with what is truly important. Its lack of crisp clarity, moreover, is consistent with the fact that religion is more a matter of being grasped than of grasping. It is also a key to religion's endless and – to the rigorous naturalist – annoying diversity.

A fourth proponent of the wider empiricism that I am promoting is Bernard Lonergan (1904–84). As I have noted all along, this great philosopher wants us to attend not only to the world "out there" but also to attentiveness itself. He proposes a general empirical method that surveys not only nature but also the acts of seeing, understanding and knowing that allow us to contact the natural world. Critical intelligence is part of nature, so any conceptualizing of nature that leaves out the fact of our cognitive interiority is woefully incomplete.[9]

Finally, Pierre Teilhard de Chardin (1881–1955) is even more explicit than the aforementioned scholars in turning our attention to a kind of *seeing* that refuses to leave out the facts of interiority and subjectivity in nature, and of teleology in cosmic evolution. I shall discuss his point of view more carefully below.[10]

STEREOSCOPIC VISION

In this brief chapter I cannot summarize the contributions of these five thinkers in any detail. Instead I shall have to be content with turning the reader's attention to their shared invitation to bring a richer empiricism to bear on the question of what is going on in evolution and in the cosmos. I invoke their names for the following reasons: (1) they are all respectful of and thoroughly familiar with the work of science; (2) they are appreciative of evolution and the fact of an emergent universe; (3) they are aware of the limits of normal science and of the need for human cognition to take into account what the sciences leave out; (4) although profoundly respectful of

---

9   See, especially, Bernard Lonergan, SJ, *Insight: a Study of Human Understanding*, 3rd
    edn. (New York: Philosophical Library, 1970), pp. xvii–xxx.
10 See, for example, Pierre Teilhard de Chardin, *The Human Phenomenon*, translated by
    Sarah Appleton-Weber (Portland, Oreg.: Sussex Academic Press, 1999), pp. 3–7.

natural science, they all consider what I have been calling scientific naturalism to be unduly narrow in its epistemological assumptions and ontological scope; (5) they all fervently agree that symbolic expression, metaphor and analogy are absolutely essential to putting the human knower in touch with the most fundamental features of the universe; (6) they would also accept the distinction I made in chapter 3 between theoretic knowing as used by science, and the primal ways of knowing that allow us to encounter dimensions of reality that the various sciences leave out.

In this collective body of wisdom what stands out is a way of *seeing* that is much more sweeping and penetrating than that practiced by conventional science and absolutized by scientific naturalism. Bergson, Polanyi, Whitehead, Lonergan and Teilhard all propose that there is available to human experience a supplementary and more radical kind of empiricism than scientific method follows. This richer empiricism is fully respectful of science, but it proposes that one can look at life and evolution by way of a wider and more piercing kind of perception than that employed by the natural sciences alone.[11] This way of contacting the universe takes a binocular, or *stereoscopic*, view of things, looking not only at the data of science but also at a much fuller range of phenomena that impress themselves upon our experience.

Most significantly, a rich empiricism refuses to leave out of its portraits of reality the experience of our own critical intelligence with its irrepressible anticipation of intelligibility and truth. To understand and know the *real* world, our rich empiricists all insist, we must attend carefully not only to the objective world but also to our own intelligent operations. Since the inner world of critical intelligence is part of nature, careful attentiveness to and reflection on our own cognitive "insideness" may be able to tell us something crucial

---

[11] Earlier the philosopher William James (1842–1910) had made a similar proposal under the heading of "radical empiricism." *Essays in Radical Empiricism* (Cambridge, Mass.: Harvard University Press, 1976).

about the evolutionary process and the cosmos that gives it domicile. Our own experience and consciousness are not alien to nature, but are nature's "inner side," as Teilhard repeatedly points out. Unfortunately, however, evolutionary naturalism has done its best to keep the domain of subjectivity and anticipation out of its field of vision. Its restricting of consciousness to humans and perhaps a few other kinds of life, Teilhard complains, has only served as a pretext for purging subjectivity from the rest of nature. Evolutionary naturalists have looked upon human consciousness as "a bizarre exception, an aberrant function, an epiphenomenon." They have taken it to be an "isolated case and of no interest to science."[12] They have even espoused the strange and ultimately magical view that unintelligent material entities and processes are a sufficient explanation of intelligence.

Of course, both dualists and materialists will object to a richly empirical attempt to embed subjectivity in nature. Dualists assume in effect that subjectivity is separable altogether from the objective universe. However, naturalists cannot consistently accept such an idea since they have already explicitly renounced dualism as a form of supernaturalism. Their creed formally forbids situating consciousness in an arena completely split off from the rest of nature. As far as their official beliefs are concerned, no such region actually exists, since nature, as science understands it, is all there is. And yet, even as they refuse on the surface to take comfortable refuge in dualism, naturalists generally forget in effect that nature has an unobjectifiable insideness accessible only by way of a deeper mode of perception than the kind that anchors scientific understanding. I personally consider it methodologically appropriate for *scientists* to leave out any considerations of subjectivity, as long as they remain aware of this omission. Naturalists, however, usually ignore the inner world *from* which each of us attends *to* the world "out there," even though this tacit dimension belongs to the universe just as fully as the objective

---

[12] Teilhard, *The Human Phenomenon*, p. 24.

world. And by refusing to take note of subjectivity from the inside, they fall back implicitly on the very dualism they have explicitly banished.

On the other hand, our more wide-ranging empirical method makes room for subjectivity at the very center of its picture of nature and evolution. It embraces both the inside and the outside of things in a single stereoscopic vision of the whole. The effect of this dimensionally deeper perspective is that the vein of subjectivity in nature can be viewed, at least in principle, as the carrier of a general cosmic meaning or purpose that remains inaccessible to science's distant and theoretically objectifying gaze. Nature's insideness, most immediately evident in the experience of our own critical intelligence, as well as in our intersubjective encounter with other sentient beings, is not a desperate human projection but a palpable reality directly accessible to each of us. It is only by decrees such as Lewontin's that naturalists exclude from their conception of life the element of subjectivity that they cannot fail to experience immediately in their own cognitional performance.

The richer empiricism I am proposing here insists that our own subjectivity is an *objective* aspect of evolution, not an excess item floating in from outside. Whitehead rightly emphasizes that every mental event is fully part of nature. Yet, as he also points out, scientific reasoning is completely dominated by the presupposition that mental functioning is not properly part of nature. And even though science's self-restricting method of ignoring subjectivity is entirely justifiable, it is fruitful in the long run only if scientists and philosophers remain fully aware of the limitations involved in the scientific way of seeing.[13] Unfortunately, scientific naturalists tend to suppress awareness of the cognitive limits of science, and this is why the naturalist's cosmos seems *essentially* devoid of the insideness we all experience most directly in our own critical intelligence. A universe purged of mind has thus become the point of departure for

[13] Alfred North Whitehead, *Modes of Thought* (New York: The Free Press, 1938), p. 156.

the naturalist's attempts to understand everything, including minds. And, of course, an essentially mindless universe is easily emptied of purpose as well.

Once we acknowledge that our own critical intelligence is a reality intrinsic to nature, and no longer a phantom dualistically split off from it, the barriers erected by naturalism against the notion of purpose in nature begin to fall down. Purpose may then be no longer exclusively "on the brain" of deluded religious persons, but a quality of the whole life-process. Indeed purpose (understood as a process of bringing to actuality something of lasting and intrinsic value) may itself be coextensive with, though not reducible to, the long story of intensifying subjectivity in the cosmos – and, along with it, freedom and critical intelligence. This mind-making project is one that astrophysics has now shown to have been in the works since the earliest moments of cosmic becoming. Of course, there is much more to life's meaning and cosmic purpose than the emergence of subjectivity. But, speaking minimally, any process that gives rise to increasingly intense modes of subjectivity – and eventually to our own undeniably valued critical intelligence – may plausibly be called purposeful. Purpose is not a projection but something we can see once we learn to become fully obedient to the mind's first imperative.

8 Cosmos

Lord how thy wonders are displayed,
Where e'er I turn my eyes;
If I survey the ground I tread
Or gaze upon the sky.

Isaac Watts, 1715

And nature's patterns are displayed
To my observant eye,
The small by microscopes arrayed
By telescopes the sky.

Kenneth E. Boulding, 1975[1]

In the preceding chapters I have been trying to show, first, that life, emergence and evolution all share in the *anticipatory* bearing of nature that came into bud most visibly in our own desire to know. Secondly, I have been arguing that there is need for a rich (stereo-scopic) empiricism that takes seriously the fact that critical intelligence is inseparable from the rest of nature. And thirdly, these first two considerations have led me to emphasize that the *whole* picture of nature changes dramatically from that of naturalism once we view life, emergence and evolution in terms of a representation of nature inclusive of critical intelligence. I have been led to conclude that scientific naturalism is finally incoherent since its formal view of nature is not large enough, logically speaking, to encompass either the fact of critical intelligence or the infinite horizon of being and truth anticipated by the desire to know.

Having looked at life, emergence and biological evolution in their actual continuity with the desire to know, it is now time to reach out and draw the whole cosmos more explicitly into our

---

[1]   Kenneth Boulding, "Toward an Evolutionary Theology," in *The Spirit of the Earth: a Teilhard Centennial Celebration*, edited by Jerome Perlinski (New York: The Seabury Press, 1981), pp. 112–13.

subjectivity-enriched picture of nature. If we truly intend to understand the *universe*, we can no longer pretend that it has no essential connection to critical intelligence. And once we re-establish the connection between the latter and nature as a whole, it will be possible to see more clearly that the same horizon of truth and being that arouses the imperatives of the mind has also been hiddenly involved in *cosmic* history throughout. The work of fashioning the cerebral apparatus that underpins human consciousness has been going on, as it now appears, for some fourteen billion years, so the emergence of critical intelligence must be located within the context of the larger cosmic epic. Likewise the cosmic story cannot be told well if we leave out any mention of the recent eruption of a restless desire to know.

Modern naturalism, however, fails to explore in sufficient depth the intimate connection between critical intelligence and its cosmic matrix. In a crudely physicalist sense, of course, naturalists agree that mind is part of nature. But they seldom look closely at what is implied about the *cosmos* in the actual performance of critical intelligence. Indeed naturalism's typical portrait of the cosmos is one in which critical intelligence is virtually absent from the seamless web of natural phenomena. The philosophical difficulty arising from this virtual exiling of critical intelligence from nature is that it leaves naturalism with no illuminating explanatory categories to account precisely for what is most obvious in the experience of each of us – our actual intelligent performance. After imaginatively sweeping the cosmos clean of subjects, the explanatory program of naturalists, including many neuroscientists and cognitive scientists today, is to show how subjective consciousness – which we all know performatively to be quite real – can come into existence out of a natural process divested from the start of any traces of mind. To set the problem of mind's existence up in this way, as do all materialist theories of mind, is to prepare the stage for magic rather than explanation.

By thinking of nature as primordially unintelligent, naturalistic materialism makes nature's recent secretion of human mentality seem more alchemical than natural. Of course, the impression of mysticism and magic is the last one that naturalists want to give, so they must take measures to prevent it. The measures are drastic, however, indeed almost violent, and their implications for human life and thought enormous. In order to avoid falling into an embarrassing pit of paranormality, naturalists often deny that subjective consciousness has any substantive being at all. They are tacitly aware that the later-and-more of critical intelligence cannot be accounted for solely in terms of a purely insensate starting point. So they treat subjectivity as virtually nonexistent, or at best epiphenomenal. And if they do admit to the moreness of mind, they refer to it verbally as the result of "emergence," which upon close examination often turns out to be a tag for either reductionism or magic. Recently some philosophers of mind have tried to fit mental phenomena into what they call "non-reductive physicalism,"[2] but the structure and subjectivity of critical intelligence, in my opinion, remain unilluminated by contemporary physicalist theories of mind. That the reality of mind – which the great wisdom traditions considered more real and more valuable than anything else in our experience – could ever have become so diminished by what we call the intellectual world today is the calamitous consequence of a shrunken empiricism that refuses steadfastly to attend fully to the fact of subjectivity at the beginning rather than at the end of its inquiry into nature.

The naturalistic habit of looking away from the subjectivity near at hand, as though it does not really exist in nature, is today being shored up by a Darwinian naturalism that regards only the historical or algorithmic past as adequate for the understanding of the present.[3] However, without denying the importance of historical or evolutionary accounts, the richer empiricism that I laid out in the preceding chapter surveys the history of life and the natural world

---

2   Jaegwon Kim, *Philosophy of Mind* (Boulder, Colo.: Westview Press, 1996), pp. 211–37.
3   Daniel Dennett's work is the most explicit example: *Darwin's Dangerous Idea: Evolution and the Meaning of Life* (New York: Simon & Schuster, 1995).

without ever turning its eyes, even for a moment, away from the present actuality of our own cognitional performance. Any adequate explanation of nature must explain *all* of its outcomes, and in doing so it does not help matters to place in brackets the novel features of emergent phenomena, especially those associated with mental existence, and then try to account for these solely in terms of what is already known. This diminishment only hides from the novelty that caused us to take note of such emergent realities as critical intelligence in the first place.

A richer empiricism, on the other hand, is so sensitive to the mind's imperative to be open to the full range of experience that it always keeps critical intelligence in the foreground as it looks into natural history. Scientific naturalism sidesteps this stereoscopic approach. This is why, in the end, it finally has to resort to magic in its own accounts of intelligence. Expelling subjectivity completely from its visual field at the outset, naturalism can only meet defeat when it approaches the irreducible subjectivity of consciousness.[4] Scientific naturalism does not possess the conceptual tools to bridge the gap between the third-person language about physical or evolutionary causes on the one hand, and the first-person discourse of intelligent subjects about their own experience on the other. As the naturalist philosopher John R. Searle admits, these disparate perspectives point to two different modes of existence: "Conscious states have a subjective mode of existence in the sense that they exist only when they are experienced by a human or animal subject. In this respect they differ from nearly all the rest of the universe," which is devoid of subjectivity. It is not helpful, however, when Searle goes on to suggest that a scientific study of mind can in some sense bridge the gulf between the subjective and objective. After all, the sciences, including neuroscience, are inevitably third-person approaches. Scientific objectivity can help to explain why minds fail, and it can uncover the

Colin McGinn resignedly admits as much in *The Mysterious Flame: Conscious Minds in a Material World* (New York: Basic Books, 1999).

physical conditions required for mental functioning. But an objectifying study of mind can never lead incrementally to the subjective experience of being a critically intelligent subject.[5]

Instead of stretching and straining a fundamentally materialist naturalism to fit the amazing feats of mind, as Searle does, I suggest that it is time for philosophers of mind to look for a worldview that can encompass both critical intelligence and the entire cosmic process in a way that avoids the *de facto* dualism to which many of them, including hard materialists, have become resigned. The perspective I am laying out here is one that starts by looking closely at the structure of critical intelligence. Only after undertaking a general empirical survey inclusive of subjective existence can one expect to understand the cosmos in its fullest dimensions. Attempting to explain how intelligence arises out of unintelligence without citing a proportionate cause for such a prodigious feat can only come off as superstition. Simply reciting the usual evolutionary factors is scarcely enough to help us understand how mindless objects can be transformed into sentient, intelligent and critical subjects. A richer explanatory toolbox is needed to avoid the appeal to miraculous leaps. Explanatory adequacy must somehow make the categories of intelligence and subjectivity fundamental to the makeup of true being rather than derivative aspects of an originally senseless reality.

Naturalism, of course, will not agree to my proposal. It cannot give up its belief that the fundamental causes of intelligence are themselves completely unintelligent. This means, however, that naturalists are compelled to explain critical intelligence in terms of processes and events that lack both intelligence and subjectivity. How then can the appearance of sorcery be avoided? If the naturalist's picture of the universe were completely correct, and the universe *fundamentally* unconscious, then it might seem that the appeal to magic could be avoided by making the actual emergence of mind

5   John R. Searle, *Mind: a Brief Introduction* (Oxford: Oxford University Press, 2004), pp. 135–36.

simply an accident of evolution. Perhaps critical intelligence is not itself the immediate result of adaptation at all, but one among many unintended byproducts of adaptations preserved by blind selection over the course of an extensive period of time. Critical intelligence, like the universe itself, could be said to be one of those things that "just happened" for no reason at all. It is no more than a fluke, as many an evolutionist has concluded.

Once again, however, such an "explanation," if taken as adequate, is contrary to reason. A series of blind and unintelligent causes of mind, no matter how temporally prolonged and gradual in cumulative effect, would never add up to a sufficient reason for putting the kind of confidence in their own intellectual functioning that naturalists in fact do when they offer such an account. Given the story they tell about the unconscious physical foundations and mindless evolutionary fashioning of their own minds, naturalists must look elsewhere to justify the colossal confidence they place in the mind. Calling mind a fluke will hardly suffice. As long as they ground their own critical intelligence *ultimately* either in blind natural selection or in a series of accidents, or both, I can see no reason why anyone, least of all they themselves, could ever trust so unflinchingly the operations of their own minds. Naturalists will tell me that their position is true and mine is false. They are completely confident that the mind can be naturalized, that is, fully explained in terms of what is physically or cosmologically earlier and simpler than mind. But what is there in this fundamentally unconscious cosmic background, or in the cultures that this unconscious foundation brought into being through the mediation of minds, that could have instilled in them their cognitional confidence?

After many years of looking at naturalistic writings I have yet to find a reasonable answer. Instead I find magic and alchemy everywhere. In almost every case, to put it bluntly, the naturalist's account of the origin of mind is one in which I am asked to believe that the lustrous gold of critical intelligence "emerges" from the dross of pure mindlessness without also being shown how such alchemy actually works. As I indicated earlier, invoking the ideas of deep time and emergence to explain how matter can become minds does nothing to dispel the aura of miracle that hovers over the whole show. The naturalist's actual, here-and-now intellectual performance is so utterly discontinuous with the set of materials out of which it is said to have been processed that it places in serious doubt any claim that naturalism is a reasonable philosophy of nature.

Notice once again, however, that I am not at all denying the power and importance of evolutionary explanations. I am only questioning the coherence of scientific naturalism. I have said nothing to discredit or discourage the ongoing scientific search for the details of the story that led up to the birth of life, intelligence, language, morality and religiousness. Evolutionary accounts are essential to adequate understanding of all living phenomena. But unless a stereoscopic empiricism and a layered method of explanation are allowed to supplement the conventional scientific way of seeing and understanding, evolutionary accounts will still sound like sheer divination. A more radically empirical method of inquiry and a proportionately expansive metaphysics are needed.

To put all of this another way, the problem with the naturalistic picture is that it is not natural enough. Interestingly, it cannot even stick to its own program of explanatory gradualism, but has to make gratuitous leaps, especially when it comes to the fact of critical intelligence. It rightly avoids any appeal to supernatural interventions in the earlier and simpler chain of efficient causes. But without leaving large explanatory gaps it cannot show how unintelligent stuff turns into subjective thought. Naturalists end up paying only lip service to their axiom that nature does not make leaps (*natura non facit saltum*). By leaving out at the beginning of its explanatory program a whole dimension of nature, that of our own critical intelligence, and then treating it in effect as though it were an unnatural interloper, naturalism has been forced time and again to resort to miraculous saltations to account for subjectivity in any sense.

Nothing, I repeat, could be more unnatural. The naturalist's temptation to necromancy could easily be avoided by adopting – along with and not contrary to science – a more capacious empiricism, one that integrates the categories of intelligence and subjectivity deliberately into a more realistic worldview. A richer empiricism, in obedience to the mind's first imperative, strives to leave nothing out of the field of our attentiveness. This includes an awareness of the anticipatory character of mind, and the corresponding idea of a cosmos seamlessly connnected to the mind's reaching out toward an endless horizon of meaning, goodness, beauty and truth.

I have made no secret of my belief that a fuller explanation of nature, one that can account for the element of anticipation in life, emergence, evolution and intelligence, requires, in addition to scientific study, the illumination of a theological worldview. The place of theological explanation is to make ultimate sense of the anticipatory aspect of nature and mind. It can give a good reason for the existence of a realm of *potentiality* that allows the world to be anticipatory. This potentiality is not the same as sheer nothingness, so it must have a ground or explanation. Theology gives the name "God" to the source and reservoir of all possibilities. It is the abiding presence of possibilities on the horizon of the cosmic and evolutionary future that arouses our own sense of anticipation, and at least in some analogous way the leaning of all things toward the future. Rather than reducing the fact of our own subjective anticipation to a ghostly shadow hovering over a mindless universe, theology can make anticipation fundamental to *everything* going on in nature. Anticipation is what bears the universe along as it reaches out toward fuller being. No doubt, the actualizing in cosmic history of explicitly conscious instances of anticipation is all very uncertain and frothed with contingency. Historically speaking, there is no doubting that the cosmos was devoid of actual intelligent subjects until recently. From the point of view of natural history the road from primal radiation to the emergence of thought has not been smooth or devoid of setbacks. But the domain of possibilities that eventually drew forth conscious anticipation has been present always.

Of all phenomena, our minds are perhaps the most fragile from a physicalist point of view. But their fragility is in direct proportion to their splendor, and their splendor is inseparable from the fullness toward which they aspire but cannot fully attain. Like a flower blossoming for a moment in bright sunshine, critical intelligence feels the call of being, meaning, goodness, beauty and truth only for a season. But in its response to this transcendental environment the restlessness of the whole universe rushes to the surface. In the mind's anticipation of truth, goodness and beauty the entire cosmic process is drawn toward the goal it has silently sought perpetually.

To the naturalist, obviously, the appeal to such a theological understanding will seem to be an unwarranted leap. But here the leap, if you want to call it that, consists only of ensuring that all necessary and relevant categories for robust explanation are loaded in at the beginning rather than invented in midstream. We are obliged after all to understand *the totality* of nature, and this includes critically intelligent subjectivity. The merit of theological explanation is that it has no need to invent *ad hoc* concepts to explain critical intelligence. Something causally proportionate to this inestimable phenomenon has always been quietly, persuasively and noncoercively proposing new possibilities to the cosmic process. When critical intelligence does eventually arise in cosmic history it is ultimately because the universe has been charged with the ingredients for its arrival from the moment of creation – "in the beginning was the Word." Moreover, the advantage of a theological understanding is that it can explain, in a way that naturalism cannot, why the intelligent subject spontaneously puts so much trust in the desire to know. Trust, after all, can flourish only where there is something to value, and value has to be rooted in what is imperishable. I can conceive of no fuller justification of the trust underlying cognitional performance than a theological vision of reality that attributes to truth, meaning, goodness (and beauty) something of the eternal.

Scientific naturalists will persist in claiming that they have already included human intelligence in their very nontheological picture of nature. Darwin, they will insist, has done so in his sweeping vision of life, explaining intelligence as a product of natural selection. But Darwin never claimed to have explained critical intelligence as such; and even in *The Descent of Man* he limits his study to objectifiable behavioral traits. No objectifying science has ever yet penetrated the world of the subject, nor can it. Naturalism still pretends that the "insideness" of intelligence is irrelevant as far as enlightened thought is concerned, but in doing so it has exiled the most stunning of all emergent cosmic phenomena from the range of those data that are essential to a full understanding of nature. As I have often emphasized before, there is nothing to complain about in such a procedure as long as one remains aware of how much it leaves out. I have no objection to the fact that science itself cannot talk about subjectivity. It is only when scientific method, which justifiably abstracts from notions like subjectivity and intelligence, is taken as the sufficient foundation for an entire worldview that objections must be raised.

THE MIND'S COSMIC HABITAT

It is hard to understand how naturalism, a vision of the cosmos that intends to be comprehensive, can appropriately suppress attentiveness to anything so empirically accessible as the mind's anticipation of truth. So it is all the more worthy of attention that recent developments in the fields of astrophysics, scientific cosmology and biochemistry now render such an exclusion much more dubious than it may have seemed only half a century ago. Those naturalists who are aware of recent studies of the early universe can no longer sever our own critical intelligence from the cosmos as casually as they did earlier in the modern period. It now turns out that the precise physical conditions that would allow intelligent, truth-seeking beings to emerge came into play at the first moment of the Big Bang universe itself.

In an anticipatory way the cosmos, it now appears, was always enveloped by the potential to become subjective. Even at a time when there were no actual intelligent human subjects around to understand and know it the universe was already infused with a mind-arousing intelligibility that would become the congenial evolutionary habitat for critical intelligence. This pervasive cosmic intelligibility must have had something to do with the fact that critical intelligence eventually arose in cosmic history. Just as the existence of photons had something to do with the evolutionary emergence of eyesight many times in terrestrial evolution, so also an environing cosmic intelligibility had to have been a causal factor in the emergence of intelligent subjects able to adapt to that environment.

Moreover, this intelligibility is inherently resistant to ever being fully "naturalized." Unless there has always been an intelligible arrangement of cosmic stuff, critical intelligence could never have come about in this or any other universe. At some point, therefore, a *full* account of the emergence of critical intelligence has to look for an ultimate explanation of why the universe is intelligible at all. A candid openness to that question cannot exclude theology as the source of a reasonable response. Astrophysics gives no good reason itself for assuming that the universe had to give rise to critical intelligence. There is an air of contingency about the actual cosmos. An indefinite array of alternative setups were possible, but the cosmos "chose" just those that would eventually lead to minds able to seek truth. What principle purged all other possible sets and allowed the universe to settle on the one that would lead to inquiring intelligence? It now seems to many investigators, after all, that only a very limited set of physical conditions could have opened the gateways to the emergence of both life and critical intelligence in our universe. So it is not inappropriate to inquire what principles may have pruned out other conceivable physical alternatives. Why did the Big Bang universe start out with just that suite of conditions and physical constants that would lead to beings endowed with a desire to know? Nature has figuratively tossed aside alternative sets that would have kept the cosmos out cold forever. Why so?

Or is this one of those questions that naturalist philosopher Owen Flanagan tells us we just should not be asking?[6] Unlike Flanagan, who arbitrarily slams the lid on inquiry whenever questions arise that challenge his naturalistic belief system, I do not believe that it is in the interest of truth-telling to be so repressive of the mind's imperative to keep seeking deeper intelligibility. It is no surprise that Flanagan has constructed his picture of nature in such a circular way as to stall any questioning that would burst that system open at the seams. However, the unrestricted desire to know that has emerged from cosmic process must not be prevented from asking how such an insatiable longing could ever have been allowed to emerge at all. Critical intelligence, whose recent appearance in the universe is dependent on a very specific cosmic habitat, now lawfully wants to understand why the cosmic environment has *always* anticipated the appearance of a desire to know the truth. And the possible existence of a multiverse would do nothing to lessen the relevance of this inquiry.

The salient question is whether the improbable paving of the cosmic path toward the creation of minds could ever be explained adequately in a purely naturalistic way. Naturalism's answer, of course, is a clear affirmative. "Nature is enough" will be the refrain here in cosmology as it has been in biology. The mindless interplay of accident and impersonal physical necessity across immensities of time in a multiverse can account adequately for the improbable set of cosmic conditions and constants that give the appearance of having been set up for mind. The Darwinian exposé of living design as only *seemingly* intelligent has now begun to shape even the naturalist's cosmology. These days Down House is casting its shadow over naturalists' thoughts about the universe as well as life.[7]

6   Owen Flanagan, *The Problem of the Soul: Two Visions of Mind and How to Reconcile Them* (New York: Basic Books, 2002), pp. 208–209.
7   Lee Smolin, *The Life of the Cosmos* (New York: Oxford University Press, 1997); Martin Rees, *Our Cosmic Habitat* (Princeton: Princeton University Press, 2003).

Yet if one takes critical intelligence as a fact of nature, the appeal to *cosmic* Darwinism as an ultimate explanation only drags the naturalist project down deeper into the alchemical vortex. The upshot is that everything in nature still emerges out of an original, though now vaster, mindlessness. Such a setting exacerbates the incongruity between the supposed unintelligibility of the larger cosmic laboratory and the emergent mind that is cooked up in it. And wherever enormous explanatory gaps show up, the temptation to magic lags not far behind. The naturalist hope is that by multiplying universes and extending the amount of time available for accident to become explanatory, it is possible to build a universe whose environmental conditions are suitable for intelligent subjects. Yet at bottom such a universe still remains ultimately unintelligible, and that means it can never be an adaptive habitat for an *unrestricted* desire to know.

What is needed is an understanding of the universe, or perhaps the multiverse, in which the desire to know can be taken as a smoothly natural extrusion of nature rather than the gnostic intrusion for which the naturalist's austere picture of the cosmos inevitably prepares the way. Falling back time and again only on the combined notions of chance, temporal amplitude and physical necessity, naturalism has not made the actual existence of mind any more intelligible – rather, much less so – than before. For naturalism to succeed as ultimate explanation it must be able to link critical intelligence and its anticipation of a fullness of truth and being to the cosmic process in a way that is more credible, less loaded with leaps, and more intuitively rational than those of its theological adversaries. So far it has not done so.

9 Morality

In the struggle for existence, according to Darwin, some organisms win and others lose. Those that win are called "fit" in the sense that they have a higher probability of surviving and reproducing than the losers. In the struggle to exist and reproduce, life involves competition, and the winners in the contest are those that can adapt to their environments long enough to bear offspring. Still, no species can survive on competition alone. If life is to last for many generations there must also be cooperation among the members, and even among separate species. Evolution entails at least as much cooperation as competition. It even requires self-sacrifice. When an organism forfeits its own reproductive opportunities for those of its family, group or species, biologists call it "altruism."

In the human sphere of life, altruism and self-sacrifice are generally considered the highest expressions of "morality." But according to much contemporary evolutionary thought, human "virtue" has its origin in the cooperation and altruism that already show up in pre-human forms of life. Some biologists and social scientists now locate the birth of morality in the fascinating process by which genes are passed on from one generation to the next.[1] Darwin himself knew nothing about genes, and he thought of evolutionary selection as taking place primarily at the level of individual organisms. But prominent evolutionists have concluded that selection applies more precisely to arrays of genes shared by many

---

[1] See Robert Wright, *The Moral Animal: Evolutionary Psychology and Everyday Life* (New York: Pantheon Books, 1994).

members of a species than to individual organisms alone.[2] Thinking of selection in terms of populations of genes makes evolution statistically measurable, thus satisfying the quantitative interests of science. Evolutionary "fitness" still means the probability of reproductive success. But such success is not so much a property of individual organisms as of groupings of genes. As long as a sufficient number of adaptive genes are present in an overall population, they have a relatively strong probability of surviving aggregately even if some individuals perish before having the opportunity to reproduce. So it is not necessarily the fittest individual organisms that survive, but instead the fittest sets of genes. Looking at evolution this way, it seems that genes rather than individual organisms are the determiners of biological destiny.

In today's gene-centered biology "altruism" has a technical definition. It means putting one's own genetic future at risk for the sake of the survival of the larger population of genes shared with one's kin. According to the standard example, a young prairie dog may possess altruistic genes that some of its siblings or kin do not, so because of these genes it is more likely than the others to sacrifice its life and any opportunity for its own reproductive success. Suppose it stands up out of its hole to warn relatives that a predator is near and then gets eaten up in the process. That unfortunate individual turns out to be "unfit" in the older Darwinian sense, but the genes it shares with others may still be fit in the sense that they will make their way into future generations. This is called "kin-selection" as distinct from individual selection, and it makes possible *inclusive* rather than

---

[2] Matt Ridley, *The Origins of Virtue: Human Instincts and the Evolution of Cooperation* (New York: Penguin Books, 1998), p. 94; George C. Williams, *Adaptation and Natural Selection: a Critique of Some Current Evolutionary Thought* (Princeton, N.J.: Princeton University Press, 1996); William D. Hamilton, "The Genetical Evolution of Social Behavior," *Journal of Theoretical Biology* 7 (1964), 1–52; John Maynard Smith, *The Evolution of Sex* (New York: Cambridge University Press, 1978); Robert L Trivers, *Social Evolution* (Menlo Park, Calif.: Benjamin Cummings, 1985); Richard D. Alexander, *Darwinism and Human Affairs* (Seattle: University of Washington Press, 1979).

individual fitness. It should be noted, however, that among biologists there are still strong opponents of this view.

CAN MORALITY BE NATURALIZED?

To those biologists who now accept the notion of inclusive fitness, however, it is tempting to conclude that there is no *real* moral heroism involved either in the lone prairie dog's self-sacrifice or in human expressions of love. This is a startling view since the capacity to sacrifice oneself out of love for another is a quality customarily associated with the highest virtue. Theology has even insisted that the rarer forms of love require a special influx of divine grace. From a religious point of view, self-sacrificial love among humans scarcely seems natural at all, or else it would be more commonplace. Yet among other mammals it now seems that exceptionally heroic acts are purely natural, so why would this not be the case with human mammals as well?

Altruism and self-sacrifice apparently emerged much earlier in evolution than we did. Something that looks like morality is evident in the mutual "cooperation" that allows any particular species to exist over a long period of time. Worker ants, for example, do not reproduce, but their selfless labor serves the larger cause of reproduction in the colony as a whole. Their self-sacrifice contributes indirectly to the passing on of the collective genes in an anthill. "A single ant or honey bee," the evolutionist Matt Ridley notes, "is as feeble and doomed as a severed finger. Attached to its colony, though, it is as useful as a thumb. It serves the greater good of its colony, sacrificing its reproduction and risking its life on behalf of the colony."[3]

One could multiply examples of altruism or cooperation in the animal kingdom. But in every case, at least according to some of our most respected evolutionists, the "force" that underlies such seemingly virtuous conduct is the striving of genes to get passed on to future generations. Morality, it would now appear, can be accounted

[3]   Ridley, *The Origins of Virtue*, p. 12.

for in a purely natural, indeed a physicalist, way. Displays of altruism and cooperation are merely the visible expressions of the need that *genes* have for reproductive success. Science has now made it possible to view altruism and cooperative activity as really neither virtuous nor sacrificial in any religious sense. They are simply the working out of blind laws of nature.[4]

The implication seems to be that ethics no longer has to be grounded in theology if biology can account for the origin and survival of moral instincts more efficiently and deterministically. After all, what is the point of multiplying explanations unnecessarily? Our moral habits are apparently due to the fact that, on average, cooperative human genes have been better at getting into the next generation than uncooperative ones. And as for our less noble urges? Well, evolution can account for them too. They are leftovers from the asocial instinctual endowment we have inherited from our animal ancestry. They may have been adaptive at one time but are out of place in contemporary social environments.[5] In any case, the moral ideals that have led people to cooperate with one another do not reflect a Platonic heaven. The whole idea of an eternal realm of values is ultimately an ingenious, although somewhat circuitously devised, construct of human genes also. Although we may think of morality as a participation in the transcendent goodness of God, our virtuous conduct can be more smoothly explained by the fact that ethically unrestrained behavior has, on average, proved to be nonadaptive. Cooperation, heroic altruism and, for that matter, any inclination to moral behavior among humans are purely natural consequences of a process now brought to the surface by Darwinian-Mendelian science.

There is a lot more to evolutionary accounts of morality than all of this, but for the limited purposes of the present book the above summary will suffice. What I wish to highlight here is the

---

[4]   Alexander, *Darwinism and Human Affairs*, p. 38.
[5]   See the essays in Jerome H. Barkow, Leda Cosmides and John Tooby (editors), *The Adapted Mind: Evolutionary Psychology and the Generation of Culture* (New York: Oxford University Press, 1992).

evolutionary naturalist's conviction that morality no longer requires the support of religion or theology. Further, I want to note that as far as Darwinian naturalism is concerned, religion itself is *ultimately* also an invention of our genes, devised ingeniously but purely naturally to shore up the moral codes essential for cooperation and survival. Through its promises of reward and its threats of punishment religion has been serving the cause of gene survival all along, even though religious and moral people have not been aware that this is what has *really* been going on. Religions and theologies mistakenly think of codes of behavior as having been given on stone tablets or planted in our hearts directly by God. But science has now provided a more economical picture of where values come from. And if altruism, the salient example of moral conduct, turns out to be purely natural, then so also do all the other virtues.

It may seem to the ethically upright person that he or she is acting selflessly in the name of eternal values, but the evolutionary naturalist knows better. Genes are manipulating the entire charade. Being good makes one feel good, and feeling good is essential to sustain the cooperation that serves reproductive success. No doubt cooperation among humans is more complicated than among other living species, and cultural factors are operative as well as biological. But the ultimate roots of cooperation are nonetheless purely natural *rather than* divine in origin.

The point of this brief summary is not to cover all the complexity in biological accounts of ethical orientation, but merely to illustrate how easily morality can be naturalized if one looks at life solely in terms of evolutionary biology. Keep in mind that the starting point of naturalism is that "nature is all there is." It follows that there can be no divine commands planted in our minds, and no transcendent goodness calling humans to a life of self-sacrifice. Why, then, are most humans inclined to be good, at least much of the time? If theology has been ruled out a priori as an explanation, then there has to be a purely natural accounting. There is no other choice as far as the naturalist is concerned. Culture and socialization may be part of the account, but the *ultimate* explanation can be found only in nature (since culture and human society are themselves part of nature). And, so far, no more plausible natural explanation of morality has been given than that provided by evolutionary biology. To many a naturalist, evolutionary accounts of morality have been more decisive than any other modern ideas in wiping the ethical horizon clean of transcendence.

But can evolutionary science ever fully naturalize morality? I have argued in earlier chapters that an adequate understanding of critical intelligence requires our going beyond the naturalist's explanatory framework as far as human knowing is concerned. If truthfulness means fidelity to the desire to know, then each of us must search for a habitat wide and deep enough to accommodate fully the mind's imperatives to be open, intelligent and critical. I have maintained, by way of a Lonerganian method of self-understanding, that the naturalist worldview cannot provide the needed breadth for the desire to know to function integrally. In this chapter I hope to show, by a similar method, that *the naturalist's own moral aspirations* cannot be explained fully in naturalistic terms any more than can critical intelligence. Evolutionary accounts of the development of a moral sense can be illuminating in a secondary way, of course. But they cannot account in an ultimate way for goodness or our attraction to goodness any more than a study of the evolution of mind can account for the universe's intelligibility or for truth and our love of truth. If my proposal proves to be correct, then it will be seen that morality cannot be fully naturalized after all.

In fact, it is not difficult to show that the naturalist is personally guided by lofty moral ideals that could not possibly function as incentives to ethical conduct if that same naturalist consistently took these ideals to be ultimately explicable in evolutionary terms. As long as one maintains that moral ideals can be accounted for ultimately in a purely natural – and that means an evolutionary – way, they can be neither lofty nor ideal. They cannot even function to provide the cooperation essential for the reproductive success of the human species. In section A immediately below I will bring out more fully the logical self-contradiction involved in any attempt to provide a purely naturalist derivation of what scientific naturalists take to be the highest ethical ideal of all, that of adhering faithfully and unconditionally to the demands of objective knowing. Then, subsequent to that discussion, I will argue in section B that evolutionary accounts of morality are especially feeble in their attempts to account for what religious and metaphysical traditions have taken to be the highest levels of moral existence. Evolutionary discussions of ethics are generally blind to the fact that there can be qualitatively distinct stages or levels of human moral development. So, even if naturalistic arguments seem compelling when accounting for one or two levels of ethical responsiveness, they may not be able to account fully for others, including the level at which the naturalist's own ethic of knowledge operates. Evolutionary insights into ethics are not unimportant, but they do not work well when taken as final explanation.

A. Morality and critical intelligence

My first point is this: the naturalist's own implicit appeal to lofty ethical principles, including what has been called the "ethic of knowledge," is enough to refute logically the claim that gene-centered evolutionary biology – or for that matter any other purely naturalistic account – can lead us to the ultimate ground of all human moral aspiration and conduct. Most scientific naturalists adhere passionately to certain values whose power to motivate would be immediately deflated if their own naturalistic accounts of the origin of virtue were applied to these values.

To drive home this point, however, I need to consider more carefully a fourth imperative of the mind, one that I alluded to only fleetingly in chapter 2. It is the imperative to "be responsible." This fourth imperative, felt to some degree by all of us, lies at the foundation of all morality and ethics. It leads to the distinct cognitional act of *decision*. Of course, the naturalist will try to show that the imperative to be responsible is one that can be explained quite easily in purely scientific, and today especially Darwinian, terms. But it will not be hard to show that the naturalist's own ethic of knowledge is curiously exempted from any such debunking.

So a fuller understanding of critical intelligence than the one we have been following up to this point could be represented as follows:

(1) Be attentive! —> experience
(2) Be intelligent! —> understanding
(3) Be critical! —> judgment
(4) Be responsible! —> decision

In addition to leaving out the imperative to be responsible and the correlative act of decision, I have also refrained so far from emphasizing how much each level interacts with the others. Each of the four cognitional acts is distinct from the others, but it is *functionally complementary* to them.[6] Being intelligent, for example, is different from being attentive or critical. But being intelligent can still function to make one *more* attentive and critical. Being critical is not reducible to being more attentive or intelligent, but it can lead one to become *more* attentive and intelligent, and so on. Each of the mind's imperatives leads to a qualitatively distinct cognitional act, but the cognitional imperatives and acts still mutually support one another. There is a dynamic interplay going on constantly among them.

What this means in the present discussion, therefore, is that being responsible improves the quality and depth of cognition. At the same time, being responsible requires that one first be attentive, intelligent and critical. It is irresponsible, in other words, to make uninformed ethical decisions. But what I want to highlight here is that one cannot be truly attentive, intelligent and critical without also being responsible. The life of virtue is not at all incidental to appropriate cognition. The more humble one is, for example, the

---

6   Bernard Lonergan, SJ, "Cognitional Structure," *Collection*, edited by F. E. Crowe, SJ (New York: Herder and Herder, 1967), pp. 221–39.

more likely one will forsake any pretense to omniscience and will, therefore, be more inclined to surrender to the imperatives of the mind, no matter where these imperatives take one. Humility, contrary to the old maxim, is not the same as truth, but it does facilitate the mind's access to truth. Likewise, the more altruistic one is, the more likely it is that one will be open to the cognitional perspectives of other persons. In this way love can function intersubjectively to make our minds more open and attentive to the real world. The desire to know is liberated most fully, in other words, when it flows forth from a subject whose character is shaped by a deep sense of the good. "Genuine objectivity," Lonergan says, "is the fruit of authentic subjectivity."[7]

Naturalists themselves provide a fair example of how inseparable the life of virtue is from knowing. The imperative to *be responsible* in the exercise of observation, intelligence and knowing undergirds the whole naturalistic project. Naturalism, as it turns out, is rooted in a profoundly ethical belief system. If you have ever read Richard Dawkins or Owen Flanagan, for example, you cannot miss the moral idealism that pervades their work. They scold their opponents for not adhering to a *responsible* way of looking at the world. Religious believers come in for especially harsh criticism not only for their cognitional but also their ethical slackness. The naturalistic ethic is demanding, almost puritanical in its moral rigor: the responsible knower is one who becomes detached from pre-scientific ways of seeing and understanding. Right knowing requires not just cognitive growth but also a painful process of moral development.

As a more venerable example, consider also how the renowned biochemist and naturalist philosopher Jacques Monod calls upon his readers to learn obedience to the "ethic of knowledge."[8] Correct cognition requires that one learn a new kind of moral responsibility,

7   Bernard Lonergan, SJ, *Method in Theology* (New York: Herder and Herder, 1972), p. 292.
8   Jacques Monod, *Chance and Necessity*, translated by Austryn Wainhouse (New York: Vintage books, 1972), pp. 175–80.

in obedience to the fourth imperative. Monod asks readers to submit to the demands of what he calls the *postulate of objectivity* – according to which only objectifying (or what I have been calling "theoretic") knowledge employed by scientific method is valid for true knowing.[9] Monod is highly critical of our moral timidity in failing to embrace the moral discipline essential for right knowing. Clearly he is asking all of his readers to follow the imperative to be responsible.

Likewise, Owen Flanagan insists that we have a moral duty to abandon what he calls the "manifest image" of common sense and classic religious piety, and instead conform our minds to the "scientific image" of exclusively theoretic knowing. Not to do so is irresponsible and will lead to many evils, including those done in the name of religion. And, of course, there is the unforgettable 1877 decree by the philosopher W. K. Clifford that "it is wrong always, everywhere, and for anyone, to believe anything upon insufficient evidence."[10] True knowledge can be based only in the proper moral disposition.

This is all deeply ethical exhortation. However, my own mind's imperatives urge me to interpose a critical question at this point. Since Monod and Flanagan, both evolutionists, are compelled to embrace a fully naturalistic account of why we humans have a fourth imperative (the one that urges us to be responsible) at all, then what reasons can they give me why I should adhere to the severe demands of their own ethic of knowledge? Since naturalism denies the existence of any transcendent criteria of rightness, there can certainly be no eternal reason why I should follow their postulate of objectivity. So what ground are the naturalists standing on when they issue their demanding decree that I must submit to their ethic of knowledge?

---

9 Ibid.
10 As made famous by William James' important essay "The Will to Believe," in *The Will to Believe, and Other Essays in Popular Philosophy* (New York: Longmans, Green, and Co., 1931).

Is it possible in principle to give a fully naturalistic account of the mind's imperative to be responsible and at the same time declare in effect that the rest of us must adhere to the naturalist's rigid ethic of knowledge? Why is not the ethic of knowledge underlying the whole naturalistic project no less subject to naturalistic debunking than a religious ethic? The catch is that if the roots of the imperative to be responsible are ultimately biological, then the ethic of knowledge and the postulate of objectivity are themselves also exposed as purely adaptive, derived ultimately, for example, from selective pressures on gene populations. If biology provides the deepest available justification for the postulate of objectivity and the naturalistic ethic of knowledge – and to the evolutionary naturalist why would it not? – then, once again, I want to know why I should pay any attention to it at all. The irony here is obvious, and it is fatal to the whole enterprise of naturalism. For why should anybody obey the postulate of objectivity if, like all other ethical postulates, science has figured out that the ultimate source of the imperative to be responsible is an unconscious drive by our genes to get into the next generation, or if not precisely that, at least some other purely natural process?

Some evolutionists, as I have already pointed out, admit that Darwinism cannot ground human ethics in a normative way either. Perhaps evolutionary biology can help to explain the *origins* of virtue, but it cannot *justify* any particular course of action. In fact, many naturalists today confess that evolution itself provides a poor model for human behavior, so they have to look for other ways of supporting morality in general and the ethic of knowledge in particular. Jacques Monod, more honest than many others, admits straight out that the postulate of objectivity is purely *arbitrary*, rooted in a leap of faith with no objective foundation.[11] But he is not consistent enough to admit that such a confession takes any real starch out of the ethical injunction itself.

11   Monod, *Chance and Necessity*, p. 176.

Once the logical contradictions in naturalistic accounts of ethics become obvious, it does not help the naturalistic cause to leap suddenly from biology into culture and history in order to place the ethic of knowledge on an allegedly steadier foundation. Evolutionary, historical, social and cultural factors are undoubtedly operative in the shaping of ethical life, but knowledge of these factors alone is not enough to justify my commitment to any particular set of ethical directives. Historical information about the background of Monod's ethic of knowledge cannot tell me why, for example, I should privilege theoretic, objectifying knowledge over other modes of experience. By itself socio-historical analysis of the roots of ethics, including the ethic of knowledge, can serve only to relativize the moral postulate of objectivity as well as all other moral postulates. Moreover, if evolutionary, social and historical factors were fully determinative of my actions, then there would be no point in talking about ethics or morality at all. Without the assumption of freedom, ethics could be replaced completely by disciplines that describe and explain behavior in terms of inviolable constants and laws of nature.

But if an understanding of evolution, history, society and culture cannot tell me why I should follow the imperative to be responsible, then what can? Certainly natural, social and personal history, as I have already noted, are involved in the shaping of conscience. However, something in addition to *past* causal influences must be involved in the awakening of a sense of responsibility. I propose once again, therefore, that an *adequate* grounding of the imperative to be responsible can come only from a view of reality that includes a theological dimension at its foundation.

Nevertheless, I would not argue, in a Kantian sort of way, that the fourth imperative is the consequence of a divine command planted immediately in each person's mind. Nor is it based on the finite mind's faint remembrance of a Platonic realm of perfection from which it has been temporarily estranged. These are interesting proposals, and they each rightly point to the inadequacy of a purely naturalistic justification of morality. They represent, in terms of their own historical eras, the correct intuition that being responsible means *being grasped* by a dimension of reality that radically transcends nature and the human subject. However, in view of what we now know about life, intelligence, emergence, evolution and cosmology, I believe it is more appropriate to say that the imperative to be responsible is activated by the mind's *anticipation* of a transcendent goodness that encompasses and grounds both the world and our consciousness, as proposed in the preceding chapter.

With Plato, Aquinas and Kant it is still possible to agree that critical intelligence is oriented toward a transcendent *goodness*. But we need not think of this goodness as frozen in timeless perfection up above, constantly measuring the inevitable inadequacy of our efforts to imitate it. Such a grounding of ethics would be most disheartening if that were all there is to it. All the ages of moral endeavor would add up to very little if the life of virtue were only a matter of imitating an eternal goodness rather than also the ushering into our evolving world of something new and enlivening. Moral action that consists solely of emulating what is already perfect can lead only to a sense of failure. In some measure, of course, the moral life entails following exemplars of goodness, but moral aspiration comes to life most enthusiastically when there is a sense that human action can contribute something new and unique to the universe.[12] For this reason it is appropriate to think of the good life as grounded in anticipation more than imitation.

However, each of us can anticipate only what has already begun to grasp hold of us. And just as the content of our minds always falls short of the truth anticipated by the desire to know, so also our obedience to the imperative to be responsible always fall short of the horizon of goodness that awakens the ethical instinct in the first place. To the evolutionary naturalist, virtue cannot be grounded in our native anticipation of a transcending goodness. Rather, it arises

12 Pierre Teilhard de Chardin, *Christianity and Evolution*, translated by René Hague (New York: Harcourt Brace & Co., 1969), pp. 92–93.

from a chain of causes in natural history, such as gene transmission. But this enshrinement of the earlier-and-simpler as ultimate explanation cannot account fully for the present anticipation of an incomprehensible goodness without which the moral sense would have no reliable compass or incentive.

Moreover, a purely naturalistic account of anything, including morality, leaves out of the field of its vision the world of subjective and interpersonal existence. The result is that scientific naturalism, at least as I have understood the term in this book, *sees* only a world without subjects as the *real* world. It is constrained then to interpret all subjective phenomena as ghostly intrusions or as having no reality at all. And if subjects seem to have little or no reality, then this can easily be taken to mean that they have little or no value either.

The path is thus opened up to political and social programs that treat personal subjects as though they were nonexistent or even as objects to be engineered and perhaps eliminated. By emphasizing theoretic knowing (the postulate of objectivity) at the expense of the primal patterns of experience the "ethic of knowledge" and its postulate of objectivity end up leaving personal subjects virtually out of its world-picture. Consequently, there should be significant ethical implications in any attempt to widen the empirical range open to the imperative "to be attentive." The wider empiricism that I have been proposing keeps the world of subjects constantly in the foreground, never allowing the natural world to be seen or thought of as ultimately separable from them. The world open to a richly empirical vision is one that can never be fully objectified. The postulate of objectivity, on the other hand, arises from a picture of the world that is inattentive, from the very start, to the reality of subjects. It is the consequence of not being sufficiently empirical.

I need not dwell here on the fact that those who adhere to the postulate of objectivity have themselves arrived at such a secure starting point only by way of intersubjective, affective, narrative and aesthetic involvement in the community of naturalists. My main point is that the imperative to be responsible is weakened and led astray by a failure to be fully attentive, intelligent and critical. This is why it is so important that an accurate understanding of critical intelligence become part of every effort to find a solid basis for moral action.

B. Stages of moral development

The naturalistic goal of accounting fully for ethics in terms of evolution is suspect also because of its failure to distinguish carefully among the various levels of moral development. Human behavior is shaped by many different kinds of motivation, but Darwinian accounts of morality tend to overlook some of these. "Morality," after all, can refer to a whole range of dispositions and actions varying considerably from one another at different stages of personal growth from childhood to adulthood. People only gradually, and sometimes only after enormous periods of struggle, move toward what we all recognize as mature, self-sacrificing moral existence. Those who think that Darwinism holds the key to a total naturalizing of human conduct must take all stages of moral development into account. However, from what I can tell, such nuancing has yet to penetrate into the inner core of evolutionary accounts of moral responsibility. No matter what stage of moral motivation is under examination, the Darwinian explanations typically come down to the same point: either genes are trying to get into the next generation, or some other physical mechanisms are doing the work of making us moral.

It is possible, however, to delineate various degrees of moral maturation. For the sake of simplicity one may speak of three such stages: pre-conventional, conventional and post-conventional.[13] These designations are not meant to be exact, but they will prove

---

[13] The typology is based, somewhat loosely, on ideas developed by James W. Fowler, *Stages of Faith: the Psychology of Human Development and the Quest for Meaning* (San Francisco: Harper & Row, 1981); and Michael Barnes, *Stages of Thought: the Co-evolution of Religious Thought and Science* (New York: Oxford University Press, 2000).

useful as general indicators of the fact that individuals can gradually become more refined in their moral discernment. And if moral *development* is possible, the evolutionist will be obliged to nuance any naturalistic theory of human morality in such a way as to explain the differences and not just the continuities that are characteristic of each stage in the developmental process.

(a) In its most primitive or "pre-conventional" stage human conduct is shaped by a sense of rewards and punishments. At this level the moral subject has little sense of what will later seem universally and unconditionally good. The motives for action are fear of punishment if one violates an imperative, and the expectation of reward if one complies. At this elementary stage, conduct is influenced by either a need for gratification or an instinctive avoidance of pain. This level of ethical existence is typical of very young children and psychologically debilitated adolescents and adults. It is possible, however, that all of us carry at least traces of moral immaturity with us throughout our lives.

It is worth noting here that religious development can run parallel to moral development. Accordingly, people whose moral lives remain fixated on rewards and punishments may think of God primarily as the source of regulations that one must follow in order to gain paradise and avoid hell. Often it happens that people who have begun to outgrow the most primitive stage of moral awareness will also become skeptical about the existence of "God," especially if they have previously associated the deity with rules and regulations that appear now to have no immediately rational justification. Scientific naturalists often dismiss the idea of God not only because of an apparent lack of "evidence," but also because of what they consider to be religion's close connection with a childish level of moral development. The writings of Dawkins, E. O. Wilson, Flanagan and many others provide clear examples. Ironically, however, in the very act of condemning what they take to be childish religiosity and morality they appeal implicitly to a standard of uncompromisable rightness. One needs to ask, therefore, whether the ideal of goodness they are tacitly appealing to when they tell us to outgrow the immaturity of religious existence can be explained naturalistically also. If so, then what is it that makes these ideals "better" than those of the religiously and ethically immature?

For the sake of the present discussion, however, let us grant that evolutionary science can account for the earliest stages of a normal human being's moral growth. The need for gratification and the aversion to pain are surely adaptive traits without which human genes would never have been able to survive. Perhaps, then, morality does have its origins in such entities as selfish genes. Yet, even if one grants that the notion of evolutionary adaptation is sufficient to account for pre-conventional morality, is it qualified to explain the later and apparently more mature and heroic instances of moral responsiveness? Is it able to tell the naturalist, for example, why he or she should be responsible enough to follow Monod's ethic of knowledge?

(b) A second phase of moral development – let us call it "conventional" morality – is based on a natural longing to become accepted by a social group of one kind or another. This group may be one's family, gang, sorority, workmates, church community, military unit, political party, or suchlike. In all cases it seems that the natural need to belong, a characteristic of most species of life, is what shapes human conduct. This level of moral development may also seem, at least at first sight, to allow for a purely biological interpretation such as that of inclusive fitness or reciprocal altruism. The ethical behavior that humans adopt corresponds to what allows us to exist in cooperative settings that enhance overall opportunities for successful gene replication. At the level of the individual person's experience, conventional morality allows one to live comfortably alongside others who are significant to us and who fulfill our individual craving to be part of something larger than ourselves. But from the point of view of our genes, conventional morality is just one of many ingenious ways for getting themselves passed off into future generations. Once again, therefore, it appears that naturalistic accounts of morality are enough.

At the conventional stage, however, rewards and punishments are no longer enough to motivate individuals. Instead it is the need for self-esteem that binds one to the group and that determines appropriate behavior. At this level the sense of right and wrong is guided less by fear of punishment and hope for reward than by what will allow the individual to abide safely and cooperatively within a particular social unit. This means that one's moral life will consist largely of internalizing the group's mentality and behavioral patterns without critical questioning. The longing to be accepted will override individual and even rational misgivings.

For all we know, most humans remain stuck in this conventional phase of moral development. However, the cooperation required here always entails at least some degree of sacrifice, a price that is not yet exacted at the pre-conventional stage. In conventional morality we have to surrender our private disagreements and asocial instincts for the sake of belonging to cooperative arrangements. Some degree of deliberate self-sacrifice will be required as a condition of being a member of the social unit. And some members of the group, analogous to the self-sacrificial prairie dog, may be enjoined to do more than the others. For instance, a suicide bomber may be recruited and sent on a self-annihilating mission. After the act, the bomber is no longer present, but the effect of the suicide may be that of solidifying the group identity of the sect in whose name the bombing was carried out.

We may think of ourselves as highly "moral" because we have sacrificed for the group's sake, but it is this kind of self-sacrifice that evolutionary psychologists now claim to be fully intelligible in terms of the same ideas of gene-survival, kin-selection and reciprocal altruism that account for cooperativeness in other species. There is nothing terribly heroic about it at all, since the real agents of the altruistic act are the genes shared by many members of a group. Conventional morality, it would seem, is no less intelligible from an evolutionary point of view than is pre-conventional morality.

Religion can also become mixed up with conventional morality, indeed, in such a way as to become almost indistinguishable from it. Conventional morality is likely to invoke religious authority for the sake of legitimating its ethical content. The idea of "God" may imbue the historically contingent moral precepts operative in a social unit with an eternal validity that renders the precepts seemingly unquestionable. In light of this conventional, and somewhat manipulative, invocation of ideas of God, therefore, it is tempting to claim that religious belief can also be fully accounted for naturalistically.

However, if conventional morality were a purely Darwinian phenomenon one should expect that it would favor genetic diversity, which in the long run is essential for the survival and future adaptability of a species. Yet conventional morality can easily lead in the direction of genetic homogeneity, a condition hardly auspicious for long-range survival and thriving of genetic lines. The conspicuous example is Nazism, where the goal was "to purify" the human species of contaminating elements, a dubious objective from the point of view of evolutionary biology. In Germany many members of the Nazi "tribe" apparently felt no pangs of conscience about leading genetically different humans to extermination. There was very little long-range evolutionary ingenuity operative here. Many German citizens even felt ethically safe in cooperating with the authorities and their fellow citizens. There was a strong sense of bonding and belonging. Yet, at least from a long-range genetic point of view, such a program could ultimately prove to be self-exterminating because of the narrowing of the gene pool. The point is that even conventional morality may not be easy to make sense of in evolutionary terms alone.

(c) Even if conventional morality could be easily understood in evolutionary terms, however, there is still a rarer stage of moral and religious development that completely befuddles the naturalist's dream of providing ultimate explanation. We may call it the post-conventional stage. Here conduct is shaped by the anticipation of and responsiveness to what is taken to be a real but incomprehensible realm of goodness. It arises primarily from the conviction that a specific set of actions seems intrinsically and unconditionally "good," regardless of the consequences to one's self or group coherence. Obedience to such a good may even precipitate social turmoil. It is undeniable that there have been at least a few heroic individuals who have pursued an ideal even when their conduct has had the effect of bringing about disharmony within a conventional setting. Such people are sometimes anything but cooperative. They feel obliged to disturb the tranquility of smug regimes that have purchased peace by excluding diversity. "Post-conventional," prophetic individuals, often representing the outcasts of a society, typically end up being persecuted and at times killed by those who have grown comfortable with the narrowness of a conventional setting.

The prophet (a term we may use to designate the post-conventional type) testifies consciously to an experience of *having been grasped* by what is imperishably and absolutely good. The truly moral life then is a courageous response – that is, an "answering back" – to a call. The prophet would be the last to maintain that we humans are the authors of our values, as naturalism is compelled to insist (since, according to the tenets of naturalism, there is no eternal source of goodness distinct from ourselves, nature and culture). Rather, the prophet insists that universal or eternal values have placed unconditional demands on all of us. To be moral is to heed an invitation that dawns from the realm of an *anticipated* goodness. Our minds' fourth imperative – be responsible! – is possible only because there already exists an inviolable realm of values, beyond the domain of conventional moral consensus, that invites us to an unswerving commitment. The moral subject does not possess this good, but instead anticipates it – in such a way as to be possessed by it.

It goes without saying, of course, that sustaining a post-conventional moral posture is not easy since the pressures to conform are enormous. And yet, there are rare individuals who have attained and sustained a level of moral development that is indicative of their sense of being called, often against their own preferences, by an unconditional goodness. Their level of moral and religious concern, where they happen to be religious (which is by no means a necessary condition of post-conventional morality), extends beyond the conventional and pre-conventional styles of piety. The prophets in our midst may not always live cooperatively with those whose moral life is still stuck at either of the first two levels, but the disharmony they cause is motivated by compassion and hope for wider and more diverse community than conventional morality can tolerate. Their stubbornness derives from a sense that the good that we all at least vaguely anticipate whenever we feel obligation is so compelling that their personal vocation requires complete obedience to it, no matter what the immediate cost. They cannot resist the call of what they take at least implicitly to be a transcendent goodness, even if it leads them to suffering and death.

An appropriate illustration of this prophetic (post-conventional) type of moral (and religious) commitment is that of the Austrian peasant Franz Jägerstätter and his resistance to Nazism. Jägerstätter refused to serve in Hitler's army because he had become convinced that the policies of the Nazis were inconsistent with what he took to be unconditional values. His friends and advisers, including the local parish priest, counseled him to abandon his shockingly distinctive stance. In their eyes it would not have been unethical for him to go along with the Nazi movement, since the latter enjoyed such popular support at the time. Franz's friends and acquaintances expected him to do his "duty" as conventionally understood. But he stood firm. Subsequently, he was arrested and executed as a traitor to his country and the Nazi cause.

History holds the memory of many other martyrs who have followed the more demanding post-conventional moral path. Almost all of them, including some prominent scientists, witnessed to what they considered the call of a time-transcending goodness. None of them would have accepted the naturalist belief that we humans are the sole authors of what we value. The story of Jägerstätter makes it clear that what passes as ethically acceptable at one level of moral development may be looked upon as morally unacceptable at another. What seems morally upright at the post-conventional level may be condemned as immoral by people whose ethical lives are stuck in the conventional or pre-conventional. Furthermore, the idea of God plays a correspondingly distinct role at each level. For pre-conventional morality God is the upholder of taboos. For conventional morality God is the sanctifier of the status quo. But for post-conventional morality God is the vaguely anticipated mystery of goodness that calls us to transcend the conventional and pre-conventional levels of morality.

It goes without saying that the most innovative figures in the history of ethics and religion have been decidedly post-conventional, their ideals contested especially by the more conventional types. It is also evident that religious and ethical traditions that are originally built on the ideals of a great prophetic figure can often decay into conventional or even pre-conventional spin-offs. When this occurs it is likely that internal clashes will develop within a particular tradition among adherents to the different stages of moral and religious development.

THE NATURALIST RESPONSE

Of course, evolutionary naturalists are ready with a rebuttal of the ideas I have sketched here. People like Jägerstätter, they will claim, are the human equivalents of the altruistic prairie dog. Heroic individuals sacrifice their own reproductive opportunities, but the final result nonetheless is that a wider population of human genes is passed on because of the prophetic valor. The human gene pool makes allowances for exceptional conduct only because without it the more comprehensive set of genes will be in jeopardy. Yet it is still the genes, ultimately speaking, that drive the self-sacrificial acts of prophetic individuals. So the theory remains intact.

Of course, there is insufficient empirical evidence available to support such a guess. But that is not the only difficulty. By definition a naturalistic account has to have sweeping success. In the present instance it must be able to account for *everything* in the varieties of conduct that occur at all the levels of moral development. Otherwise it will have to be judged a failure since it will not have explained everything about moral behavior after all. Thus, if any of the three levels of moral development does not lend itself to an exhaustively evolutionary account, then morality will still be a mystery open to other kinds of understanding, including theological.

Let us ask, then, whether the moral instincts of children, the conventional conduct of adolescents and most adults, as well as the moral idealism of martyrs like Franz Jägerstätter are all subject to a covering theory that accounts naturalistically for all the grades of morality without exception. A consistently naturalistic understanding of morality would have to search out a principle general enough to be equally illuminating at all levels of moral activity. It would have to be no less explanatory of Jägerstätter's idealistic intransigence than of the Nazi's sense that it is good to purify the race. In terms of evolutionary naturalism this would mean that gene survival would have to be the explanation of mutually contradictory motivations and actions.

However, as we have seen in every chapter so far, logical inconsistency is not a deterrent to the persistent naturalist. The gene-survival theory of morality is indeed logically flawed. For if one kind of motivation can be explained by the need of genes to have immortality, then an opposing kind of motivation cannot be adequately understood by appealing to exactly the same chain of causes. Most people, in any case, will not find it very helpful to be told that both the Nazi and Jägerstätter acted the way they did because of the need for gene survival. A theory that explains everything explains nothing. Even if both kinds of behavior contribute to gene survival (which is not impossible in the short run at least), citing this fact does not explain the differences. The principles of thermodynamics are operative whether the temperature is hot or cold outside today, so perhaps in one sense it is not wrong to say that heat exchanges are the explanation of the weather in both instances. It is not wrong, but it is empty. If this were all that needed to be said about the weather, we would not have meteorologists. Physicists would suffice. Similarly, genetic transmission is going on whether people are being bad or good, cowardly or heroic. Something other than gene-survival – or other evolutionary causes – will have to be called upon to account for the differences.

CONCLUSION

Moral aspiration, as rooted in the fourth imperative, is one of many modes of cosmic emergence. But emergence, as I argued in chapter 5, cannot become intelligible apart from a worldview in which *anticipation* is taken to be fundamental. *Ultimately* it is the anticipation of an absolute goodness that entices the mind to issue the imperative to be responsible, just as it is the anticipation of a fullness of truth that activates the desire to know. Intelligence, life, emergence, evolution, cosmic process and, now, morality are all seen to be anticipatory at heart. That is, they make complete sense only in terms of a worldview in which nature at all levels is being drawn toward an infinite horizon of mystery that remains hidden from any present comprehension. Anticipation is as elusive, but as real, as subjectivity. Conventional science, as I have argued, does not *see* this anticipatory aspect of nature any more than it sees the obvious fact of subjectivity. In order to highlight the fact of anticipation that underlies all stages of emergence, I have first had to make the case for a richer empiricism, one that takes note of aspects of the world that are discreetly passed over by the narrower – because more abstract and quantitative – methods of conventional science.

Finally, we arrive at the same conclusion as before. Although evolutionary and other scientific accounts must be part of any adequate understanding of morality, these cannot function coherently as *ultimate* explanation without subverting the whole naturalistic project. The project itself, as I noted earlier, is inseparable from the naturalist's own submission to the imperative to be responsible. Here responsibility means submission to an ethic of knowledge that takes scientific-objective-theoretic knowing as unconditionally normative. But any claim to be able to explain this exacting ethic in purely naturalist terms would be to render it conditional rather than unconditional. Naturalism therefore cannot lead the intelligent and responsible subject to any secure foundations for either intelligence or responsibility.

10 Suffering

One of the main reasons why religion and theology are so appealing to their followers is that they provide answers to the problem of suffering. Today, however, the traditional answers do not always seem believable, and suffering, no less than death, seems to be just one more fact of nature. Especially after Darwin all aspects of life, including suffering, can apparently be understood in natural terms. To the strict naturalist this means that, as far as life's suffering is concerned, there is no need to fall back on obsolete religious interpretations, nor is there any good reason any longer for invoking the idea of a redeeming God. Humans, with the aid of science, can understand and respond to the fact of suffering all by themselves.

From Darwinian biology's point of view, suffering (which in this chapter I shall take to be inclusive of the sensation of pain by all sentient life)[1] is simply an adaptation that enhances the probability of survival and reproductive success in complex organisms. How then could theology plausibly add anything of explanatory substance to the Darwinian naturalist's account? Darwin himself observed that suffering is "well adapted to make a creature guard against any great or sudden evil."[2] Suffering, he surmised, is life's warning system, and if at times the torture it brings seems exorbitant, the excess is still consistent with a purely naturalist understanding of life.[3] A follower of Stephen Jay Gould

[1]   Although some writers do not attribute "suffering" to nonhuman forms of life, reserving for the latter only the term "pain," I consider the distinction somewhat arbitrary, unnecessarily anthropocentric and fundamentally Cartesian, as the following reflections will try to make clear.

[2]   Nora Barlow (editor), *The Autobiography of Charles Darwin* (New York: Harcourt, 1958), pp. 88–89.

[3]   However, deadly viruses can invade organisms painlessly, so the warning system, like other evolutionary adaptations, is not perfect. See John Hick, *Evil and the God of Love* (London: The Fontana Library, 1968), pp. 333–38.

and Richard Lewontin might even suggest that the surplus of suffering is a byproduct of adaptation rather than an adaptation itself.[4] In any case, when compared to Darwin's understanding, religious and theological views of suffering may seem to have little if any explanatory value.

Nowadays, of course, some evolutionists go beyond classical Darwinism by accounting for the suffering of sentient life in terms of genes striving to make their way into subsequent generations. Genes somehow sense that they will not get passed on to the next generation unless they fashion for themselves organic vehicles endowed with sensory feedback equipment that can alert living beings when their survival is in jeopardy. So, for their own good, genes have to take it upon themselves to engineer delicate nervous systems that will secure their immortality. Such machinations may seem intelligent and even ingenious to those who are unaware of how evolution works, but to Darwinian naturalists there is nothing intelligent about it at all. The process is, at bottom, blind and impersonal.

Still, it seems to be nothing short of remarkable that the life-process, however one explains it, has gradually woven into organisms more and more delicate and pain-sensitive nervous systems. It is impossible not to remark at how an allegedly unintelligent evolutionary process, no matter how much time it takes and how gradually it all unfolds, could turn out to be so ingenious. And yet Darwinians endowed with a sense of deep time have no difficulty at all in conceiving of a purely natural, *because very gradual*, emergence of sensitive organisms. Furthermore, at least for some people, the haphazard way in which pain is distributed in the organic world is a most disturbing challenge to religious interpretations of life. Although he was not a scientific naturalist himself, Sir Charles Sherrington, in his 1940 Gifford Lectures, offers a poignant portrayal

---

[4]   S. J. Gould and R. C. Lewontin, "The Spandrels of San Marco and the Panglossian Paradigm: a critique of the Adaptationist Programme," *Proceedings of the Royal Society of London*, Series B, vol. 205, no. 1161 (1979), pp. 581–98.

of how the lowly fluke-worm, for example, secures its existence at the expense of excessive suffering in higher organisms:

> There is a small worm (Redia) in our ponds. With its tongue-head it bores into the lung of the water-snail. There it turns into a bag and grows at the expense of the snail's blood. The cyst in the snail's lung is full of Redia. They bore their way out and wander about the body of the snail. They live on the body of the snail, on its less vital parts for so it lasts the longer; to kill it would cut their sojourn short before they could breed. They breed and reproduce. The young wander within the sick snail. After a time they bore their way out of the dying snail and make their way to the wet grass at the pond-edge. There amid the green leaves they encyst themselves and wait. A browsing sheep or ox comes cropping the moist grass. The cyst is eaten. The stomach of the sheep dissolves the cyst and sets free the fluke-worms within it. The worm is now within the body of its second prey. It swims from the stomach to the liver. There it sucks blood and grows, causing the disease called "sheeprot."

The worms then produce eggs that travel down the sheep's liver duct and finally exit into the wet pasture. "Thence as free larvae they reach the meadow-pond to look for another water snail. So the implacable cycle rebegins."

What does it all mean? To Sherrington

> it is a story of securing existence to a worm at cost of lives superior to it in the scale of life as humanly reckoned. Life's prize is given to the aggressive and inferior of life, destructive of other lives at the expense of suffering in them, and, sad as it may seem to us, suffering in proportion as they are lives high in life's scale. The example taken is a fair sample of almost countless many.[5]

---

5   Charles Sherrington, *Man on His Nature* (Cambridge: Cambridge University Press, 1951), p. 266.

Even if there is a fascinating ingenuity to such phenomena, it seems silly to attribute it to a beneficent divine designer. Darwin himself was led to reject the idea of divine design, at least in the biological world, after learning about such indecencies as ichneumon wasps laying their eggs inside living caterpillars so that their larvae will have fresh meat rather than decaying flesh upon which to nourish themselves. Those of us who take the idea of a good and powerful creator seriously must also wonder if there is anything in such performances that theology could possibly illuminate. What holy message can we wrest from the book of nature as we read about fluke worms and ichneumon wasps?

For centuries religions and theologies have been explaining suffering without the benefit of Darwinian expertise. They have been persuasive to most people not only because their sacred stories seem to account quite satisfactorily for the origin of suffering, but even more because they offer hope of release from it. Religious salvation, although it means much more than final release from suffering, means at least that much. Religions generally encourage people to trust that in the end all tears will be wiped away and pain and death will be no more. But now that evolutionary biology has graced us with an elegant "naturalistic" answer to the question of why suffering occurs in sentient life, what are we to do with all the convoluted but apparently healing and adaptive perspectives of our religions? After Darwin, can religious myths about the origin and end of suffering have either explanatory power or salvific efficacy?

Any plausible theological response to suffering cannot simply overlook ichneumon wasps, fluke worms and countless other instances of nature's indifference to suffering. Clearly the natural world has *never* been a paradise, contrary to what a literal reading of Genesis may suggest. The emergence and evolution of life have been rather messy. As we now realize, suffering, death and mass extinctions have been constitutive of, and not just accidental to, the ongoing creation of life on earth. Religious belief encourages people to hope that "alas far off" all tears will be wiped away and death will be no more.[6] And for people of faith it should not be a terribly uncomfortable doctrinal stretch to extend such extravagant hopes, as Buddhism does, to the release of *all* life from suffering. But our theologies, with only a few exceptions, generally avoid the issue of why God's universe would be the theater of so much evolutionary struggle, travail and death in the first place. Theology still needs to consider in depth what biology tells us about God, sin, evil, redemption and especially the meaning of suffering. And it needs to ask more sincerely than ever whether a purely naturalist – and that means evolutionary – understanding is not the best answer to the question of why life brings so much suffering.

The question "why suffering?" is irrepressible, and, along with the prospect of death, it has been the main stimulus to the countless stories about the origin and end of evil that humans have been telling one another for thousands of years. Myths about how suffering came about have provided reassurance that life is not absurd. And religious conjectures about how suffering can be redeemed have carved out the spiritual space in which most peoples have lived, hoped and aspired to ethical goodness. Is it wise, then, to ignore these venerable accounts, as naturalism would propose? Or can we repossess them, even after Darwin, as a great treasury of wisdom deserving of ever deeper exploration? Whatever answer one gives, it is at least necessary to admit that none of the ancient myths of evil and suffering said anything about evolution. That they did not do so is entirely forgiveable, of course, but it is no mark of theological courage that so many religious thinkers even today still touch only lightly on Darwin's science if they mention it at all.

I shall propose in this chapter, then, that it is entirely appropriate to keep telling the old stories about the origin and end of suffering, but that our religions and theologies should not recite them any longer as though Darwin never lived and evolution never happened. Evolutionary biology clearly requires the widening of theological

6   Alfred Lord Tennyson, "In Memoriam."

reflection so as to take into account the enormous breadth and depth of nonhuman pain and the unfinished character of the universe. Even if theology is a reasonable alternative to naturalism it must not be seen as an alternative to good science.

EVOLUTIONARY NATURALISM AND THE SUFFERING OF SENTIENT LIFE

To the evolutionary naturalist, religious stories about suffering lack the explanatory economy of evolutionary science, so they will be of little interest to the intellectually enlightened. Any supernormal accounts of human suffering, indeed the whole panoply of religious mythology and doctrine, appear to the naturalist to be at best nothing more than empty, though perhaps occasionally heartwarming, illusion. This impression applies especially to "theodicy." Broadly speaking, any attempt to understand or explain suffering may be called a theodicy. In theistic contexts theodicy is the theoretical attempt to "justify" the existence of God given the facts of evil and suffering. If God is all-good and all-powerful, then God must be able and willing to prevent life's suffering. But suffering exists. Why? Theodicy is the branch of theology that tries to answer this question. Many theodicies are highly philosophical, and their rarefied speculation does little or nothing to remove actual suffering. For that reason today the whole business of theodicy often seems useless even to the devout. Yet finding an answer to the question of suffering is an irrepressible concern of most people, so *any* intelligible explanation of suffering can be a kind of theodicy.[7] Even Darwinism itself now functions, at least for scientific naturalists, as an ultimate answer to the ancient question of how to locate and understand the fact of suffering.

Evolutionary theory, in fact, is satisfying to so many people today because it proposes in effect to have found a "theodicy" that surpasses all previous ones in clarity and simplicity. For many

---

[7] Following the broad usage of the term by sociologist Peter Berger in *The Sacred Canopy* (Garden City, N.Y.: Anchor Books, 1990), pp. 53ff.

thoughtful people, Darwinism, employed as a kind of Occam's razor, has made the ideas of God, sin, punishment, demons – and perhaps even human guilt – worthless as far as the understanding of suffering is concerned. Nobody pretends that Darwinism can wipe away all tears and do away with death. To those who find evolutionary accounts of suffering sufficient the universe still remains pointless, and hope for redemption an idle dream. But the price of surrendering religious hope seems well worth the intellectual luminosity that Darwinism brings to an issue that has befuddled humanity for so many centuries.

Nevertheless, religious theodicies still persist, and Darwinism is having a tough time dislodging the venerable sources of comfort.[8] Is this persistence of religion simply due to recalcitrant human irrationality and poor science education? Or to an all too human refusal to grow up and face reality? Whatever the answer, Darwinian naturalism, with its promise to provide a complete explanation of life,[9] is now obliged to account not only for suffering but also for the tenacity with which most people still adhere to allegedly obsolete religious and theological myths about suffering. If the Darwinian answer to the question of suffering is so easy to understand, then why do religious myths and theodicies still captivate the minds of most people, including many who are scientifically educated and fully up to date with evolutionary biology?

A simplistic Darwinism might reply that religious myths of suffering still have an adaptive function.[10] Religions trick people into *believing* that their lives are worthwhile. Religion promotes

8   See Robert Hinde, *Why Gods Persist: a Scientific Approach to Religions* (New York: Routledge, 1999); Walter Burkert, *Creation of the Sacred: Tracks of Biology in Early Religions* (Cambridge, Mass.: Harvard University Press, 1996); Pascal Boyer, *Religion Explained: the Evolutionary Origins of Religious Thought* (New York: Basic Books, 2001).

9   For examples and extended discussion, see my book *Deeper than Darwin: the Prospect for Religion in the Age of Evolution* (Boulder, Colo.: Westview Press, 2003).

10 See, for example, Edward O. Wilson, *Consilience: the Unity of Knowledge* (New York: Knopf, 1998).

gene survival, and that is why God will not go away for good. Religion, according to at least some Darwinian naturalists, is in fact a "noble lie," but it is still adaptive. Its illusory projections help to keep individuals and communities together so as to allow their genes to get into future generations. Recognizing the evolutionary effectiveness of religion, some disciples of Darwin even propose that we should never let the deceptions of religion die out completely, lest our species perish from having abandoned one of its most adaptive inventions.[11]

However, a more chastened Darwinism now admits that religious theodicies may not necessarily be adaptive *per se*. Rather, religious ideas and aspirations are only "parasitic" upon cerebral modules which themselves can be accounted for in terms of evolutionary adaptation originally for other purposes than that of providing religious consolation. This hypothesis modifies earlier and cruder Darwinian interpretations of religion's persistence. It concedes that humans will always have a propensity for religion as long as they continue to carry around the same kind of brains that our ancestors acquired during the Pleistocene period. Pascal Boyer and Scott Atran, for example, find the roots of our "counterfactual" religious ideation not so much in culture as in the kinds of hominid brains that became adept at "agent detection," starting several million years ago.[12] Ideas about invisible supernatural beings, Atran claims, "are, in part, by-products of a naturally selected cognitive mechanism for detecting agents – such as predators, protectors and prey – and for dealing rapidly and economically with stimulus situations involving people and animals."[13] Such mechanisms are ready-made for the religious enterprise of looking for unseen deities to soothe our suffering.

[11]   E.g. Loyal Rue, *By the Grace of Guile: the Role of Deception in Natural History and Human Affairs* (New York: Oxford University Press, 1994), pp. 82–107.

[12]   Boyer, *Religion Explained*; Scott Atran, *In Gods We Trust: the Evolutionary Landscape of Religion* (New York: Oxford University Press, 2002).

[13]   Atran, *In Gods We Trust*, p. 15.

In response to this Darwinian debunking of religion and theodicy, I believe theology would be well advised to make two moves. First, it must undertake a thorough critique of the naturalist conviction that Darwinism provides an exhaustive and adequate explanation of the suffering of sentient life. The Darwinian naturalist's virtual claim to complete and final understanding of suffering in evolutionary terms, after all, is an exceptionally audacious one. If justifiable, it would bring down the entire classical edifice of ethics, religion and theology. However, just as the Darwinian naturalist's claim to be able to explain critical intelligence and moral responsibility fully in evolutionary terms has proven to be inflated and even self-subverting, so also the belief that Darwinism can at last make suffering *fully* intelligible will also prove to be groundless. It is groundless, as I will show, because of its failure to understand fully the intimate connection between suffering and the more mysterious fact of subjectivity that is required to register both pain and pleasure.

The second theological move, however, is to attend carefully to the evolutionary accounts of the suffering involved in pre-human and nonhuman forms of sentient life. Without embracing scientific naturalism, theologians can still accept the discoveries of evolutionary science, one of which is that suffering occurs much more extensively in nonhuman life than religions had previously noticed. My proposal is that by looking closely at evolution, theology may be aroused to find fresh and profound meaning in many of the classical religious myths and teachings about suffering. What follows can be no more than a sketch of the two theological assignments I have just laid out.

Can Darwinism fully explain the suffering of sentient life?

Scientists are not yet close to understanding the origin of life on Earth, but in the notion of adaptive fitness Darwinian biologists can claim at least to have found a powerful explanation of life's morphological diversity. Moreover, the notion of evolutionary adaptation can also at least partly explain why life became sentient to the point of suffering. The capacity to have feelings, both physical and affective, has given complex organisms an adaptive advantage over those not so endowed. And even though the capacity for suffering is as imperfectly developed as other evolutionary adaptations, it can often signal quite accurately just when an organism is in danger, allow it to move out of harm's way, and thus promote the cause of survival and reproduction. To the Darwinian naturalist, adaptive fitness is the *ultimate* reason why suffering occurs. Of course, the degree of intensity of suffering by sentient beings is often out of proportion to the minimum that would be adaptive (as Darwin himself noted), but to the pure naturalist this surplus is simply another indication of the universe's fundamental impersonality.

Nevertheless, one may still wonder whether Darwinian naturalism accounts *fully* for the emergence of either sentience or suffering. For there can be no suffering without sentience, and there can be no sentience without *subjects* able to experience either pain or pleasure. So any attempt to naturalize suffering in a complete way will sooner or later bump into the fact of subjectivity. And for the naturalist program to claim final victory science must be able to show why there are any subjects at all. Yet, as previous chapters have shown time and again, scientific method lacks both the rich empiricism and the layered explanation essential to take the fact of subjectivity fully into account. By virtue of its own methodological self-restriction, science, including biology, has no cognitive access to those centers of feeling or awareness that we intuitively recognize as subjects. Here is another point at which scientific method is not nearly as empirically open as its practitioners generally assume. It leaves out any consideration of the inner worlds of living, experiencing centers, confining itself impersonally to what is objectively or publicly accessible. The organic interiority without which neither sentience nor suffering could purchase a foothold in this world necessarily eludes objectifying inquiry. It follows that if science, including Darwinian biology, cannot comprehend the subjectivity that underlies sentience and suffering, then evolutionary naturalism – which takes biological science as ultimate explanation – cannot plausibly claim to encompass or explain the totality of organic beings as such.

This limitation applies especially to critical intelligence, but by analogy it extends across the board to *all* kinds and shades of subjectivity, anywhere in the universe. Even the most rudimentary instances of subjectivity already place the universe at least partly beyond the boundary of what can be captured cognitionally by conventional scientific method.[14] Annoyed at nature's resistance at this point to complete objectification, some scientists completely dismiss subjectivity from the realm of being, classifying it as a purely contingent offshoot of natural processes in a world where accidents happen abundantly. Of course, evolutionary biology may elucidate at one level of understanding the slow *intensification* of sentience in natural history, taking it to be a consequence of the gradual complexification of nervous systems over the course of abundant time. But, as we have seen already in the case of our own intelligence, science can never provide an adequate understanding of what it cannot even "see," namely, the "insideness" of subjectivity as such.

Moreover, only sentient subjects are able to *strive*. Only a subjective kind of being would be able to *aim* intentionally at a specific goal. And only a striving being could experience success or failure – or pain. As I noted earlier, one of the main characteristics that makes living beings distinct from nonliving ones is what philosopher Michael Polanyi calls the logic of achievement.[15] Living beings, unlike nonliving, can strive, and therefore either achieve success or experience failure in their efforts. The experience of suffering is tied into this logic in a way that usually goes unnoticed. It is because organisms are anticipative that they can suffer at all.

---

[14] Pure Whiteheadians claim that the physical universe was *never* devoid of subjectivity, even prior to life. "Apart from subjects," as Whitehead says, "there is nothing, nothing, nothing, bare nothingness." Alfred North Whitehead, *Process and Reality*, corrected edition, edited by David Ray Griffin and Donald W. Sherburne (New York: The Free Press, 1978), p. 254.

[15] See Michael Polanyi, *Personal Knowledge* (New York: Harper Torchbooks, 1964), pp. 327ff.

Scientists themselves are living, striving centers (personal subjects), able to experience success or failure in their endeavors. And it is especially their own experience of striving, succeeding and failing that allows them to intuit, by way of a tacit kind of knowing, that other sentient beings are also striving, subjective and (often) suffering centers as well. Science as such cannot "see" the dimension of sentient, striving subjectivity in nature. It can deal explicitly only with what can be objectified.

The resistance of subjectivity, sentience and striving to objectifying control is so unsettling that some scientists, especially eliminative materialists, actually deny that these are even real at all.[16] But the stipulation that subjectivity should vanish altogether from the realm of being makes it all the more ironic that contemporary gene-centered Darwinism cannot expurgate even from its own discourse a presupposed element of subjectivity. Nor does its formal bracketing of all considerations of teleology prevent the theme of striving from intruding into the neo-Darwinian's gene-centered explanations – through the backdoor, as it were.

In *The Red Queen* the widely respected Darwinian Matt Ridley, for example, in effect concedes that biology cannot function without the categories of subjectivity and striving. Many contemporary biologists, he notes, "think of genes as analogous to *active and cunning individuals.*"[17] Ideally, he admits, scientists would avoid the language of subjectivity and intentional striving, but when biologists talk about genes today they find it hard to follow such a puritanical principle. In contemporary biological parlance, genes, which according to scientific naturalism are just impersonal segments of mindless DNA, curiously take on the traits of intentionality and even

---

[16] See, for example, Paul Churchland, *The Engine of Reason, the Seat of the Soul* (Cambridge, Mass.: Bradford Books, 1995) and Daniel Dennett, *Consciousness Explained* (New York: Little, Brown, 1991). For a critical discussion I recommend especially Alan Wallace, *The Taboo of Subjectivity: Toward a New Science of Consciousness* (New York: Oxford University Press, 2000).

[17] Matt Ridley, *The Red Queen: Sex and the Evolution of Human Nature* (New York: Penguin Books, 1993), pp. 92–93 (emphasis added).

personality. They are said to *cooperate* and *aim* for "survival." "A gene," Ridley says, "has only one criterion by which posterity judges it: whether it becomes an ancestor of other genes." And it must *achieve* that "at the expense of other genes."[18] Genes even form *strategies* to avoid extinction as they make their passage through time.[19] Genes (or arrays of genes) are said to strive, and hence, just like biologists and other striving centers, they can either succeed or fail in this enterprise. The logic of achievement tacitly dominates a discourse that otherwise emulates physics in its pursuit of impersonal laws of causation.[20]

The main point I am making here is that Darwinian science may be able to help us understand that suffering has adaptive significance, but it cannot tell us what subjectivity is or why subjectivity – and eventually critical intelligence – came into the universe at all. Nor can it explain why sentient, subjective centers tend to strive. Here again nature gives evidence of carrying a fundamentally *anticipatory* orientation that overflows the boundaries of the naturalist philosophy and calls out for an alternative worldview. The aspect of anticipation – by which I mean openness to new possibilities – that has always undergirded cosmic emergence comes to the surface most explicitly in the phenomena of subjectivity, sentience and striving. Hence it is not natural selection but something much more fundamental, namely, nature's anticipatory deportment, that provides the deepest subsoil of both life and suffering. To account for suffering in a substantive way requires, at least at some point, that we reach an understanding of why nature is so habitually anticipatory in the first place.

The fact that religious persons are also striving subjects places them in continuity with a whole succession of subjective, striving centers acting throughout the story of life. Yet it is characteristic of

---

18   Ibid., p. 94 (emphasis added).   19   Ibid., *passim.*
20   For a fuller discussion see my book *Deeper than Darwin*, pp. 103–119.

evolutionary naturalism to look away from the subjectivity, affectivity and centered striving that religious persons *actually* experience from the inside. In the world of religion, human subjects, usually as part of a group, are involved in the kind of striving that theologian John Bowker calls "route-finding."[21] Religious persons, usually with the help of a tradition's symbolic and doctrinal stimuli, strive to make their way beyond the ultimate limits imposed by nature, death and suffering. Darwinians strive (another irony) to reduce all religious expression, or at least the cerebral components underlying religion, to evolutionary adaptations. But their naturalizing zeal leads them to ignore the obvious fact that religions are composed concretely of striving, sentient subjects involved in a most earnest kind of anticipation.[22] And, since all striving arises from a mysterious region of subjectivity inaccessible to science, Darwinian naturalism could never, even in principle, penetrate to the core of religion or theodicy either.

Theodicy after Darwin

What surplus of theological meaning, though, can we make out in life's suffering after Darwin? And what shape will theodicy assume in an age of evolution? Theodicies, I am convinced, cannot remain exactly the same after Darwin as before. Our relatively new awareness of the millions of years of life's suffering prior to human emergence challenges all predominantly human-centered theological traditions. Since there is suffering in all of life, as Buddhism emphasizes so clearly, theodicy must encompass this larger biological whole. What would happen to theology, then, if it brought all the pre-human epochs of innocent suffering, death, predation, disease

---

21 John Bowker, *Is Anybody out There?* (Westminster, Md.: Christian Classics, Inc., 1988), pp. 9–18, 112–43.

22 We need not enter here into the theological question of whether by its own efforts our religious striving can ever be successful. In fact, religious striving by itself risks the greatest of failures, and according to some interpreters of religion it is in moments of failure that the religious personality is finally in a position to surrender to "grace."

and extinction to the center of its systematic reflections on evil. And what would theology look like if it considered in a sustained way the evolutionary fact that the universe is an anticipatory – and that means still unfinished – creation. Even though out of the corner of its eye theology may have occasionally looked at (1) the suffering of the wider life-world and (2) the unfinished state of the cosmos, it has yet to integrate these two evolutionary themes fully into its thoughts about God, suffering and redemption.[23]

Theodicy, at least in its classical formulations, has dwelt almost exclusively on *human* suffering and has typically construed it as the penalty for sin. One advantage of this selective reading is that it seems to safeguard the idea that God cannot be an accomplice or cause of evil. But evolutionary science now envisages suffering and death as constitutive of creation; so how can the wider panorama of life's undeserved suffering make theological sense? Often theology has avoided the issue by in effect denying that a larger arena of innocent suffering even exists at all. One assumption has been, for example, that nonhuman animals do not *really* suffer.[24] But common sense and reflection on evolution make this belief highly questionable. Moreover, theodicy must address not just the issue of suffering, but also the *perishability* of all life, a discussion that I shall take up in the following chapter. Here I can deal with the question of suffering only in the context of Western theology, although I hope my reflections will have implications for religious thought more generally speaking.

Ignoring the nonhuman story of suffering, the dominant Western theodicies insinuate that in paying the price for human guilt there might come an end to suffering. With Paul Ricoeur, one may call this

---

A very recent and clear example of a theodicy that ignores nonhuman suffering is John Thiel's otherwise insightful book *God, Evil, and Innocent Suffering: a Theological Reflection* (New York: Crossroad, 2002).

24 For example, Thiel, ibid., pp. 1–31, tends to downplay animal pain as a theological issue.

the "ethical vision" of evil.[25] Unlike the "tragic vision" of suffering, which maintains that suffering just happens to be part of the way an impersonal world works, the ethical vision looks for a redemptive meaning in suffering. Seeking to preserve the idea of divine justice, the ethical vision assumes that suffering cannot be separated from freedom and human fault. "All we, like sheep, have gone astray" (Isaiah 53:6). In Christianity the one exception to such straying is Jesus, in whose free surrender to crucifixion a completely guiltless suffering somehow pays the price for our own sin. Ricoeur recalls that the Suffering Servant theology of Second Isaiah, developed centuries before the era of Christianity, already prefigured the Christian intuition that undeserved suffering can be a gift of love for others, thus subverting the idea that suffering is always punishment.[26] However, what Ricoeur does not bring out is that this radical transformation in principle calls for a theology in which the suffering of *all* of life is taken into account.

The suffering of most sentient life is purely innocent, and where there is no guilt suffering cannot make sense as expiation. Perhaps then, one might counter, suffering is pure meaningless tragedy to be combatted wherever possible, but otherwise courageously endured because there is no ultimate healing in store. Maybe the best we humans can do is simply resign ourselves to the prospect that there is no meaning in suffering. Certainly many a naturalist has settled into this tragic "realism." To the sober naturalist, for example, if there is any meaning in suffering at all, it is that tragedy provides individual persons with the opportunity to experience a sense of honor at facing the harshness of existence (Weinberg), or to

---

[25]   Paul Ricoeur, *The Conflict of Interpretations: Essays in Hermeneutics*, edited by Don Ihde (Evanston, Ill.: Northwestern University Press, 1974), pp. 455–67. According to the ethical vision of evil, "punishment only serves to preserve an already established order." Paul Ricoeur, *History and Truth*, translated by Charles Kelbley (Evanston: Northwestern University Press, 1965), p. 125.

[26]   Paul Ricoeur, *The Symbolism of Evil*, translated by Emerson Buchanan (Boston: Beacon Press, 1969), pp. 324–26.

feel that they are somehow superior to their fate (Camus).[27] It seems that Darwin himself shifted gradually toward such fatalism, and one of the traits that makes him seem so endearing is the undeniable courage that accompanied his own experience of pain.

Sober naturalism is notable for the courage it exhibits in the face of what it takes to be a meaningless universe. But wherever there is courage, as theologian Paul Tillich has persuasively argued, there is also vitality.[28] In any exercise of human courage there is a spontaneous commitment to life for life's sake. There is a refusal to cease *striving*, even when striving seems futile. It is this resurgent, undefeatable vitality, with its anticipation of *more and deeper* life in the face of absurdity, that we need to make sense of in a conceptually consistent way. Naturalism, in my opinion, cannot do so. Even in the depths of tragic resignation, after all, there is a tacit assumption that life is a gift that should not be squandered but instead intensified. An irrepressible gratitude for life lurks beneath even the most tragic forms of pessimism. Thinkers such as Schopenhauer, Nietzsche and Camus, all of whom formally judged the universe to be meaningless, nonetheless continued in their own oblique ways to affirm life as incontestably meaningful and worth living. Unfortunately, as philosophers, they did so in such a way as to manifest the same kind of inconsistency we have seen in contemporary scientific naturalism: they persistently denied in their philosophies what they affirmed in their hearts and in their every act of courage. All the more, then, is it incumbent upon responsible thinking to articulate a worldview that is logically consistent with the implicit valuing of life that becomes manifest even in the lives of tragic pessimists.

A more logically consistent alternative to the tragic vision, I believe, is one in which life's suffering and sacrifice can be interpreted in terms of the anticipatory, unfinished state of the universe.

---

27 Steven Weinberg, *Dreams of a Final Theory* (New York: Pantheon Books, 1992), p. 256; Albert Camus, *The Myth of Sisyphus, and Other Essays*, translated by Justin O'Brien (New York: Knopf, 1955), pp. 88–91.

28 Paul Tillich, *The Courage To Be* (New Haven: Yale University Press, 1952), pp. 78–84.

Most of life's suffering makes sense neither as punishment nor reprisal. Nor is it ultimately absurd. It is part and parcel of a universe still in the making. Suffering, which at one level of understanding may simply be information about the dangers to an organism's existence, at another level is information about the unfinished state of the universe. The response to suffering, therefore, should not be to justify it theoretically or scientifically, but to strive to conquer it in hope of its final vanquishing. Science over the last two centuries has been demonstrating, at least to those who have bothered to look, that life's suffering spills out far beyond the boundaries of the ethical vision of evil. To some naturalists the excessive suffering of sentient life is final vindication of the ancient tragic interpretations of life, and I suppose that this interpretation will always have a following. But there is available another conceptual space in which to situate life's innocent suffering – that of a universe being drawn toward a future fulfillment. It is *expectation*, not *expiation*, that constitutes the most consistent setting for theodicy after Darwin.

And yet the suspicion that suffering is *essentially* punishment persists. It still lives on, not too far beneath the surface, in psyches and societies. The expiatory bias of the ethical vision still festers at the heart of legal systems, public policy and international relations. It even quietly colors evolutionary naturalism's understanding of morality.[29] The expiatory outlook still shows up whenever we suspect that any good fortune that comes our way must be paid for. And, of course, it seems to have found a lasting abode in theodicies that view suffering as primarily satisfaction for our sinful dishonoring of God's glory.[30]

---

[29] Life seems to many Darwinian naturalists to be essentially about selfish genes and competitive struggle rather than gene-sharing and cooperation, whereas the latter are more central to evolution. See Holmes Rolston, III, *Genes, Genesis and God: Values and Their Origins in Natural and Human History* (New York: Cambridge University Press, 1999), pp. 47–50.

[30] For an insightful discussion of traditional themes of expiation and satisfaction see Gerard Sloyan, *The Crucifixion of Jesus, History, Myth, Faith* (Minneapolis: Augsburg Fortress Publishers, 1995), pp. 98–122.

The expiatory understanding of suffering is so deeply embedded in our sensibilities that it seems nearly ineradicable. It first took verbal shape in ancient stories about how an original cosmic perfection was spoiled by free human acts of rebellion. In the biblical world the Adamic myth, with which Paul Ricoeur associates the ethical vision of existence, represents the intuition that suffering exists mostly because of human freedom and sin.[31] The offshoot of this influential theodicy has been that even today, in secular as well as deeply religious societies, whenever suffering or misfortune occurs, people are inclined to look for culprits.[32] The assumption that a price in suffering must always be paid for the ancestral defiling of a primal purity of creation has underwritten social habits of looking for victims to blame for the mess we are in. It has legitimated a history of scapegoating that exacerbates misery on our planet.[33]

The penal view of suffering has also damaged the reputation of Christianity in the eyes of many who have tried to make sense of suffering. In 1933 the Jesuit paleontologist Teilhard de Chardin wrote:

> In spite of the subtle distinctions of the theologians, it is a matter *of fact* that Christianity has developed under the over-riding impression that all the evil round us was born from an initial transgression. So far as dogma is concerned we are still living in the atmosphere of a universe in which what matters most is reparation and expiation . . . This accounts for the importance, at least in theory, of the idea of sacrifice, and for the interpretation almost exclusively in terms of purification.[34]

---

31   Even in the Adamic myth, however, the figure of the serpent represents the intuition that evil is much more than a human product. Ricoeur, *The Conflict of Interpretations*, pp. 294–95.

32   Pierre Teilhard de Chardin, *Christianity and Evolution*, translated by René Hague (New York: Harcourt Brace & Co., 1969), p. 81.

33   Ibid.   34   Ibid.

Teilhard is not denying that there is something sacrificial about life and evolution. There is. Nor is he denying the fact of human guilt. What he is questioning is our habit of associating sacrifice primarily with expiation rather than with expectation. Instead of resigning ourselves to suffering as though it were tragically necessary, or trying to make sense of suffering in terms of punishment, suffering may be understood informationally as a kind of negative feedback at a level deeper than the Darwinian notion of adaptation can excavate. Life's suffering is information about the discrepancy between an actual and an ideal state of cosmic being. Suffering, then, is best thought of in terms of an unfinished, anticipatory universe in which the possibility of something completely new – an eschatological plenitude – awaits it up ahead.

Unfortunately, theology still exaggerates the idea of an hypothesized primordial offense, an idea that usually implies that God's original creation was one of rounded-off perfection. Too often theology has situated suffering in the context of myths that emphasize the primordial purity of an original creation. This only makes the original fault seem all the more enormous, hence liable to unleash bloodthirsty, demonizing expeditions to find someone or something to blame. The logic implicitly operative in the penal vision of suffering is that if a state of paradisal wholeness had preceded the original fault, then the fault itself could be no trivial matter. Thus an expiatory view of suffering and sacrifice would always be calling for us to make things right by piling more punishment on those we suspect to be somehow complicit in despoiling the primordial perfection. What is worse, however, setting things right would mean at best the *restoration* of what has already been, rather than an opening to the future of a completely new creation up ahead.

It is important to ask, therefore, just what theological consequences would follow if the universe, as evolution implies, has emerged only gradually from a state of relative simplicity, a universe that still remains unfinished. What need would there be for expiation or scapegoating if nothing significant had been lost in the beginning? And what if the perfection for which humans ache were envisaged as a future state of (new) creation instead of a lost past? What if the path of restoration were permanently closed off by the very logic of evolution? Would not an evolutionary view of life logically call instead for a theology that purges sacrifice of its motifs of expiation and situates life's suffering and sacrifice once and for all within the horizon of expectation – eschatology, in other words – where the whole emergent universe is understood as anticipating a healing, renewing future?

I am asking, in other words, what might be the consequences for theology if it thought out fully and conclusively the implications of the evolutionary claim that *a state of complete cosmic integrity has never yet been an actuality.* By ruling out any past epoch of created perfection, our religious aspirations may henceforth be turned more decisively from regret and remorse and more decidedly in the direction of hope. A worldview that takes anticipation seriously could make better sense than tragic pessimism does of the irrepressible vitality underlying all of life, including the courage of fatalists. Such a cosmic vision would in no sense be a reversion to vitalism since it makes anticipation a feature of the whole universe and not of life alone. The *universe*, along with the life it carries, has emerged only gradually, and there has never yet been any actualized epoch of paradisal perfection. If this is true – and science seems to confirm it – then our religious aspirations, in consonance with the general cosmic anticipation out of which they have emerged, may now turn irreversibly toward the wide openness of an infinitely resourceful Future, the only arena in which the fulfillment of life's longing for perfection or release from suffering could conceivably become actualized.

After Darwin and contemporary cosmology it is difficult for educated people to believe that there has ever been any point in past cosmic history when the universe was pristinely perfect. Accordingly, there could never have been any literal "fall" from a cosmic paradise into the state of imperfection. Imperfection would have been there from the start, as the shadow side of an unfinished universe.[35]

---

[35] Ibid., p. 40.

Hence, it would follow that there can be no cosmological justification for purely expiatory interpretations of suffering, nor for self-punishment, resentment and victimization, since no loss of primordial perfection has ever occurred that could provide the rationale for resentment at such an imagined loss. Scapegoating violence, moreover, would make no sense in an anticipatory universe whose essential or ideal implementation is still coming into being, still dawning on the wings of an ever arriving Future.

Unfortunately, however, the story of human religiosity has often been more one of nostalgia for an imagined past perfection than anticipation of new creation.[36] Even in religions descended from the biblical environment a longing to restore or recover some idyllic past has suppressed the spirit of Abrahamic adventure that looks to an indeterminate future opened up by a God of promise. The central, but often forgotten, thrust of biblical faith is to look for the anticipated realm of perfection in the not-yet-future instead of in a remote mythic past or, for that matter, in a Platonic realm of present perfection hovering eternally above the flow of time.

SUMMARY AND CONCLUSION

It is not natural selection alone but, even more fundamentally, the universe and life's anticipation of a fullness of being up ahead that allows suffering to show up wherever and whenever perfection still remains out of reach. Suffering is the dark side of any universe that remains unfinished and in which anticipation remains alive. The thread of anticipation that our richer empiricism has located as the dynamic core of critical intelligence, life, emergence, evolution, cosmic process and moral aspiration is inseparable from the occurrence of life's suffering as well. For wherever there is anticipation

---

[36]   I believe that contemporary naturalism, with its eyes always turned to the earlier-and-simpler as the region of what is most fully real has also been shaped by a religious history of looking only to the past for the realm of perfection.

there will also be frustration. And although a Darwinian look at life will be able to see suffering as adaptation, at another layer of understanding suffering is information about the unfinished status of an anticipatory universe.

At the end of this chapter's reflections, however, a big question still remains. No doubt the scientific naturalist has been raising it all along. The question is this: why is it that the universe, if it is indeed grounded in something other than itself, remains unfinished? Why does the universe have an anticipatory bearing at all? What sort of creator would have failed to round nature off into final perfection in the beginning, or at least by this time in cosmic history? Why not create the universe fully and finally in the beginning, so as to avoid all suffering, struggle and even striving. Why all this fooling around for fourteen billion years and the trillions that may lie ahead?

Here the only answer that makes sense to me is that any notion of an originally completed cosmos would be theologically incoherent. As Teilhard and others have already suggested, there is no plausible alternative, theologically speaking, to an unfinished initial creation. An originally perfect creation – an idea that seemed tenable before we became aware of the unfolding, unfinished character of the universe – is theologically inconceivable. Why? Because if a creator, in the beginning, made a perfectly finished, fully completed world, such a world would not be distinct from its maker. It would not be *other* than God. If the world were created perfectly in the beginning, then this world would be nothing more than an extension of God's own being, an appendage to a dictatorial deity. It would not be a world at all.

Not just Christianity, but Islam and Judaism also, have always emphasized that God is not the world. They have persistently rejected pantheism along with materialist monism. This means that, theologically speaking, the world must in some sense be radically other than God. But for the world to be truly other than God it has to be given the opportunity to *become* itself. In other words, it has to be given permission to experiment, often unsuccessfully perhaps, with new possibilities of being. And this experimental self-actualizing may take a long time – deep time.[37]

Try to imagine the alternatives. An originally perfect world might be a world without suffering. But it would also be a world without a future because everything would have been fixed in place once and for all. It would also be a world without freedom, since all events, including human actions, would be determined from the very start to be just what they are. There would be no indeterminacy or contingency, essential ingredients in any world open to the newness of the future. And an originally perfect world would be one without life. An originally perfect universe could anticipate – nothing. Theologically speaking, there can be no reasonable alternative to an unfinished initial creation.[38] For that reason theology should be completely comfortable with an evolutionary understanding of nature as essentially anticipatory.

---

[37]   For a much more extended development of this perspective see my book *God after Darwin: a Theology of Evolution* (Boulder, Colo.: Westview Press, 2000).

[38]   These thoughts are based on my reading of the many works of Pierre Teilhard de Chardin, but especially his essays in *Christianity and Evolution.*

11 Death

And all that borrows life from Thee
Is ever in thy care,
And everywhere that man can be
Thou, God, art present there.

Isaac Watts, 1715

However fragile life may be
'Tis in the system's care,
And everywhere that man can be
The Universe is there.

Kenneth E. Boulding, 1975[1]

According to much modern thought, the natural and most intelligible state of the universe is one in which life and mind do not yet exist. Life and mind are puzzling exceptions to the fundamental lifelessness of the cosmos. However, people did not always look at things this way. To most of our ancestors, as Hans Jonas points out, life was the fundamental reality, death the unintelligible exception.[2] Naturalistic belief, however, has supplanted the earlier panvitalist view of reality in which everything throbbed with life. The naturalistic agenda is now that of explaining how life, and eventually mind, emerged from the earlier and simpler lifelessness of the cosmos. Both Jonas and Paul Tillich have even referred to modern scientific naturalism as favoring what may be called an "ontology of death."[3] What they mean by this designation is that over the course of time the universe has literally died in our hearts and minds. This is a severe assessment, but there is no denying that scientific materialism typically assumes that the

[1] Kenneth Boulding, "Toward an Evolutionary Theology," in *The Spirit of the Earth: a Teilhard Centennial Celebration*, edited by Jerome Perlinski (New York: The Seabury Press, 1981), pp. 112–13.

[2] Hans Jonas, *The Phenomenon of Life* (New York: Harper & Row, 1966), pp. 9–10.

[3] Ibid.; Paul Tillich, *Systematic Theology*, vol. III (Chicago: University of Chicago Press, 1963), p. 19.

fundamental being of the cosmos is lifeless. And this assumption is the result of "expurgating from the physical record our own felt aliveness."[4] The alienation of subjectivity from the physical universe has rendered nature vulnerable to being drained of life as well.

To the Darwinian materialist, in particular, lifeless matter is the ground state of being. Somehow nature is endowed with prodigious creative powers which the passage of time can gradually release, but the starting point and ultimate basis of evolutionary creativity is mindless material stuff and blind physical processes. From an evolutionary point of view, of course, death is an important part of the creative process. In order for new and more adaptive forms of life to emerge, the perishing of individual organisms, and sometimes entire species, is a biological necessity. If natural selection is to work, abundant diversity is needed, and there are never enough organisms alive in any present generation to provide the requisite variety. Each present generation must eventually die off if sufficient numbers of variations are to become available for the selection process. Given the spatial limitations of the terrestrial environment, the perishing of organisms is compulsory over the course of virtually limitless time if there is to be a gradual increase in life's versatility and complexity. For example, the emergence of primate life and eventually critically intelligent subjects could never have occurred except on an enormous mound of mortality.

Furthermore, if one follows the tenets of naturalism, not only do all organisms, including ourselves, have to die but our perishing will be final. All of life will return to the primordial state of being: lifelessness. Naturalists seriously doubt that even critical intelligence can escape the finality of death, so they make no plans for an afterlife. Science, they point out, has shown that we are purely material beings. Mentality and morality may seem at first to be signs of our substantially spiritual nature, but there is no "evidence" of the existence of spirit, souls or immortality. Naturalists believe that life

---

4   Jonas, *The Phenomenon of Life*, pp. 9–10.

and mind are explainable ultimately in physical terms. Thought, desire, ethics and even religion are at bottom purely material in their makeup and motivation. They are so intimately connected to a physical brain and central nervous system that when the body dies, critical intelligence and all that goes with it vanish forever. Naturalists concede that human hope for life after death may be adaptive, but this does not make it any the less illusory. When we die, our minds and memories dissolve into the eternal silence that awaits menacingly beneath the feeble flickering of life. Eventually the whole universe will decay into energetic immobility, and nothing or nobody will be left to remember anything that went on during its long pilgrimage to nonbeing. Many billions of years from now, after the physical universe has lapsed into flame or frost (probably the latter according to the latest physical theories), everything to which it has given birth will be greeted by undying nothingness.

It is hard even for most naturalists to look unblinkingly into such an abyss, but the eventual annihilation of life, mind and culture is nonetheless an inescapable logical consequence of the naturalist creed. The philosopher William James has expressed the bleak implications of this worldview as candidly as anyone:

> That is the sting of it, that in the vast driftings of the cosmic weather, though many a jeweled shore appears, and many an enchanted cloud-bank floats away, long lingering ere it be dissolved – even as our world now lingers for our joy – yet when these transient products are gone, nothing, absolutely *nothing* remains, to represent those particular qualities, those elements of preciousness which they may have enshrined. Dead and gone are they, gone utterly from the very sphere and room of being. Without an echo; without a memory; without an influence on aught that may come after, to make it care for similar ideals. This utter final wreck and tragedy is of the essence of scientific materialism as at present understood.[5]

---

[5]   William James, *Pragmatism* (Cleveland: Meridian Books, 1964), p. 76.

As I noted in chapter 1, sober naturalists find nothing in this desolate picture to lift the human heart. According to Steven Weinberg, for example, the most one can do if naturalism is true is to salvage a sense of honor at not running away from its obvious implications. I find Weinberg's sober strain of naturalism more intellectually appealing than the prevalent sunny varieties since at least it tries hard to remain obedient to the imperatives of the mind. Weinberg does not ignore, for example, the fact that naturalism is bad news for most people, including naturalists. If the universe is pointless – and here I believe James would agree with Weinberg – we should have enough courage and respect for truth to admit it. If the end of all things is "utter final wreck and tragedy," then clothing nature in a mantle of "mysterious" benevolence, as sunny naturalists do, is a failure of nerve as well as logic.

Sober naturalists seem willing to swallow what they take to be the poisonous implications of their creed, and they want no part of sunny naturalism's facile compromises. They frankly acknowledge that science in all its splendor can never make the universe responsive enough to satisfy the human longing for meaning. In fact, they are convinced that science, especially after Darwin, provides solid reasons to question whether the universe could ever be called kind. It is not surprising then that sober naturalists are few, far outnumbered by their more buoyant counterparts. Nor is it unexpected that they themselves seldom stay perfectly true to their grim cosmological assumptions.

Sunny naturalists, however, make even less of an effort to be consistent. They officially endorse scientism and (usually) materialism, and they admit to the finality of death and the perishability of the cosmos, but their general outlook on life remains one of resilient sanguinity. As such, they are the kind of skeptics that a Nietzsche or a Sartre would have denounced for the timidity of their atheism. If the universe is meaningless, and ethics groundless, then truthfulness demands that one pass through the fires of nihilism before finding a post-religious comfort zone. But sunny naturalists have not yet looked down into the bottom of the abyss they have opened up. Instead they have nestled into the cultural and ethical worlds nurtured for centuries by worshipers of God.

Surely naturalism has to have more disturbing implications than sunny naturalists are willing to entertain. If science has in truth dissolved the transcendent ground that formerly upheld nature and morality, then the sober naturalist wins the contest of candor hands down by at least trying to field the full implications of an essentially lifeless world.

However, in my view neither sober nor sunny naturalism has opened its eyes wide enough, either to the universe or to the blinding reality of critical intelligence. Both sets of naturalists in fact begin their reflections on the world by looking only at a very limited range of data. They generally assume that scientific experiment is our deepest access to true being and that the real world, at least as far as serious reflection is concerned, terminates at the limits of what science can potentially see. Some naturalists are willing to admit that science is not the only way of seeing or knowing, and they even make room for affective, intersubjective, narrative and aesthetic patterns of cognition. But, in the end, they still arbitrarily enshrine the theoretic field of science in a position of supremacy over the primal modes. Naturalism, moreover, is not accustomed to a stereoscopic visualization that allows for different dimensions of the world to come into view (see chapter 7). It knows nothing of the wider empiricism that takes in both the data of scientific experiment *and* the fact of critical intelligence in a single sweep. Nor, when it comes to following the mind's second imperative, is it at home with a richly layered approach to explanation.

Furthermore, naturalism does not attempt to draw out the full implications of the undeniable fact that critical intelligence is tied into the cosmos in such an intimate way that the whole notion of "cosmos" must be radically transformed in the light of this inclusion (see chapter 8). Instead, it persistently envisages nature as something foreign to both intelligence and subjectivity, a presupposition that can lead in extreme cases to an ontology of death and then to magic in lieu of explanation when it comes to understanding the actual emergence of mind in natural history. Embracing the modern habit of tearing critical intelligence out of the universe at the very start of its inquiry into nature, naturalists are bound logically to construe the world "out there" as inherently mindless, lifeless and often valueless as well. Then, building on the assumption that this fully objectified universe is "naturally" devoid of anything like life and mind, they are led to the view that the entire cosmos is purposeless also. The outcome of the modern divorce of nature from mind is that the intelligent, meaning- and truth-seeking human subject is left stranded in some indefinable place outside an apparently unconscious universe. It is not surprising then that critical intelligence, having been uprooted from nature, seems almost indistinguishable from "nothingness." And then, when death swallows up this chimera, little is lost because there was never much there to begin with.

Given the way it looks at the world – screening out all traces of subjectivity from the start – sober naturalism at least has the merit of trying to be philosophically consistent with its grounding assumption. If the cosmos is indeed essentially mindless and lifeless it would be cowardly to assume that our meaning-seeking subjectivity can ever find a home there. Sunny naturalism, on the other hand, while having the merit of keeping hope alive, has not yet been able to show convincingly how its zest for life is consistent with naturalism's dismal picture of the universe.

The position I have been developing has a different starting point. Heeding the imperative to be open to the *full* range of experiences, and recognizing the primal as well as theoretic fields of meaning in relating to the real world, I have proposed that critical intelligence is a natural phenomenon to which we must attend before going on to construct our philosophies of nature. A widely empirical contact with the real world cannot ignore the fact that nature is the matrix of mind and that mind is in some way cosmic in scope. Even astrophysics and astrobiology are now challenging on scientific grounds the ironic naturalist suspicion that mind does not belong fully to the natural world. The roots of life and human intelligence coincide with cosmic origins, so the cosmos has never been intrinsically alien to mind and life. These facts, if thought through consistently, can make a great difference not only to how we understand nature and subjectivity but also how we think about death.

IS DEATH FINAL?

By expelling critical intelligence from the universe that gave rise to it, modern naturalism has led not only to a diminished view of human life, but to a trivialization of death as well. For there can be nothing terribly consequential about the perishing of mind if mind is merely the ethereal wisp that modern thought has taken it to be in the first place. As long as mind is separated from the universe, what happens to the subject can have little bearing on the cosmos and vice versa. When consciousness disappears, the mindless world remains unshaken. Yet today even natural science is demonstrating that critical intelligence, reliant as it is on the proper functioning of brains, is deeply dependent on specific physical features pertaining to the history of the whole universe. The emergence of each intelligent subject has a dramatic cosmic prelude that we knew very little about until recently. When a mind emerges, the event is more than a local disturbance of indifferent matter. It is a cosmic eruption. Likewise, when a subject dies, something happens to the whole universe. If the physical constituents of consciousness extend historically back to the birth of the universe itself, then the death of every cell and every organism is something more than just another Darwinian inexorability. Death may indeed be biologically inevitable, but in some sense, as both animal and human instinct tell us, it is also a lessening of the universe.

If subjectivity were truly alien to the cosmos, as it is taken to be in naturalism's modernist (and ironically dualistic) outlook, then thoughts about our own death would make little difference to a full understanding of nature. However, the stereoscopic outlook I have been following changes the whole picture. We cannot properly *see* the universe if we fail to look simultaneously at the critical intelligence to which it has lately given birth. Looking hard at the cosmos without keeping our own minds in view flattens out the field of vision, obscuring its real depth. A more dimensional empiricism, on the other hand, ties its vision of the world's remotest physical origins tightly to an awareness of the critical intelligence that has come to birth in the foreground of natural history. By linking matter intrinsically to life and mind, this richer empiricism avoids the conclusion that lifeless matter, purged of subjectivity, is the fundamental reality. Finally, our stereoscopic vision proposes that the perishing of each subject – and not just human subjects – somehow reverberates throughout the universe. So it follows that if there is any hope for our own subjective survival of death, the universe that remains forever the root system of our subjectivity may in some sense be destined to escape final nothingness as well.

However, the question is whether there is any hope for our own survival as critically intelligent subjects. Naturalists will only scoff at such an idea. According to philosopher Owen Flanagan, there is no basis for the belief that anything about us could survive death since science has destroyed the idea of immortal souls.[6] Nevertheless, he goes on, once we have resigned ourselves to this harsh fact, our lives do not have to be sad. Flanagan is the epitome of a sunny naturalist. The universe is pointless, and death final, but that is no reason to deny that human life can be meaningful and happy. When we die we are gone for good, but in the meantime we can live fulfilling lives anyway. Flanagan concedes that most people believe they have souls and that their souls, or some remnant of conscious life, will live on after death. But, in typically naturalist fashion, he rejects belief in immortality as "irrational."

---

6   Owen Flanagan, *The Problem of the Soul: Two Visions of Mind and How to Reconcile Them* (New York: Basic Books, 2002).

Why irrational? Because there is no *scientific* evidence to support it. One might respond that belief in immortality is at least harmless even if untrue. But not in Flanagan's opinion:

> The beliefs in nonnatural properties of persons, indeed of any nonnatural things, including – yes – God, stand in the way of understanding our natures truthfully and locating what makes life meaningful in a nonillusory way . . . Furthermore, historical evidence abounds that sectarian religious beliefs not only lack rational [i.e. scientific] evidence or support, but they are at least partly at the root of terrible human practices – religious wars, terrorism, and torture. Yes, I know the answer; such calamities come at the hands of fanatics. Even if this is true, the fact is that fanatics are fanatics because they believe that what they believe is indubitably true.[7]

The majority of the world's people, on the other hand, would consider the final extinguishing of mind and "soul" to be the greatest of evils. The possibility that anything as luminously real and palpable as consciousness could end up in the pit of final nothingness is simply unthinkable. Humanity's instinctive revolt against such a prospect, of course, is no proof that the naturalist is wrong. But it still seems extremely audacious for Flanagan and other naturalists to dismiss as irrational so enduring a consensus of human wisdom simply because empirical science, which is not wired to detect subjectivity even in its present state let alone after death, can find no "evidence" of it.

Most people, both in the past and even in an age of science, have believed in some form of subjective survival beyond death – in spite of the absence of present evidence. Some have anticipated reincarnation culminating in final release from the wheel of rebirth. Others have expected bodily resurrection, and still others the survival of their souls in a state of final liberation from the mortal limits

---

[7] Ibid., pp. 167–68.

imposed by the physical world. Theistic religions have based their hope for life after death on the foundational conviction that God is powerful and faithful and will fulfill the divine promise to defeat death in due time. God, according to a saying of Jesus recorded in the Gospels, is "a God of the living and not of the dead," so the everlasting aliveness of God can surely bridge the wide abyss that now divides the living from the dead. Yet naturalism, in keeping with its physicalist assumptions and its metaphysics of the past, cannot fathom how any of this is remotely possible. Hope for immortality is a childish, though possibly adaptive, fantasy from which we must now awaken.

But is belief in life after death as irrational as Flanagan and other naturalists insist? I shall argue to the contrary that, far from being irrational, the expectation of subjective survival may be judged to be a most reasonable belief, precisely insofar as it is supportive of the flourishing of the desire to know. And is the prevalent human hope for survival of death as harmful as Flanagan contends? Granted that terrorists, emboldened by belief in an eternal reward, can do horrible things, does this say anything one way or the other about either the reasonableness or the wholesomeness of the belief itself? Flanagan, speaking with all the confidence of a true believer, consigns most of his fellow humans to the status of madness and potential criminality because they cannot give up their hope for eternal happiness. I have to confess surprise that so esteemed a philosopher seems unaware that almost anything can be twisted to serve evil purposes, and that he considers it necessary to tell us that "fanatics are fanatics because they believe that what they believe is indubitably true." Perhaps the fanatics could reply that Flanagan is a naturalist because he *believes* (as he clearly does) that naturalism is indubitably true.

In this chapter, however, I am concerned less with whether hope for immortality is harmful than whether it is consistent with the truth. When I use the word "truth" I mean it in two senses. First, truth is simply another word for being or *what is*; and, second, truth is a property of all warranted propositions. I am using the term in both senses. My point is that our minds cannot work without anticipating truth. Even in moments of confusion and extreme skepticism our minds still know that it is *true* that we are confused and in doubt. Truth stands there permanently as the inescapable horizon, standard and goal of all intellectual performance, even when we explicitly deny the possibility of attaining it. Minds are aware also, at least at some level, that truth cannot perish. "It fortifies my soul to know that, though I perish, truth is so," says the poet Arthur Hugh Clough. I would propose, accordingly, that the expectation of subjective survival of death is completely consistent with and supportive of our performative appeal to the everlastingness of truth. If so, then this belief can be called reasonable, for it fulfills the fundamental criterion of truth: fidelity to the desire to know. Let me now unpack the proposal.

First of all, there is something imperishable about truth. For example, it is *still true* that dinosaurs once inhabited Earth, even though the dinosaurs themselves are now gone. And it *will still be true* trillions of years from now that dinosaurs, you and I did live at one time on Earth, even though we and the dinosaurs will have perished long since. Even though this planet, the solar system and the Big Bang universe will be gone, all of these facts will still be true. But since *we* will be gone, *where* will it be true? Where will the totality of truth be registered if we are not around to acknowledge it?

Theology has always identified the ultimate repository of truth with the eternal mind and memory of God. Numerous religious texts and teachings express the sentiment that we ourselves are like grass, but that God is forever. The naturalist, on the other hand, is compelled to claim that truth also is like grass. For if truth exists only in our own minds it will perish along with our minds – since there is no eternal registry of what is or what has been. However, if the truth of *that* claim is a product only of the mind that makes the claim, then it need not be taken seriously. For any truth-claim to be taken seriously the basis or criterion of its truthfulness must reside somewhere other than in the perishable truth-affirming mind alone. To affirm the truth of any proposition the human mind is formulating here and now, critical intelligence must assume at least tacitly that there is something beyond its own fragile existence that can place the seal of truthfulness on its claims, or, as the case may be, judge them to be untruthful. The well-functioning mind is willing to subject its content to such a judgment.

The steady endurance of truth, however, is not something the mind can grasp or focus on, but instead something the mind *anticipates* in every act of knowing. The truth anticipated by the mind has already grasped that mind, inviting (not compelling) a kind of surrender. Even the hard naturalist must concede that truth-telling requires a surrender of the mind to what *is* the case rather than to what one would like to be the case. And only an implicit love of *what is* can be trusted to lead the mind to assent to truth. To be a truthful person one must *love* the truth. I cannot imagine that the serious naturalist would deny this. Yet the naturalist also believes that the ultimate repository of truth can only be the fragile assembly of human minds. Truth therefore will disappear once all these minds are gone.

However, if we seriously thought that it depends for its existence and survival only on the human minds that are its transient vessels I doubt that we could value truth enough to surrender ourselves to it here and now. Do you find yourself doubting what I have just said? If you do, it is only because you also love truth. But would your love of truth be justifiable if it were nothing more than a temporary attribute of your perishable mind? Or is it not the case that truth transcends your mind and that of others and invites you to surrender to it? And can you be content with anything less than such a surrender? "Naturalism is true," you will say if you are Flanagan. But is it true because you (and other naturalists) say so? Obviously not. Every judgment the mind makes about the truth of a proposition or belief (including the truth of naturalism) requires a more enduring standard and repository than the entire set of perishable human subjects. Indeed for truth to function as a goal worth seeking, it has to be imperishable. Anything less would allow me to assume that I am the author of truth. And if I honestly thought this to be true, then "truth" itself would be no firmer than the perishable mind that thought it up.

Without a more permanent dwelling place than your own mind, or even the totality of finite minds, truth cannot last forever. And a truth that does not last cannot be deeply valued or loved. It is the nearly universal experience of humans, after all, that it is foolish to trust and love things that have no lasting value. The same principle applies especially to truth. The desire to know flourishes best where truth is valued most. And truth can be more deeply loved if it is judged to be imperishable than if it is only a patina on transient minds. So it seems safe to conclude that the belief that truth never perishes is one that fulfills the fundamental criterion of truth, that of promoting the interests of the desire to know.

I propose next, then, that the almost universal human denial of the finality of death is tied in some way to the mind's intuitive awareness of the fact that truth never fades. Obviously I have no intention of trying to prove that subjective immortality is a fact in a way that would satisfy those, such as Flanagan, who believe that *scientific* evidence must underlie every claim to truth. In any case, were I to try to elicit scientific evidence of immortality I would just be capitulating to the narrower empiricism that underlies naturalistic belief. What I will say, though, is that the hope for some form of subjective survival is a favorable disposition for nurturing trust in the desire to know. Such hope is not at all irrational if it undergirds the trust required for the activation of critical intelligence. On the other hand, a belief that mental existence is destined for absolute extinction, if taken consistently, could easily lead us to underappreciate the cognitional core of our being. Such a conjecture, if taken with full seriousness, may contribute to the undermining rather than confirmation of the trust needed to activate my mind's imperatives.

My desire to know is most fully liberated to seek its goal, namely truth, only if I deeply trust this desire. And nothing that I know of encourages me to trust my desire to know more completely than a religious hope for the climactic fulfillment of this longing.

Such a hope is reasonable if it provides, as I believe it can, a climate that encourages the desire to know to remain restless until it encounters the fullness of being, truth, goodness and beauty. In my own experience nothing outside the world of religious hope comes close to providing such encouragement to embrace the unrestricted dynamism of the desire to know.

The struggle to liberate the desire to know from other desires, from longings that are content to wallow in illusions, requires a tacit trust that the mind can be fully satisfied only when it encounters the fullness of *what is*. Even the naturalist's own attempt to free our minds from the illusion of immortality is itself an implicit, though ambiguous, witness to the mind's longing for enduring truth. Otherwise there would be no good reason to try to convince religious believers that they are wrong. Furthermore, every revision of scientific understanding is undertaken in the interest of getting closer to the goal of complete truthfulness. We may conclude, then, that belief in subjective survival of death need not be an illusion after all. It may be a most reasonable expression of the same spontaneous trust that energizes the desire to know. The ageless religious trust that the core of our critical intelligence is in some sense imperishable is of a piece with an unquenchable trust in the permanence of truth.

"Evidence" for immortality, it goes without saying, could never show up in the naturalist's picture of reality. However, our wider empiricism and layered explanation have exposed this picture as incomplete. The naturalistic worldview cannot even support a belief that the mind is real here and now, let alone that it will be able to exist beyond death. It refuses, at least in any systematic way, to include the fact of critical intelligence as part of the real world. But once nature is more realistically understood to be the matrix of mind, and mind in turn is acknowledged to have cosmic extension, the landscape on which we inquire about the finality of death changes dramatically. The question of critical intelligence's ultimate destiny is no longer separable from the question of the universe's destiny. Here again, mind and the universe are a package deal.

HOPE

Let me summarize, in yet another way, what I have been saying. The free unfolding of critical intelligence requires a trust in the complete intelligibility of the universe and the imperishability of truth. The desire to know intends or anticipates a *fullness* of being, meaning and truth. Anything short of this plenitude makes the intelligent subject restless for more. Hence, the naturalistic belief that the universe is essentially and primordially mindless, and that truth will perish along with our minds, would hardly make the world an adaptive habitat for critical intelligence. Only a belief that the world ultimately makes sense through and through, and that truth will not perish, can keep the spirit of inquiry alive indefinitely. If I thought seriously that at the margins of the universe, or beneath its origins and beyond its final destiny, there lurks an environing unintelligibility, sooner or later this picture of things would have a paralyzing effect on my natural incentive to ask further questions.

However, the core of each person's critical intelligence performatively refutes such a belief. Even though the naturalist may subscribe formally to the materialist view that intelligence is rooted in unintelligence, every act of his or her mind nonetheless tacitly subscribes to a belief in the complete intelligibility of being. This silent anticipation of a fullness of truth is inconsistent with the naturalist's explicit worldview. Moreover, to deny what I have just said would be to destroy the credibility of *all* claims, including those of naturalism. The only consistent or coherent worldview is one that lines up our thoughts about the world with what *actually* goes on in the invariant structure of our thinking and knowing.

My point is that religious hope proves itself to be more consistent with the mind's anticipation of meaning and truth than naturalistic pessimism does. The desire to know, which cannot function without subordinating the human mind to *what is*, is not frustrated but buoyed by the sense that the world ultimately makes sense and that there is something imperishable about truth. Moreover, critical intelligence thrives in an atmosphere of trust that all things will be made clear in a climactic moment of illumination when the ground of the world's intelligibility "will light up all that is hidden in the dark" (1 Corinthians 4:5). Hope for final clarification can give undying zest to the long adventure of inquiry. And a sense that the world is rooted in limitless intelligibility and truth can even serve to give science itself an indefinitely prolonged future.

I would suggest to naturalists such as Owen Flanagan, therefore, that any belief that consistently supports the desire to know – whose goal is nothing short of truth – is by definition realistic rather than illusory or irrational. Consequently, if religious hope supports the mind's confidence in the worthwhileness of the quest for truth, then such hope cannot be dismissed out of hand as illusion. Unless the world is completely absurd – in which case the quest for intelligibility and truth would be pointless – those beliefs that most fully support the desire to know and that excite the mind's imperatives cannot simply be discarded as unreasonable.

According to Darwinian naturalists, of course, the *real* cause of our instinctive hope, including our defiance of death, is natural selection. We possess hope, a Darwinian might say, because it is adaptive, or perhaps it is the byproduct of other adaptations. Belief in an ultimate state of happiness is a fiction that supposedly increases our reproductive fitness directly or indirectly. Hope in life after death has been adaptive at the level of genes, individual human organisms and even religious groups. Darwinian naturalism, by undertaking a genealogy of religious anticipation, proposes thereby to have debunked all hope for immortality. Even though sound logical argumentation demands that the justification of beliefs be undertaken independently of speculation about their origins, most Darwinian critics of religion believe that evolutionary accounts of human religious anticipation should also cast doubt on the existence of whatever it is that is being anticipated.[8]

[8] For a critique of this peculiar leap in logic, see Holmes Rolston, III, *Genes, Genesis and God: Values and Their Origins in Natural and Human History* (New York: Cambridge University Press, 1999), p. 347.

My response to this reductive debunking of hope is to turn the attention of the naturalists, once again, to the very minds that are doing the debunking. In exposing religion's "irrational" longing as adaptation, Darwinian naturalists may be logically subverting the confidence that undergirds their own desire to know as well. What is it that would make their own confidence in intelligibility and truth immune to the same critique that they direct toward the trust that anticipates ultimate fulfillment beyond death?

It seems to me that the mind's instinctive longing for complete clarity is brought to its most significant expression in the quest for a meaning and truth that will redeem the intelligent subject from the threat of extinction. Hope is one of those virtues that provides support for the desire to know in its anticipation of intelligibility. Hope delivers critical intelligence from the obsession of needing to understand everything here and now. Hope widens out the world in the foreground of critical intelligence, inviting the desire to know to unfold ever more expansively.

But, the naturalist will persist, how do we know that the mind's performative trust in reality's intelligibility and its anticipation of a fullness of truth are not just futile stabs in the dark? Perhaps trust in truth too is an irrational belief, convenient for the sake of luring the mind into ongoing inquiry, but lacking any foundation in reality? Is not the mind's anticipation of intelligibility and truth an adaptive fiction, a trick it plays on itself to avoid facing the ultimate absurdity of the world? Well, once again, I would not have to take this question itself seriously if that were the case, since the mind that issues such a proposal would be merely "adapting" rather than seriously searching for truth. The fact is, however, that such a question is sincerely in search of understanding and truth, and as such it is an exemplification of the very point I am trying to make: each mind, in order to work at all, anticipates intelligibility and truth. To reduce our anticipation of truth to psychic illusion or Darwinian adaptation would be to negate the trustworthiness of all human thought.

It deserves repeating that I am appealing here to what Lonergan calls the *fundamental* criterion of truth: fidelity to the desire to know. And I am saying that hope in the face of death for final redemption and fulfillment of the desire to know is truthful in that fundamental sense. Naturalism, on the other hand, fails to provide any comparable support for critical intelligence. It confronts each intelligent subject with the prospect of an ultimate extinguishing of both subjectivity and intelligence. According to this mostly modern kind of belief, not only will individual minds perish for good, but minds of any sort will be dissolved into the elemental stupor from which they arose. One cannot help wondering therefore how such a picture of things could ever be a nourishing environment for critical intelligence.

Naturalism, I am convinced, would be a cognitionally ruinous belief system if it were ever taken consistently – which it almost never is because of the innate trust in being and truth that empower even the minds that profess to follow that creed. On the other hand, a theological perspective, being explicitly aware of the limits of nature, enlarges the picture of reality as a whole to make a home proportionate to the mind's full deployment. Religious hope provides a satisfactorily adaptive atmosphere for organisms endowed with an *unrestricted* desire to know. Critical intelligence, after all, is at home only in a world whose horizons are limitless. To be fertile and coherent, therefore, a philosophy of nature must allow the world to be large and supportive enough to contain intelligent and critical subjects. I have been arguing that only a worldview that locates the natural world and critical intelligence within a wider than natural environment can fulfill this requirement.

12 Anticipation

> Our world contains within itself a mysterious promise of the future, implicit in its natural evolution . . . that is the final assertion of the scientist as he closes his eyes, heavy and weary from having seen so much that he could not express.
>
> Pierre Teilhard de Chardin[1]

As I reflect on my own desire to know and try to follow its instinctive orientation toward a *fullness* of being, truth, goodness and beauty, I can expect to find a satisfactory setting for this desire only in some version of a theological – and specifically eschatological – understanding of reality. Such a worldview could be declared illusory by definition only if it frustrated or failed to support the unfolding of my desire to know. But religious hope, including belief that my critical intelligence is in some sense imperishable, serves to shore up my natural inclination to *value* the mind in such a way as to encourage me to surrender humbly to its imperatives. Hope can serve the cause of truthfulness if it encourages me to remain faithful to my desire to know in the face of all apparent frustrations. I have proposed, therefore, that anticipation of subjective survival beyond death is much more consistent with, and supportive of, the spontaneous trust I place in my critical intelligence than naturalistic pessimism could ever be.

Therefore, looking forward to conscious life beyond death is not necessarily harmful to, but coincides with, the search I have been undertaking in this book for an adequate justification of the spontaneous trust each of us places in the desire to know. I have concluded that a *sufficient* foundation for this trust cannot be found exclusively by looking back to the causal past but only by taking into account the mind's innate anticipation of a fullness of being, truth, goodness and beauty looming on the horizon ahead. Minds are naturally and

[1] Pierre Teilhard de Chardin, *Writings in Time of War*, translated by René Hague (New York: Harper & Row, 1968), pp. 55–56.

irremediably anticipatory, oriented toward a fulfillment that only an endlessly open future can bring. Moreover, critical intelligence is embedded in a long unfolding of life, emergence, evolution and cosmic becoming whose own orientation has always been deeply anticipatory. The forward thrust of nature as observed in its various phases of emergence is not a fiction that humans wishfully invent. Rather it is a general hallmark of cosmic process. It comes to light most explicitly in the emergence of the desire to know, but a leaning toward the future is a fundamental feature of all of nature, one that finds a full flowering in religious hope for a final fulfillment of nature, persons and history.

Natural occurrences, not to mention human creativity, become intelligible only if one does more than just take note of the causal history that leads up to them, or of the atomic constituents ingredient in them. To appreciate the full reality of emergent phenomena it is necessary to attend also to their present openness to future transformation. Everything in nature, as a recently chastened physics now has to admit, is open to future outcomes that defy scientific prediction on the basis of what has already occurred in the realm of the earlier-and-simpler.[2] This freedom from absolute determination by the past is part of their identity just as it is part of our own. Why, ultimately, nature has this general openness to possibility the natural sciences do not say. Scientific method has characteristically understood things primarily in terms of what has led up to them or, reductively, in terms of the allegedly "fundamental" physical units that make them up. It has been able to make only very general – though technologically useful – predictions based on the past habits or present structures in nature. But it has not laid out in fine-grained specificity what actual future, and especially long-range, outcomes will be like.

[2] Robert B. Laughlin, *A Different Universe: Reinventing Physics from the Bottom Down* (New York: Perseus Books, 2005).

What science deliberately leaves out is the question of why the universe is open in the first place to the dawning of new possibilities. This may not be a properly scientific question in any case, but theology at least has an appropriate explanatory role to play here, not only in accounting for why the universe exists at all, but also in speculating about why nature remains open to future transformation. In saying this I am not making room for a god-of-the-gaps that would ever compete with scientific understanding. My approach challenges naturalism, but in no sense does it compete with science. The hard work of science still remains to be done, and theology can never be a substitute for this effort.

My point is simply that the later-and-more of nature, as the present reflection on critical intelligence has already shown, cannot be fully understood by telling the scientific story of how it arose out of the earlier-and-simpler. Learning how mind appeared in the history of nature is fascinating in its narrative content. But if nothing else were involved in explaining the reality of mind than conceptually and imaginatively cobbling together a series of mindless antecedents and components, then the essential feature of critical intelligence will still have been overlooked, namely, its *present* anticipatory openness to a fullness of meaning and truth up ahead. And by leaving this dimension of anticipation out of our understanding of mind we would also have diminished our understanding of the wider universe.

Of course, one can always deny verbally that there is anything "more" involved in critical intelligence than its material constituents. Perhaps minds, like everything else in life, are *really* just simplicity masquerading in the guise of complexity, as Peter Atkins claims.[3] However, as I have already stated in other contexts, any such claim is self-refuting since it implies logically that the complex mind that makes such a claim is itself *really* nothing more than the earlier and simpler mindless stuff from which it arose. And if the roots of

---

[3] P. W. Atkins, *The 2nd Law: Energy, Chaos, and Form* (New York: Scientific American Books, 1994), p. 200.

Atkins' own mind have such a physically lowly status, where then did he acquire the colossal *trust* in his mental powers that allows him to assume now that we should listen to him? Tracing the causes of present phenomena all the way into the remotest past and all the way down to the elemental levels of cosmic stuff, leads the mind toward the incoherence of sheer multiplicity.[4] Only by looking toward future syntheses of the world's elemental units does intelligibility start to show up. Complete intelligibility therefore coincides with the arrival of an Absolute Future, a goal that we can approach here and now by taking on the virtue of hope.[5]

Temporal passage, physical determinism and Darwinian selection, though essential to the ongoing creation of life and mind, are not alone enough to account for the anticipatory bearing of critical intelligence, nor for that of the entire natural world in which mind is embedded. Each natural entity, in addition to comprising physically simpler and historically antecedent factors, is also open, though not without constraints, to being transformed by a realm of new possibilities looming on the horizon of the future. I have called nature's openness to possibility *anticipation*, a concept that each of us can understand immediately since it is the dynamic core of our own critical intelligence. And although scientific discourse understandably shies away from such terminology, a stereoscopic empiricism is obliged to employ analogies like anticipation in order to arrive at a realistic and expansive understanding of nature. A wider empiricism allows that the earlier and simpler phases of natural process have a less intense anticipatory openness than we experience in our own consciousness. But at least some degree of anticipation – that is, openness to possibility – is a *fundamental* feature of nature, and not something that drops in out of the void only after the emergence of the human mind.

---

[4]   A point that Teilhard de Chardin makes throughout his works.
[5]   Karl Rahner, SJ, *Theological Investigation*, vol. VI, translated by Karl and Boniface Kruger (Baltimore: Helicon, 1969), pp. 59–68.

Since I have made anticipation fundamental to all natural occurrences, my understanding of nature does not have to invent magically a completely new set of categories when it comes to interpreting that region of nature known as critical intelligence. Critical intelligence is the flowering of a straining intrinsic to nature at all times and places. But the naturalistic alternative, with its metaphysics of the past, purges the cosmos of subjectivity and anticipation from the start of its program. Thus, it has nothing in its explanatory arsenal that can account adequately for the emergence of critical intelligence. Consequently, it is compelled either to deny that intelligence or subjectivity is *real* or to "explain" it in terms more appropriate to an ontology of mindlessness.

For a while the naturalist worldview seemed to be successful, at least as long as it could get by with the assumption that critical intelligence is not part of nature. But that assumption has been destroyed even by scientific discovery. Especially after Darwin the human mind can no longer be reasonably separated from the rest of nature. At the beginning of the modern age the scent of dualism in the cultural atmosphere was still strong enough to encourage both scientific and religious thinkers to imagine that there is a natural world "out there" in which all traces of subjectivity and anticipation are absent, and in which nature lies passively waiting to be mastered by minds intrinsically estranged from it. And this way of looking at the world still lives on in the commonly accepted belief that nature is altogether devoid of teleology, or that purpose exists only in human brains.

However, science itself has now in principle destroyed the dualism that allowed philosophers of nature to invent this construct in the first place. Evolution, cosmology and even physics have recently returned the intelligent subject to its proper home in nature. If so, then anticipation, attributed analogously to all stages of emergence, is not an inappropriate term to employ in a richly empirical view of nature as a whole. Although it is not necessary for conventional science itself to think in these terms, it is essential that any philosophy of nature that proposes to be based on a broad range of experience do so.

EXPLAINING ANTICIPATION

But then the quality of anticipation in nature needs an explanation also, and it is here that I would locate the relevance of theology to my inquiry. Such an explanation would focus on the notion of *possibility*. Possibility, in Latin, is *potentia*, a term that can be translated as potency or power. Power, though, is not limited to efficient or mechanical causation. There is also the *power of the possible* that allows room in nature for anticipation, cosmic emergence and eventually the desire to know. Without an inherent openness to future possibility everything would be frozen in its present status and nothing new could ever happen. Unlike naturalism, which views the future as a void to be filled in by the forward rush of events out of the past, a theology of nature refuses to take for granted the openness of the world to surprising new modes of being. The world's openness to novelty is due not to an absolute emptiness stretching up ahead, but to an array of possibilities that come to greet the present, as it were, from out of the future, luring it away from entrapment in what has been. There is a "power of the future" whose best name is God, and whose central action is the "arrival of the future."[6] It is the same power of the possible that ultimately arouses the intelligent subject to look toward a climactic fulfillment beyond death.

The naturalist will still object that there is no physical evidence to support such a prospect, but I have attempted to show that this protest is rooted in a narrow empiricism that looks only to *what has been* as the all-determining explanation of what will be. All the naturalist needs to do to *see* the anticipatory side of nature, however, is attend directly to the imperatives that ground his or her own critical intelligence at this very moment. The relevant evidence

6   Wolfhart Pannenberg, *Faith and Reality*, translated by John Maxwell (Philadelphia: Westminster Press, 1977), pp. 58–59; Ted Peters, *God – The World's Future: Systematic Theology for a New Era*, 2nd edn. (Minneapolis: Fortress Press, 1992).

consists of the experience of *being grasped by* a fullness of being, intelligibility, truth and goodness that summon forth the imperatives to be attentive, intelligent, critical and responsible. The best reason for bursting through the boundaries erected by naturalism is right there in front of each one of us if we would but turn and take a look at it.

Then, after taking a look at the ineradicably anticipatory orientation of our own critical intelligence, the next step is to try to make sense of it. Which worldview gives the better account of the anticipatory thrust of our desire to know? Naturalism, with its reduction of mind to the earlier-and-simpler, and its predicting the eventual obliteration of subjectivity and truth? Or a theological worldview in which the mind's anticipation is aroused by an infinite fullness of truth and goodness that grasps hold of each of us even here and now, luring our minds, and hearts, to enter more completely into it?

Religious hope, I dare say, arises from the same anticipatory desire to know that underlies all conscious intentionality, including scientific inquiry. Even in all its ambiguity and even crudity, religious anticipation of a final end to all confusion can hardly be completely alien to a critical intelligence whose very definition is a search for ever deeper intelligibility and truth. The widespread religious longing for ultimate fulfillment and a destiny beyond death does not contradict, but arises simultaneously with, the unrestricted desire to know. Indeed, the cognitional ancestry of our irrepressible trust in the desire to know is intertwined with the religious tendency to look for ultimate fulfillment. To disentangle the two desires, I believe, runs the risk of killing them both.

Index